Outline of
The Principle

Level 4

Outline of
The Principle

Level 4

Holy Spirit Association for the Unification of World Christianity

Scriptural quotations are from the Revised Standard Version of the Bible, copyrighted 1946, 1952, 1971, 1973 and used by permission of the Division of Christian Education of the National Council of Churches.

Printed in the United States of America
Reprinted 1983
Reprinted 1984

Holy Spirit Association for the Unification of World Christianity
4 West 43rd Street
New York, New York 10036

Library of Congress
Card Catalog No. 80-50226

ISBN 0-910621-41-1

TABLE OF CONTENTS IN BRIEF

TABLE OF CONTENTS IN FULL

2 The Fall/47

5 Resurrection/107

6 Predestination/125

7 Christology/137

8 Overview of the Principles of Restoration/147

9 Adam's Family in the Dispensation for Restoration/171

10 Noah's Family in the Dispensation for Restoration/179

11 Abraham's Family in the Dispensation for Restoration/187

12 Moses in the Dispensation for Restoration/205

13 Jesus in the Dispensation for Restoration /235

14 Dispensational Time Identity/255

15 Preparation for the Second Coming/271

16 The Second Coming/293

Introduction

We are entering a new age. We are living in a time of rapid transition; yet, for all the changes that are taking place in individuals and families, in society, in the nations, and in the world, many worry about the direction that these changes are taking and feel that there is still some fundamental change needed.

The Principle*, which is outlined in this volume, is a vision and a guide that offers hope to those who want to find the essence of life and live righteously. All of us have at some time asked fundamental questions about God, ourselves, and the world. We have also often wondered what our futures would be. Such questions are common to everyone. However, the answers that have been given often have been inadequate. In answering these questions, we need to think of them from a new perspective that will give us answers we can all be satisfied with. *Outline of The Principle* is directed toward this purpose.

The Principle is the teaching revealed by God to the Reverend Sun Myung Moon. Reverend Moon did not study theology or philosophy in school or with any teacher. God chose him to express His Will. Yet, revelation from God does not rush down easily, like water over a waterfall, nor is it given all at once. There are certain stages in its unfolding, and a proper response by man is essential for that unfolding to proceed.

Sun Myung Moon was first called by God when he was sixteen years old. He then wandered through the invisible (spirit) world, which is the world of cause, seeking to solve all of the fundamental questions about life and the universe. He

---

* When printed in roman type, 'The Principle' refers to the revelation received by the Reverend Sun Myung Moon. (See also the footnote on page 35.)

had to overcome tremendous obstacles in the spirit world. In search of the truth, he walked a path of suffering and fought a bloody battle against the forces of Satan. Only God really knows the kind of path he travelled. He freely communicated with Jesus and the saints in Paradise. In his spiritual communication with God, Sun Myung Moon received revelation concerning the fundamental aspects of God's Will for man's life.

In order to systematize and teach this knowledge, he spent countless hours in prayer and in study of the Bible. In 1950, he began to teach formally the most important parts of The Principle to his disciples. However, much of The Principle received by Reverend Moon is still unpublished. More of The Principle revelation will be released according to the progress of the dispensation and the development of the foundation on earth.

Two texts, titled *Wol-li Hae-sul* [Explanation of The Principle] (Seoul, Korea: Segye Kidokyo Tongil Shillyong Hyop-hwe, 1957; untranslated) and *Wol-li Kang-ron* [Discourse on The Principle] (Seoul, Korea: Segye Kidokyo Tongil Shillyong Hyophwe, 1966; published in English as *Divine Principle*, Washington, D.C.: HSA-UWC, 1973) have been used as the official doctrine of the Unification Church. They were written by Hyo Won Eu, the first president of the Korean Unification Church, who served Reverend Moon in the early years of his ministry and was taught directly by him.

At Reverend Moon's request, this series, *Outline of The Principle*, is being written, based on *Wol-li Kang-ron*, to help readers understand The Principle and to be used as a lecture outline. I* have studied and lectured on The Principle for over twenty years under the guidance of Reverend Moon. Nevertheless I still lack a complete understanding of The Principle and the ability to perfectly express it. Not wanting to lessen the precious value of The Principle itself, I have written this book with prayer. If there is any confusion in the expression of The Principle, it is my responsibility alone.

According to The Principle, God is the origin of love and

---

* This text was written in Korean by Chung Hwan Kwak.

heart. God's motive in creating is to realize his ideal of love—to realize his ideal of love is the Purpose of the Creation. In the world where God's ideal is realized, man and all things are to live in happiness and harmony, with God's love as the source of their life and happiness. The world where the sphere of God's ideal love is complete is the Kingdom of Heaven. God created man on earth, not in heaven. God's ideal when realized on earth is thus called the Kingdom of Heaven on earth. Man is to live in God's kingdom on earth, and then his spirit self is to enter God's kingdom in the spirit world, where he will live for eternity (the relationship between these two worlds is similar to that between the mind and the body in human beings). The Kingdom of Heaven is the place where an individual who has completely experienced God's love lives happily for eternity in an ideal relationship of love with God and other people.

In God's ideal world of love, there cannot be any sin, unrighteousness, injustice, or restraint. However, the first man and woman did not fulfill their responsibility, and as a result, they did not perfect themselves, and they left the realm of God's love. This was the Fall, and its result was that sin and evil entered the world, and Hell, which is the realm outside God's love, came to exist.

Could God abandon this world, full of sin, unrighteousness, and suffering? No; he could never do so. As he said in Isaiah 46:11, " 'I have spoken, and I will bring it to pass; I have purposed and I will do it.' " God will restore man to be as He promised in the blessings that He gave after man's creation (Gen 1:28). So God's dispensation for salvation is the Dispensation for Restoration, in which he will establish the ideal kingdom of love, which was his original Purpose for the Creation.

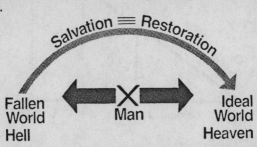

God is a living and active God. Both throughout history and in the minds of people, God's active providence has left its mark. Then, what of man, the object of this living God's dispensation; what has man been like throughout history? At each stage in history, God has had to deal with man according to man's spiritual state and intellectual level. Has man always remained the same internally, or has he been progressing and constantly improving? If man had not fallen, he would have reflected God's character (Jn 14:20) and perfection (Mt 5:48), and thus God would have been able to relate to him directly. However, Adam and Eve fell and became embodiments of sin and evil instead of becoming the persons that God had originally envisioned. If we were to speak of how man's spirituality and intellect were affected by this state of separation and fall, we could say that they were reduced to a very base state.

Through God's Dispensation for Restoration, the spirituality and intellect of fallen people have gradually developed. As man's spiritual and intellectual levels have developed in each age, God has been able to revise accordingly the means of educating people and relating to them. For example, in Abraham's time, when man's spirituality and intellect were extremely low, God had to have people come closer to him through the offering of sacrifices. The people of that time were too immature to respond to laws and commandments. Several hundred years later, at the time of Moses, God

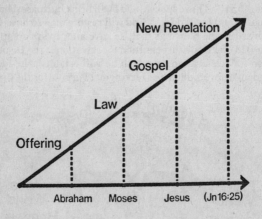

carried out the dispensation through the Law. At Jesus' time, instead of repeating the same dispensation through laws or commandments, God worked in a new way to bring the people closer to him, by giving the Gospel, on a level appropriate for the spirituality of the people of that age.

The fact that the Jewish people, who so devoutly believed in God, did not recognize his son, Jesus, as the savior is a crucial point in the Dispensation for Restoration. Why were they unable to recognize him? In that age, the people of Israel followed God through obedience to laws, but then God began to approach the people through Jesus himself, by means of the new dispensation of the Gospel. In light of these historical facts, we can see that as man's spirituality and intellect develop, God has always adopted a correspondingly developed method to reach man. The objects of the living God and his dispensation are not like fossils, but rather are persons who are very much alive and active.

Then, who is the present focus of God's dispensation? It is not the people of Jesus' time, nor the people of Moses' age, nor primitive man still further back. It is contemporary man, living here and now. Yet we cannot deny that today most young people are not interested in the churches and that people in general are turning away from them. The rational and scientific emphasis of people today demands a clearer and deeper understanding of the truth and an explanation of the seeming contradictions in religious teachings and practices before they will take up a religious way of life. As we have seen in God's historical process of restoration, God is alive and working, so we can know that God will definitely give man a new expression of the truth, one that can lead the people of this age to salvation and a new age.

Today, many difficult questions arise during an examination of the Bible. For example, what is the proper relationship of God, Jesus, and man; what is the correct understanding of resurrection and the Last Days; why must Jesus return; and when and how will he return? Answers to all of these have been given in parables and symbols but they have yet to be clearly explained.

We read in John 16:25 that Jesus said, " 'I have said this to you in figures; the hour is coming when I shall no longer speak to you in figures but tell you plainly of the Father.' " In John 16:12,13 we read that he also said, " 'I have yet many things to say to you, but you cannot bear them now. When the Spirit of truth comes, he will guide you into all the truth; for he will not speak on his own authority, but whatever he hears he will speak, and he will declare to you the things that are to come.' " And in Revelation 10:11 we read, " 'You must again prophesy about many peoples and nations and tongues and kings.' " Each of these passages indicates that in the Last Days a new expression of the truth will be given.

However, since it will be a new revelation, there will be some aspects which may not be understood in light of conventional doctrine or tradition. For example, even though Jesus' teachings were based on the Old Testament, the people of his time were bound to such a literal interpretation of the Old Testament that they could not understand Jesus. It was for this reason that Jesus said, " '. . . new wine must be put into fresh wineskins' " (Lk 5:38); he was teaching them that they had to make themselves new if they were to receive the new words.

We know that God worked through Noah and Abraham and we know that God spoke through Moses and Jesus. Is the same God, who is alive today, unable to give a new revelation? The Church does not need another human interpretation of the Bible. What matters is how God interprets it and that we fulfill his Will by living it.

There is another reason that mankind needs a new, deeper expression of truth. We can clearly see the rapid collapse of modern civilization and of order in society with no satisfactory replacement in sight. A feeling of emptiness, loneliness, and discontent has led to despair, confusion, self-indulgence, and alcohol and drug abuse. Confusion throughout society about standards of value and conduct has caused the strong trend toward egoism, and accompanying it, the breakdown of the family and the rapid increases in crime, juvenile delinquency, and all kinds of immorality, which are unsettling the foundations of society and causing a loss of hope in the future. Violence and war, which are prevalent, and racism, the unequal distribution of wealth, the impotence of the world religions in leading the modern age, and the expansion of atheistic Communism all reinforce the doubts about the prospects for modern civilization. None of these crises can be completely or even partially solved in an instant. A fundamental and eternal solution is needed. Since God is alive, he will definitely save mankind from these crises through a new and revolutionary approach.

The key to truly solving or eliminating any of these problems is knowing and understanding their causes. It is because the causes have never been fully understood that these problems have never been eliminated. The Principle explains these causes and then presents clear and practical solutions that through education make it possible for the individual and the family (which are the core of human society) to freely and happily alter their life styles.

To fallen man, knowledge is intellectual and spiritual renewal; ignorance is death and destruction. No aesthetic sentiments can come from ignorance, nor can will or hope flourish in it. And ignorance and misunderstanding of God cause men to turn away from God and to despair. The Principle not only shows that God exists, but also explains the *original Heart of God* and the details of his dispensation as revealed in history.

Moreover, it fosters a change of character for those who sincerely want to find God through a spiritual experience with the Holy Spirit. The more we experience the true love of God through The Principle, the more we experience our own re-creation. Furthermore, we are able to develop genuine and sincere human relationships with others.

Through developments in the means of communication and travel and through trade and cultural exchanges, the world has been drawn externally so close together that now each nation directly or indirectly influences all others. However, the basic content of human relationships is still distrust and hate based on self-centeredness and mutual lack of concern. In other words, despite the external trend toward a one-world community, unity and harmony in the truest sense are not present. And God's love alone can make them possible.

The Principle teaches that the family is the basic unit needed for the realization of God's love. The Principle also affirms that only through establishing order in the home can love be planted in the dry heart of modern man, and only then can a true relationship be established between husband and wife, between parents and children, among brothers and sisters, and among neighbors. The love between an ideal husband and wife is the fundamental condition for the happiness of human beings. Only when there is such love between parents will children be able to understand and experience ideal love from their parents.

God's original ideal is for human beings to love God as their parent and live in brotherhood as one extended family. The Principle is a guide to the awakening of man's original love and to the restoring of the original human relationships that will create a one-family world society.

The Principle also leads to unification of the internal truths, which religion has sought, and the external truths, which science has sought. The reason that The Principle is able to achieve this unification is that whether one is concerned with man's inner life or the cosmos, man's effort to find truth in God's Creation is related to God, whatever the discipline or approach.

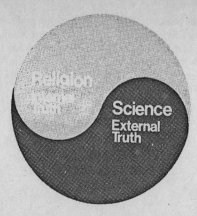

Furthermore, The Principle will prevail over the communist ideology, which denies God, and it will end the last ideological battle of history with a victory for God's side. Completion of the dispensation for salvation will include the restoration of people under communist regimes. They also are to become individuals with perfect character by means of God's love and new words.

According to The Principle, all religions throughout history which have sought and urged a conscientious way of life directly or indirectly came to exist by virtue of God's Will. It is true that today Christianity plays a central role in fulfilling the overall purpose of God's dispensation. However, God has led people of other nations by establishing religions suited to their particular time and environment in order to prepare them to receive the Messiah in the future. As John 3:16 says, " 'For God so loved the world that he gave his only Son, that *whoever* believes in him should not perish but have eternal life' " (emphasis added). God sends the Messiah not only for Christians, but for all mankind.

The revelation that God gave to Sun Myung Moon was given quietly in the East, but it has given men and women throughout the world, especially young people, new happiness and new hope, and it has given them life in the depth of their hearts. Young people from more than one hundred twenty nations, with different skin colors, cultural backgrounds, and life styles have all taken up this new life and have found new meaning and follow God's Will with a new passion. Here, we introduce an outline of The Principle, which has the vitality to deeply move the human mind and spirit and to transform a searching individual into a person of new character centered on God.

CHAPTER ONE

The Principles of the Creation

The fundamental questions about life and the universe cannot be finally resolved without understanding the nature of God, the Creator. This is so because in order to understand and solve the problems concerning any resultant being we must first understand the causal being. So in order to answer the most basic questions about all resultant beings, we must first understand the nature of God, the Creator, and the principles by which he created the world. "The Principles of the Creation" explains God's nature and these principles, and thus answers the fundamental questions about life and the universe.

I. THE DUAL CHARACTERISTICS OF GOD AND THE CREATION

A. The Dual Characteristics of God

How can we know the nature of God, who is invisible? We can know it through observing the Creation. Just as the work of an artist is a visible manifestation of its maker's invisible nature, every being in the Creation is a substantial manifestation of the invisible nature of God, its Creator. Just as we can sense an author's character through his work, so can we perceive God's nature through his Creation.

For this reason, Paul said,

> Ever since the creation of the world his invisible nature, namely, his eternal power and deity, has been clearly perceived in the things that have been made. So they are without excuse. . . .
>
> (Rom 1:20)

We will determine what God's nature is like by finding the characteristics which are common to all entities in his Creation.

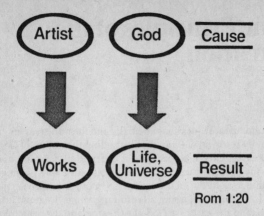

Rom 1:20

1. The Dual Characteristics Sung Sang (Internal Character) and Hyung Sang (External Form)

We find that all existing beings have both an invisible, internal character and a visible, external form. *Sung Sang* is the inner nature or character of any being, whereas *Hyung Sang* is the aspects of matter, structure, and shape of any being. Sung Sang and Hyung Sang are Korean terms which can be roughly translated as *Internal Character* and *External Form*.

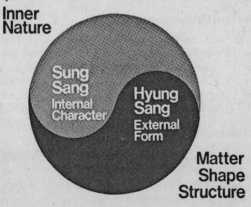

For instance, in man, simply speaking, Sung Sang is the invisible mind and Hyung Sang is the visible body. In animals, the invisible instinctual mind is the Sung Sang, while the tissues and organs forming an animal's body are the Hyung Sang. In plants, life and the various invisible internal characteristics are its Sung Sang, whereas the material part made up of the cells is its Hyung Sang. The same principle can be applied to the elements. The physicochemical character of molecules, atoms, and particles is their Sung Sang, while the visible matter and structure are their Hyung Sang. In man,

Man	Heart & Mind	Body
Animals	Animal Mind	Body
Plants	Plant 'Mind'	'Body'
Molecules	Inherent Nature	Energy/ Matter
Atoms	Inherent Nature	Energy/ Matter
Particles	Inherent Nature	Energy/ Matter

the mind is the *subject* and motivator of the body; thus the body moves according to the direction of the mind. Likewise, the Sung Sangs of animals, plants, molecules, atoms, and particles direct and control their Hyung Sangs.

The body, which is Hyung Sang, reflects and resembles the mind, which is Sung Sang. Though the mind cannot be seen, it has its own "form," and the body, which reflects and resembles the mind, assumes a corresponding form. Mind and body are simply the inner and outer aspects of the same person, with the mind being causal and in the subject position to the body. This is the reason one can perceive things about a man's mind and destiny by examining his outer appearance. From this, we can understand that Sung Sang and Hyung Sang are simply the inner and outer aspects of each being. Sung Sang is the causal aspect and stands in the subject position to Hyung Sang; Hyung Sang is the resultant aspect and stands in the *object* position to Sung Sang. Accordingly, Hyung Sang may also be called the *second Sung Sang*. Together we call them *dual characteristics*.

Since God is the First Cause of all beings and each created being has dual characteristics of Sung Sang and Hyung Sang, God must have Sung Sang and Hyung Sang (Rom 1:20). God's Sung Sang and Hyung Sang are in the subject position to the Sung Sangs and Hyung Sangs of the created beings. God's Sung Sang, which is in the subject position to the Sung Sangs of all created beings, is called the *Original Sung Sang*, and his Hyung Sang, which is subject to the Hyung Sangs of all created beings, is called the *Original Hyung Sang*. It should be emphasized that God's Original Sung Sang and Original Hyung Sang do not exist as independent entities, but in harmonious reciprocal relationship with one another. God is the subject being of harmonized Original Sung Sang and Original Hyung Sang, and he is the First Cause of the resultant world.

2. The Dual Characteristics Positivity and Negativity

We also find that throughout the Creation there is a reciprocal relationship between *Positivity* and *Negativity*.* For example, atoms are formed from the reciprocal relationship between positive and negative elements. Atoms themselves have positive or negative characteristics. Based on such characteristics, two or more atoms enter into a reciprocal relationship, forming molecules. Plants have male and female elements. Similarly, most animals reproduce through relationships between male and female. All plants and animals exist and reproduce by virtue of myriad internal and external interdependent relationships of positive and negative elements. The Bible says that God was not satisfied with man alone (Gen 2:18)—so he made a woman, Eve, as Adam's object. Then for the first time God saw that his Creation was ". . . very good." Mankind is composed of men and women, and human society exists and develops through the reciprocal relationships between men and women.

The relationship between Positivity and Negativity is similar to that which exists between internal character and

---

* Positivity and Negativity, or Positive and Negative, are used with the meaning of yang-yin (yang-um, in Korean) as in yin-yang philosophy. They in no way connote good and evil, good and bad, or constructive and destructive.

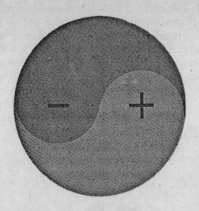

Man	man	woman
Animals	male	female
Plants	male	female
Molecules	positive	negative
Atoms	positive	negative
Particles	positive	negative

external form. Positivity and Negativity have the reciprocal relationship of subject and object, cause and result, internal and external; so Positivity and Negativity together are also called *dual characteristics*. The Creation is made in such a way that everything exists through the reciprocal relationship of Positivity and Negativity.

Then what is the source of these dual characteristics of Positivity and Negativity, which can be found throughout the Creation? Since all beings are resultant beings, the elements they have in common must have originated in their ultimate source—God, the Creator. The fact that the Creation is composed of dual characteristics of Positivity and Negativity means that God himself, who is the First Cause of all things, is the origin of the dual characteristics of Positivity and Negativity. This fact can be understood from Genesis 1:27, which says, "So God created man in his own image . . . male and female he created them."

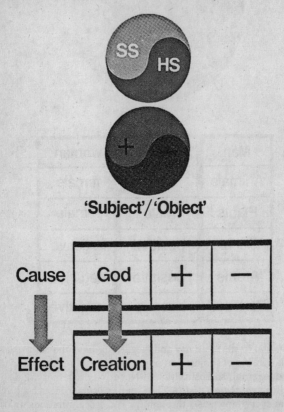

'Subject'/'Object'

Cause	God	+	—
Effect	Creation	+	—

God is the being whose Positive and Negative attributes stand in the subject position to all the Positive and Negative aspects of created beings. We call God's subject Positive and Negative aspects *Original Positivity* and *Original Negativity*.

God's Original Positivity and Original Negativity are harmonized within him; so God is the First Cause of the resultant world and exists as the being of harmonized Positive and Negative aspects.

3. The Dual Characteristics of God

What is the relationship between the dual characteristics of Sung Sang and Hyung Sang and the dual characteristics of Positivity and Negativity? In all beings the dual characteristics of positive and negative, or masculine and feminine, are attributes of Sung Sang and Hyung Sang. This means that mind and body are the most fundamental aspects of the individual human being, and masculinity and femininity are secondary aspects. In other words, Sung Sang has positive and negative attributes, and Hyung Sang also has positive and negative attributes.

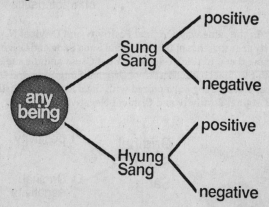

Let us look at these dual aspects in man. First, in the mind, or Sung Sang, there is positive emotion, which is bright or lively, and there is negative emotion, which is sentimental or placid. There is positive intellect, which is active, and negative intellect, which is passive. There is positive will, which initiates and takes charge, and there is negative will, which is passive, or responsive. There are also positive and negative aspects to man's physical body, or Hyung Sang. The protruding, or convex, parts are the positive aspects, whereas the sunken, or concave, parts are the negative aspects. Thus, we can see that Positivity and Negativity are attributes of Sung Sang and Hyung Sang.

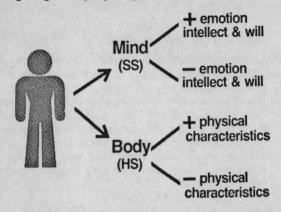

In the same way, Original Positivity and Original Negativity are attributes of God's Original Sung Sang and Original Hyung Sang. In brief, God is the First Cause and the subject with the dual characteristics of Original Sung Sang and Original Hyung Sang harmonized with the dual characteristics of Original Positivity and Original Negativity.

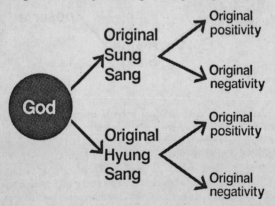

Then, what are the essential natures of God's Original Sung Sang and Original Hyung Sang? God's Original Sung

Sang is the internal nature of God and the origin of the invisible inner aspects of all created beings: man's mind, an animal's instinct, the life of plants, and the physicochemical character of the minerals and elements. Original Sung Sang is the mind of God, which includes emotion, intellect, and will, as well as concepts and law. However, the most essential of God's internal characteristics is Heart.*

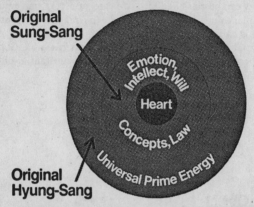

Original Sung-Sang

Emotion, Intellect, Will

Heart

Concepts, Law

Universal Prime Energy

Original Hyung-Sang

The Original Hyung Sang is God's external attributes and is the origin of the substance and form of all created beings: man's body, the bodies of the animals and plants, and the substance and form of inorganic matter. *Universal Prime Energy* (see the next section) and matter are the main attributes of the Original Hyung Sang.

B. The Relationship between God and the Creation

Every created being is God's substantial object, that is, each being is the visible and substantial expression and form of the

---

* Heart (Shimjung, in Korean) is the essence of God's personality—the essence of his Sung Sang. Heart is the most vital part of his nature, such that all other attributes in him are what they are and do what they do solely because of this attribute. Heart is the impulse to love and to be united in love with the object of its love. For this reason, Heart is said to be the source of love, and at the same time is the chief motive behind love.

God's Heart has within itself its own purpose; so it is through God's love, through his Heart, that *The Principle* (Logos) is expressed and the Creation comes into being and achieves fulfillment.

dual characteristics of God, who exists as the invisible subject. When a created being becomes a perfect object to God, the subject, the Will of God is fully realized. In other words, the completed world is like one perfect organic body which moves or remains calm only according to God's Purpose for the Creation.

Though all created beings reflect God's dual characteristics, they can be classified into two categories: (1) man, and (2) all other things. Man is created to be the image of God, and thus he is called the substantial object in the image (image substantial object) of God. All other things resemble God symbolically, and thus are called symbolic substantial objects of God.

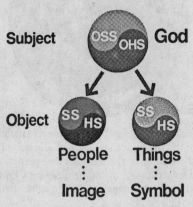

Any substantial object containing dual characteristics which resemble the dual characteristics of God is called an *individual truth body*. As we have seen, every individual truth body has within itself Sung Sang and Hyung Sang and Positivity and Negativity, which are derived from and resemble the Original Sung Sang, Original Hyung Sang, Original Positivity, and Original Negativity within God.

Let us sum up the relationship between God and the Creation as seen from the viewpoint of dual characteristics. The Creation is God's substantial object, consisting of individual truth bodies which are the manifestations of God's dual characteristics in image (man) and symbol (all other things) forms.

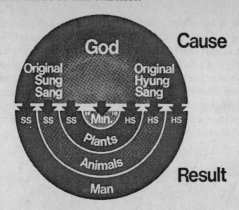

When we look at God and the Creation as a whole, the relationship between God and the Creation corresponds to that between Sung Sang and Hyung Sang. God is the invisible, internal cause and the Sung Sang, masculine subject to Creation; the Creation is the visible, external result and the Hyung Sang, feminine object of God.

II. UNIVERSAL PRIME FORCE, GIVE AND TAKE ACTION, AND THE FOUR POSITION FOUNDATION

A. Universal Prime Force

As God told Moses in Exodus 3:14, ". . . 'I AM WHO I AM.' " God existed before time and space and transcends time and space. God is an eternal, self-existing, and absolute being. Therefore, the fundamental force for his being should also be eternal, self-existing, and absolute. This original force was not created, but simply has existed within God from the beginning, transcendent of time and space. This force is called the Universal Prime Force; it is the fundamental force of God, the Creator. It is also the fundamental force of the Creation—the force with which God endows every being, or individual truth body, when it is created as God's substantial object.

B. Give and Take Action

1. The Meaning of Give and Take Action

Each being which is created by God has the essential characteristics of Sung Sang and Hyung Sang and Positivity and Negativity. Then, do these beings exist as individuals, separately and unrelated to one another, or do they have some kind of reciprocal relationship? Though each individual being seems to exist independently of all others, the entire Creation originates from the Ideal of God, who is the being of harmonized dual characteristics. Therefore, each created being does not exist independently, but is created to exist through reciprocal relationships.

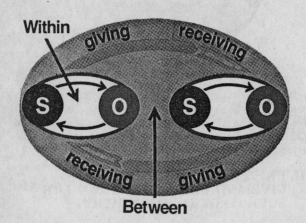

Give & Take Action

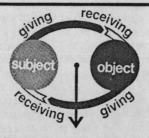

Forces for existence, development, reproduction

The ideal reciprocal relationship is established when subject and object have a good giving and receiving relationship. This good giving and receiving between subject and object is initiated by the Universal Prime Force and is called *Give and Take Action*. When the subject and object aspects within a being and between beings are engaged in Give and Take Action, all the forces necessary for its existence, reproduction, and action are generated.

Let us consider a few examples. The body maintains its life through the Give and Take Action of the arteries and veins, and of inhalation and exhalation. An individual is able to achieve his purpose of existence through the Give and Take Action between mind and body. A family or society exists through the Give and Take Action between individuals and groups. Material things come into being and maintain their existence when the subject and object elements within them generate harmonious movement and physicochemical reactions through Give and Take Action. Both plants and animals maintain their functions through Give and Take Action among their various organs and systems. And we find that even the solar system exists through the Give and Take Action between the sun and the planets in their orbital movements.

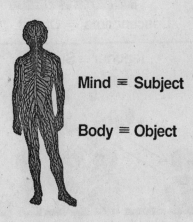

Mind $\equiv$ Subject

Body $\equiv$ Object

Parents ≡ Subject

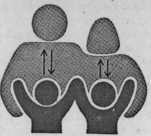

Children ≡ Object

Grandparents ≡ Subject

Descendants ≡ Object

Teacher ≡ Subject

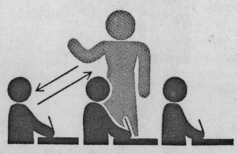

Students ≡ Object

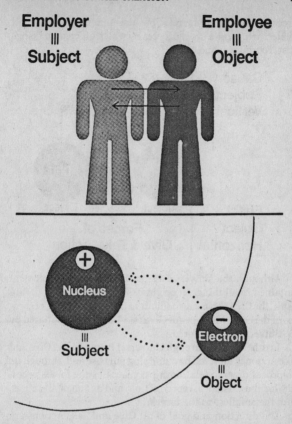

2. The Relationship between Universal Prime Force and the Forces of Give and Take Action

The *Forces of Give and Take Action* are the forces generated wthen a subject and an object have good Give and Take Action with each other. This action is initiated by the Universal Prime Force, and so the Universal Prime Force is causal and *vertical* and in the subject position to the Forces of Give and Take Action, which are resultant and *horizontal* and in the object position. The Universal Prime Force originates in God and is the force which God projects into each being at the time of its creation. The Forces of Give and Take Action are the

forces manifested in the relationships among and within all
created beings, and are the forces by which all created beings
exist, reproduce, and act.

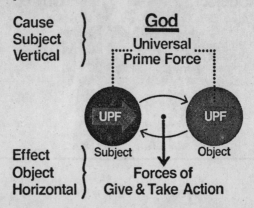

Cause
Subject
Vertical

God
Universal
Prime Force

UPF   UPF

Subject   Object

Effect
Object
Horizontal

Forces of
Give & Take Action

Although the Universal Prime Force is a basic element
contained in all things, it originates in one source, God. As a
result, the Creation is harmonious in its myriad forms, regardless of the countless types of Give and Take Action initiated by
the Universal Prime Force.

In other words, through Universal Prime Force, Give and
Take Action is directed by a unifying purpose and, through its
reciprocal organic relationships, generates the forces necessary for the existence, reproduction, and action of all things,
from the smallest to the largest.

The direction and goal of all Give and Take Actions are
controlled by Universal Prime Force. Give and Take Action
exists not only so that a subject and object can fulfill their
individual purposes, but also for the greater purpose of unifying all things. The ultimate purpose of Give and Take Action
is to have subject and object unite and develop to a greater
and higher dimension. The individual being which the subject
and object become when they unite then strives for Give and
Take Action with a corresponding counterpart of this greater
dimension, and by uniting they develop into a still higher
being. Thus, all things have both the purpose of self-
maintenance and the purpose of maintaining the whole;
therefore the universe can be said to be one huge organic body

of interpenetrating, harmonized dual purposes. (This will be explained further in the section "The Purpose of the Creation.")

3. The Relationship between God and Man in Terms of Give and Take Action

Next, let us consider the relationship between God and man in terms of Give and Take Action. The fact that God gave the first human ancestors his commandment (Gen 2:17) means that man is created to respond to God by keeping that commandment. Human beings were originally meant to maintain perfect Give and Take Action with God. An individual becomes a perfect object to God when he resembles the perfection of God and incarnates God's character (Mt 5:48). Then he automatically has a full Give and Take relationship with God and becomes one with God's Will, and God becomes the center of his thinking, behavior, and life (Jn 14:20). If the first human beings had established a vertical relationship with God through perfect Give and Take Action, their descendants also would have been able to maintain perfect Give and Take Action with him. With this perfect vertical relationship established with God himself, all individuals would have been able to maintain harmonious relationships with each other and live for the sake of each other, thus realizing the Kingdom of Heaven on earth. Through the fall of the first human beings,

this Give and Take relationship with God was cut off, and therefore each person has been unable to maintain a harmonious Give and Take relationship with God and with fellow human beings.

The Messiah is God's Son and becomes one with God through having a full Give and Take relationship. Fallen people should live a life of faith and attend the Messiah as their central subject. A fallen individual should become the object who will serve the Messiah absolutely because by Give and Take Action with the Messiah a fallen person becomes one with the Messiah, who is his mediator with God, and so can thereby restore his Give and Take relationship with God. Therefore, Jesus is called the "mediator" (1 Tim 2:5) and " '. . . the way, and the truth, and the life . . .' " (Jn 14:6) for fallen man.

As the term Give and Take Action implies, the action is first giving, and then receiving, not receiving, and then giving. The very fact that God created means that he gave of himself. In other words, he sacrificed himself for his Creation. Thus it is heavenly law that giving precedes receiving. However, fallen man fails to return even after he receives—and it is this way of life that gives rise to problems.

Jesus came to serve mankind with love and sacrifice: " '. . . the Son of man came not to be served, but to serve . . .' " (Mt 20:28). Jesus also taught directly concerning the principle of Give and Take Action when he said, " 'Judge not, that you be not judged. For with the judgment you pronounce you will be judged, and the measure you give will be the measure you get' " (Mt 7:2) and " '. . . whatever you wish that men would do to you, do so to them . . .' " (Mt 7:12).

C. Origin-Division-Union Action, the Three Objects Purpose, and the Four Position Foundation

1. Origin-Division-Union Action

The dual characteristics of God, who is the invisible, subject being, produce substantial subject and object beings. Through the action of the Universal Prime Force a subject being and an object being form a reciprocal base and engage in Give and Take Action. The step prior to Give and Take Action is that of establishing a reciprocal base. It is possible when the subject and object put priority on the *purpose for the whole* rather than on their *individual purposes*. When subject and object beings perform Give and Take Action, they become one, thus forming a union which becomes a new object to God.

This union is the substantial realization of the purpose for the whole which the subject and object hold in common. The union is the fruit or result caused by the action on the subject and object of the purpose element within the Universal Prime Force. In brief, *Origin-Division-Union Action* is the course of development of the force that begins in God (the Origin), divides, and then unites again.

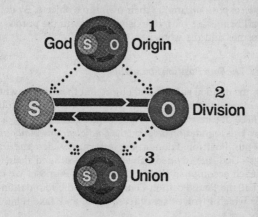

2. Three Objects Purpose

When each of the four beings—the origin, the subject and the object, and their resulting union—takes a subject position to the other three, the *Three Objects Standard* is formed. Then, through the Universal Prime Force each subject performs Give and Take Action with its three objects, and is united with each, fulfilling the *Three Objects Purpose*.

As was already explained, the basis for the existence of an individual being cannot be established by that being alone. The *basis for existence* can be established only when a being has an ideal object or subject with which it has Give and Take

Action. When a being in the subject position has three ideal
objects for the purpose of Give and Take Action it has a complete base for existence. Thus, only through fulfilling the
Three Objects Purpose can a being fulfill its purpose for existing.

If Adam and Eve had become perfect as individual embodiments of God's nature and had then become husband and
wife and borne children embodying goodness, an ideal family
of goodness would have been established. In that family,
Adam, Eve, and their children would each have fulfilled the
Three Objects Purpose. Each would consider that among its
three object beings God would be the first with whom he
should have a Give and Take relationship. That is, the divided
subject and object and their union should each set God in the
first object position among their own three objects. By doing
this, all beings are harmoniously united with the purpose of
the cosmos and the whole.

3. The Four Position Foundation

When the divided subject and object and their union, which
come into being through Origin-Division-Union Action, fulfill
the Three Objects Purpose, they form an eternal foundation of
power. This foundation is called the *Four Position Foundation*.
The Four Position Foundation is formed when the four
beings—God, the divided subject and object, and their union—each accomplish their Three Objects Purpose. We can
say that the Four Position Foundation is the foundation of
power which involves six different Give and Take relationships.

The ideal Four Position Foundation is established when
subject and object unite through ideal Give and Take Action,
which is centered on God. The Four Position Foundation is the
basic foundation upon whch God can operate. It is also the
basic foundation of goodness through which the Purpose of
God's Creation is accomplished. As will be explained more
fully later, God's Purpose for the Creation is fulfilled through
the Three Blessings which God promised to man, and this is
done by establishing Four Position Foundations.

When the mind (subject) and body (object) of a person
perform ideal Give and Take Action (centered on God (origin)), they form an ideal person, with unified mind and body

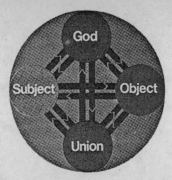

Four Position Foundation

(union), and an individual Four Position Foundation is realized. When husband and wife perform ideal Give and Take Action, they create a family which is a perfect object to God, and the family level Four Position Foundation is realized. When man and the things of the Creation enter into ideal Give and Take Action, the Creation as a whole becomes God's perfect object, and a Four Position Foundation for dominion is realized. In all cases, God is the origin and center. This means that God's Heart and Will of goodness are the center. Therefore, the Four Position Foundation is the basic foundation of goodness which acccomplishes the Purpose of God's Creation.

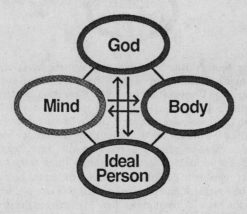

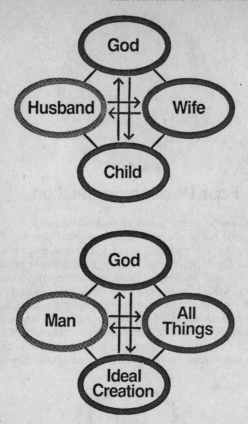

The Four Position Foundation is also the basis of the frequent use of the numbers *three, four, seven,* and *twelve* in the Bible and the Dispensation for Restoration (see Chapters 8-16). The Four Position Foundation must be established through the three-stage process of Origin-Division-Union Action. Since the realization of the Four Position Foundation is through a three-stage process, there are also three stages in the growing period (see Section IV B), and 'three' is the number that represents completion. From a structural point of view, the Four Position Foundation consists of four elements. This is the basis for the number 'four' symbolizing the structure required for the realization of God's Ideal.

Since the Four Position Foundation consists of four diffe-rent elements and is realized through a three-stage process, it is also the basis for the frequent symbolic use of the numbers 'seven' and 'twelve'. 'Twelve' is also the number of different directions of movement, in the Give and Take relationships between the four entities in the Four Position Foundation. The numbers 'seven' and 'twelve' represent perfection or completion of the Four Position Foundation.

III. THE PURPOSE OF THE CREATION

A. God's Purpose for Creating

Each being has its own purpose of existence. If a created thing loses its purpose for existing, it should be discarded. If the purpose for existing is so vital, then what is man's purpose of existence?

The purpose for existing is not determined by the created being itself; its true purpose is determined by its creator. Therefore, we must know God's Purpose for the Creation in order to understand the true purpose for man and the cosmos. Why did God, who is almighty and absolute, begin to create?

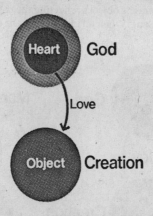

The most essential aspect of God is Heart. Heart is the impulse to love an object and is the fountain and motivator of love. It is the nature of Heart to seek an object to love. This nature of Heart is God's motive for making the Creation. That is, God, whose essence is Heart, feels joy when he can love an object that he created. If there is no object, God cannot satisfy his impulse to express care and love, which springs limitlessly from within himself. God made the Creation to be the object which he could love.

We can see in Genesis 1 that whenever God added to his Creation, he said that it was good to behold. God wanted his creations to be objects of goodness and happiness to him. The reason he wanted the Creation to be the object of his Heart is so that he could love it and receive the satisfaction and joy of loving.

B. How Is Joy Produced?

Let us think about how we feel joy. Joy is not created by an individual alone, but only through our having an object which reflects our own natures. Joy is felt through the stimulation a subject feels when its own nature is reflected in an object, whether the object is visible or invisible. For example, a painter feels joy both when he has a stimulating vision or idea as his object and when his vision or idea stands before him as a substantial painting. Joy comes about as a result of the stimulation felt from the object's reflecting the painter's Sung Sang and Hyung Sang. When an idea itself is the object, the stimu-

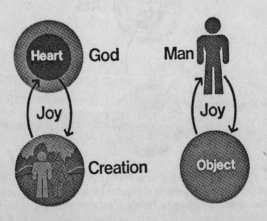

lation derived from it is not substantial; therefore, the joy derived from it cannot be substantial either. For instance, though an artist may feel joy from an inspiration or idea that he has, that joy is not as full or complete as the joy that he feels when the finished work which embodies his inspiration stands before him. We receive the strongest stimulation from relationships with concrete or substantial objects. Consequently we feel the greatest joy from objects which are substantial. This attribute in man comes from God. Thus, we can understand that God feels joy when he feels his Original Sung Sang and Original Hyung Sang reflected by his Creation.

C. Man—The Object of Heart for God's Joy
The Three Blessings

The Creation is made in the image of God's Original Sung Sang and Original Hyung Sang. Man is a substantial object in the image of God, whereas all the other things of the Creation are substantial objects that are symbols of God. Therefore, man is the object (responsive being) that is closest to God's Heart.

God gave a commandment to the first human ancestors, Adam and Eve, saying, " '. . . of the tree of the knowledge of good and evil you shall not eat, for in the day that you eat of it you shall die' " (Gen 2:17). This shows that God directly conveyed his Will and Heart of love to man. There is no reason that God would convey his Heart to man if God had created man incapable of feeling God's Heart. So we can understand that man was created as the object who is able to understand and respond to God's Will and Heart and thus is the being closest to God's Heart. Thus man was created as the object that would directly receive God's Heart and bring him joy. Man is created as God's child.

As was already explained, the Four Position Foundation is the basic foundation through which God can operate. When man completes the Four Position Foundation by fulfilling the Three Blessings, centered on God's ideal of love, he becomes the object of Heart which returns perfect joy to God. Then God's purpose for man is fulfilled. Genesis 1:28 summarizes the purpose for God's creation of man in what are called the *Three Blessings*.

Three   Blessings

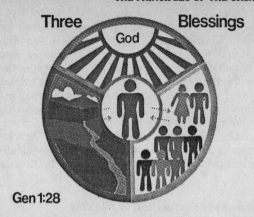

Gen 1:28

1. The First Blessing

God's First Blessing is man's ability to perfect his character. By performing proper Give and Take Action between his mind and body and uniting them centered on God, a person forms the Four Position Foundation on the individual level and becomes the temple of God (1 Cor 3:16). When such perfected individuals become completely one with God in Heart (Jn 14:20), they come to have God's character and constantly have God at the center of their thoughts and actions.

When a person achieves God's First Blessing, he will naturally share God's feelings as his own. Thus, it would be abso-

First Blessing

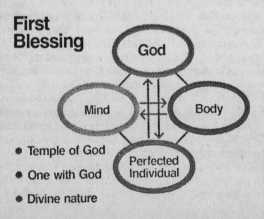

* Temple of God
* One with God
* Divine nature

lutely impossible for such a person to commit a crime, for by doing so he would feel the same grief that he would cause God. Rather, such a person would only want to be a perfect object to God. When a person accomplishes individual perfection, he becomes the complete object of God's Heart and satisfies God's impulse to love. In other words, if man had fulfilled the First Blessing, he would have become the object of Heart which God desires to love. Then he would have been the fruit of God's *vertical love*.

2. The Second Blessing

God's Second Blessing is man's ability to have an ideal family. Adam and Eve were to attain individual perfection and then become husband and wife and give birth to children with natures of goodness, forming a sinless family. This God-centered family Four Position Foundation would have fulfilled God's Second Blessing.

By becoming husband and wife on the foundation of having perfected themselves through God's vertical love, Adam and Eve would have completely realized God's *horizontal love*. From the viewpoint of Heart, the fact that God allowed man to have children upon having fulfilled God's horizontal love is a great blessing, for by having children man can feel the vertical love that God feels toward man.

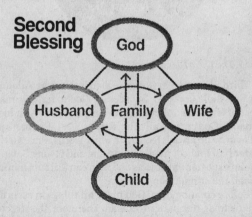

If Adam and Eve had attained perfection, formed the first family, and given birth to children with natures of goodness, they would have been the True Father and True Mother (centered on God) of all mankind—that is, they would have become the eternal True Parents and True Ancestors of all mankind, establishing the Kingdom of Heaven. The basic unit of the Kingdom of Heaven is the true family, the basic Four Position Foundation.

The true family is the basic foundation for God's vertical and horizontal love and the perfect object of God's Heart. With this true family as a base, a true society, true nation, and true world would have been realized. This is God's Will. If Adam and Eve had created such a family and world, it would have been the Kingdom of Heaven on earth.

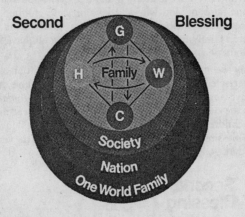

3. The Third Blessing

The Third Blessing that God gave man is the right of dominion over the whole Creation. In order for God to feel joy, man, as object of His Heart, should always experience joy in his life. Therefore, God created all things to be objects for man's joy so that man could always feel joy. In other words, since all things substantially reflect man's Sung Sang and Hyung Sang, they are man's substantial objects and man can feel substantial joy through the stimulation they give.

Before creating man, God made all things in accordance with the image (or pattern) of man. Therefore, the structures, functioning, and characteristics of animals are contained within man. In addition, man has the structure and characteristics of plants and minerals. Since all things resemble man's Sung Sang and Hyung Sang, man can love all things and feel joy through the stimulation they give. Man's dominion of love over all things and his attainment of joy from them is the realization of God's Third Blessing to man.

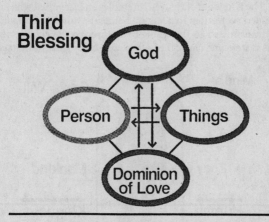

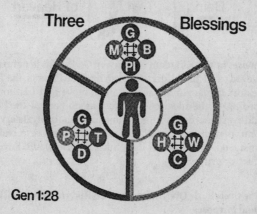

The world where the Three Blessings are realized is the ideal world in which God and man, and man and the cosmos, are in complete harmony. Such a world is the Kingdom of

Heaven on earth. As will be more fully explained later, man was created to live in the Kingdom of Heaven on earth in a life of total oneness wtih God, the source of life and goodness. When his physical self died after such a life on earth, his spirit self would leave his physical self and pass into the spirit world. There, he would live eternally in the Kingdom of Heaven, in the dominion of God's perfect love.

The Kingdom of Heaven resembles an individual who has attained perfection. In a human being, the mind's commands are transmitted to the whole body through the central nervous system and cause the body to act so as to maintain itself.

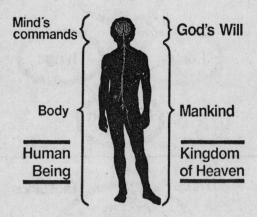

Mind's commands — God's Will

Body — Mankind

Human Being — Kingdom of Heaven

Likewise, in the Kingdom of Heaven, God's Will is naturally conveyed to all his children through the True Parents, the True Ancestors of mankind, causing all to move and harmonize according to the Ideal of God. Just as no part of the body would ever rebel against the commands of the central nervous system, perfect man would feel no antagonism or rebellion against God's dominion of love. Such a world would have no conflict or crime.

D. The Creation is One Interconnected Body of Beings with Dual Purposes

Every existing being consists of two aspects: Sung Sang and Hyung Sang. Likewise, every being has dual purposes, the

Sung Sang purpose and the Hyung Sang purpose. The Sung Sang purpose is the *purpose for the whole* and the Hyung Sang purpose is the *individual purpose*. Purpose for the whole is the purpose directed toward the preservation and development of the whole. Individual purpose is the purpose directed toward the preservation, strengthening, and development of the self. Man's individual purpose is to preserve and maintain his existence. On the other hand, he has a whole-oriented purpose of life—to make a certain contribution to his family, society, and nation as a member of these bodies.

Not only human beings, but everything from the universe to the smallest sub-atomic particle has dual purposes. The individual purpose and the purpose for the whole are not independent, but rather are related and interdependent.

The purpose for the whole is also secondarily a purpose for the betterment of the individual. The individual purpose is not separate from the purpose for the whole, and the purpose for the whole cannot continue to exist without guaranteeing the individual purpose. The Creation is an organic body intertwined with dual purposes. Therefore we call it an 'inter-connected body with dual purposes'.

Dual Aspects of Purpose

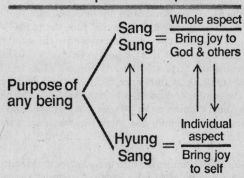

Of all the purposes directed beyond the self, the supreme purpose for all things is to serve man's needs, in other words, to give joy to man, and the supreme purpose for man is to offer joy to God. Therefore man and all things have the purpose to serve God and give joy to him.

IV. THE GROWING PERIOD FOR CREATED BEINGS

The order of creation for all things is recorded in Genesis 1. God's Creation began with his creating light out of chaos, void, and darkness, and required a period described as six "days" before culminating in the creation of man. But since 2 Peter 3:8 says that ". . . with the Lord one day is as a thousand years, and a thousand years as one day," we can understand that these days were not actual twenty-four-hour days. What Genesis 1 does tell us is that the universe did not come into being instantaneously, but was created through six gradual periods.

A. The Growing Period for Created Beings

The fact that it took time for the entire Creation to be created implies that a growing period is necessary for each created being to mature. If time were not necessary for an individual being to reach perfection, then there is also no reason why time would have been necessary in creating the universe. Let us look at some additional reasons why we can say that a growing period is necessary in order for created beings to reach maturity.

If the word "day" in chapter one of Genesis does not refer to the familiar twenty-four-hour day, then the terms "evening" and "morning" cannot be interpreted in the usual sense either. Let us consider this passage in Genesis 1: "And there was evening and there was morning, one day" (Gen 1:5). After one stage of God's creation work, lasting through evening and night, the coming of morning was regarded by God as part of the first day. Continuing in Genesis, chapter one, God said, "And there was evening and there was morning, a second day. . . . a third day. . . . a fourth day. . . . a fifth day. . . . a sixth day."

"Morning" signifies the time period when the Ideal for the Creation was first realized. "Evening" signifies the period when God finished creating. Including the morning that came after the evening and night, God counted all these as one day. God indicates the time required for his Ideal for the Creation to be realized. The period from the point where God begins creating to the point where the Ideal for the Creation is realized is a growing period for all created beings and is represented by the night, the period between evening and morning.

The Fall of man also implies that there is a growing period, for if man had been created perfect, then there would have been no possibility of his falling. If a perfect being of goodness, resembling God, were to fall, then we would have to conclude that goodness itself is imperfect and therefore question whether God is really perfect.

Prior to the Fall, man had not yet perfected himself; he was growing toward perfection and could choose either the way of life or the way of death (Gen 2:17). God's Ideal for the Creation is perfection; so he would not create man to be imperfect. Yet man fell; so he must have been imperfect. We can therefore conclude that when the Fall took place man was in an uncompleted stage, in a period in which he was growing toward perfection.

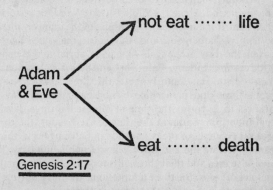

B. The Three Stages of the Growing Period

God's entire work of creation took place through three stages: evening, night, and morning. The Four Position Foundation is established through the three stages of origin, division, and union. Similarly, the growing period is comprised of three stages: *formation*, *growth*, and *completion*. So, all creatures attain perfection by going through the formation, growth, and completion stages which constitute the growing period.

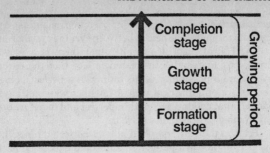

Some examples of the number 'three' which occur in the natural world are: the three kingdoms—animal, plant, and mineral; the three states of matter—solid, liquid, and gas; the three parts to most animals—head, body, and limbs; the three parts to most plants—roots, stem, and leaves; and the three layers of the earth—crust, mantle, and core.

In falling, man failed to go through the three stages of the growing period. Since the Bible is God's Word for restoring fallen man, it includes many examples of the number 'three': the Trinity—Father, Son, and Holy Spirit; the three stages of heaven; the three archangels—Lucifer, Gabriel, and Michael; the three sons of Adam—Cain, Abel, and Seth; the three sons of Noah—Shem, Ham, and Japheth; the three decks of Noah's ark; the three kinds of sacrifices by Abraham; the three days of darkness in Egypt at the time of Moses; the three days of separation from Satan at the time of the Exodus; the three forty-year courses of the restoration of Canaan; Jesus' thirty years of private life and three years of public ministry; the three wise men and their three gifts to Jesus; the three major disciples of Jesus; the three temptations; the three prayers at Gethsemane; and Jesus' three days in the tomb.

C. God's Direct Dominion

After going through the growing period, a person reaches perfection and then dwells in the realm of God's *direct dominion*. Man was created to be the *object of God's Heart*. It is in the realm of God's direct dominion that man becomes one in Heart with God (becomes the object of God's Heart) and God rules man by love. The realm of God's direct dominion is the realm of perfection, the realm which a person reaches when he perfects himself; it is the place where man is under God's direct control.

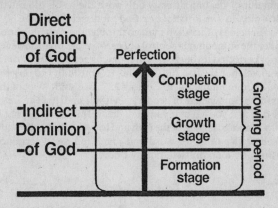

Man enters God's direct dominion as he accomplishes the individual Four Position Foundation by realizing the union of mind and body centered on God. It is in the realm of God's direct dominion that husband and wife establish the family Four Position Foundation centered on God. Thus, the realm of God's direct dominion is the realm where the purpose for creating man is fulfilled.

God created all things for man, to be ruled by man. A perfect person, who is centered on God, is to govern all things when they are mature. This is man's direct dominion over all things. God rules all things indirectly, through man.

D. God's Indirect Dominion

How does God rule people and all things while they are still in the growing period, in an immature state? God, a perfect being, can rule only perfect objects. Therefore, people who are in an imperfect state cannot be objects to God. God can rule them only indirectly, through *The Principle*.* Thus, from the viewpoint of dominion, the growing period is the realm of

---

* When printed in italics, '*The Principle*' refers to the basic active universal law that originates in God and pervades the Creation. The term 'non-Principle' refers to a violation of *The Principle*.

God's *indirect dominion*. God, as the source of *The Principle*, relates to people and things indirectly while they are still immature,† dealing directly only with the result of growth according to *The Principle*, or God's indirect dominion.

All beings other than man go through the growing period under the autonomous control of *The Principle*. Man, however, is not perfected through the autonomous action of *The Principle* alone, but by also fulfilling his responsibility to observe God's commandments. In Genesis 2:17, God said, " '. . . of the tree of the knowledge of good and evil you shall not eat, for in the day that you eat of it you shall die.' " This indicates that it is up to man to not eat of the fruit and to perfect himself. Man's disobedience of God's Word and man's fall are determined entirely by man himself, not by God.

Perfection

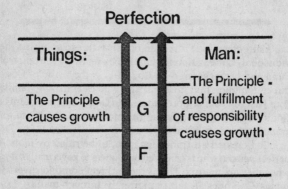

Things: C   Man:

The Principle
causes growth   G   The Principle
and fulfillment
of responsibility
causes growth

F

Therefore, man's perfection cannot be accomplished through God's responsibility alone, that is, through the autonomous action of *The Principle* (or God's control during the growing period). Man cannot think that God will take responsibility for man's perfection; man will realize his perfection only when he fulfills his own responsibility, even though that responsibility is very small when compared with God's responsibility. Man fell because he failed to obey God's commandment.

---

† When a person reaches perfection, God dwells in that person (1 Cor 3:16); so it can be said that God actually relates to the things of the Creation directly.

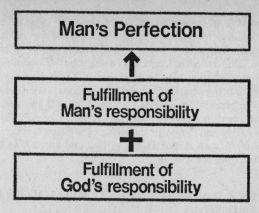

After seeing the result of man's failure to fulfill his responsibility—that is, the Fall—we may well ask why God gave man a portion of responsibility. In short, it was for man to qualify as lord of the cosmos. The true right of *direct dominion* belongs only to the creator. Nevertheless, God wanted man, a created being, to have direct dominion over all things. In order for man to rightfully have this dominion, God had to have man, who is a created being, inherit the nature of a creator. That is, God had to have man inherit His creatorship. Man is to do this by voluntarily participating in his own creation. In short, a person is not perfected by God's *Principle* and power alone. Man's own responsibility is a necessary element, although it is small when compared with that of God.

God gave this responsibility to man as the means for man to achieve perfection. So, God cannot interfere with man's responsibility. God let man participate in and cooperate with His work of creation because it is by man's doing so that man is to become God's heir. Thus, man's responsibility is a precious grace given to him by God. Yet, it is by failing to accomplish their responsibility that the first human ancestors fell. Therefore, man's responsibility is an absolutely necessary element in the dispensation for salvation, through which God restores fallen man to his original state.

God's dispensation for salvation has been prolonged for so long because the central persons in his Dispensation for Restoration have repeatedly failed to accomplish their responsibility, with which even God cannot interfere. As expressed in

John 3:18, no matter how much blessing and love God may grant, salvation cannot come to those who have no faith. Matthew 7:21 says, " 'Not everyone who says to me, "Lord, Lord," shall enter the kingdom of heaven, but he who does the will of my Father who is in heaven.' " This tells us that a person's doing what his Heavenly Father desires is entirely his own responsibility. Why can't a merciful God give even to those who do not ask? Why can't God enable those who do not seek to find and those who do not knock to enter? It is because it is man's own responsibility to seek and knock, and God cannot interfere with it.

V. THE INVISIBLE SUBSTANTIAL WORLD AND THE VISIBLE SUBSTANTIAL WORLD, CENTERED ON MAN

A. The Invisible Substantial World and the Visible Substantial World

It is very important for our life of faith that we correctly understand the issues concerning life after death and man's *spirit self*. Let us examine these questions: Does man have a spirit self? If so, what does it look like? What is the *spirit world* like? What is the relationship of the spirit world to the *physical world*? What principles govern the spirit world?

Much information is being collected these days in relation to the spirit world. However, it does not seem possible to explain systematically or to understand clearly these apparently complex phenomena. As a result, the important questions mentioned above have confused and even dismayed many people, and this has affected their religious lives. Some logical explanation is necessary for the many descriptions of a spirit world that appear in the Bible, such as the three stages of the spirit world mentioned in 2 Corinthians 12:2, the appearance of Moses and Elijah with Jesus on the mount of the Transfiguration, and the many examples concerning heaven that are recorded in the Book of Revelation.

The Creation is not composed of only the Visible Substantial World, which may be compared with the human body; it also consists of the Invisible Substantial World, which may be compared with the human mind. The Invisible Substantial World is the Sung Sang part of the cosmos and is called the spirit world; the Visible Substantial World is the Hyung Sang part of the cosmos and is called the physical world. We can understand the relationship between these two worlds by considering the relationship between mind and body. Our physical body is limited by time; it cannot transcend the present moment. Our physical body is a being of the moment; it eventually becomes old and returns to the soil. Our mind is not limited by time; no barrier of time can stop it. It can freely reflect on the past and long for the future, if it wishes to do so; it is eternal.

The physical body is also limited by space. It occupies a specific place at each moment and cannot be in another place at the same time. The mind, however, is not limited by space. The mind does not leave any visible traces in the world of space and can exist in any place, if it desires to. The mind is so limitless that it can embrace the universe, if it expands its dimensions.

So, man consists of a body, which is limited and transitory, and a mind, which is limitless and eternal. The sphere of action for the limited, transitory body is the Visible Substantial World, and the sphere of action for the limitless, eternal mind is the Invisible Substantial World. Just as man's mind is subject and motivator of the body, the Invisible Substantial World is subject and motivator of the Visible Substantial World (Heb 8:5).

B. The Position of Man in the Cosmos

Then what is man's relationship to these two worlds? In Genesis 2:7, it says, ". . . the Lord God formed man of dust from the ground . . ." which means that God created man's *physical self* with the basic elements of the Visible Substantial World. That God ". . . breathed into his nostrils the breath of life" (Gen 2:7) means that he fashioned man's spirit out of the basic elements of the spirit world to form what in The Principle is called the spirit self.

The position of man in the cosmos is as follows. First of all God planned man as the microcosm of the cosmos. God created the cosmos first, but he created it based on the pattern of the Sung Sang and the Hyung Sang of the ideal human being, whom he planned to create later. Man's spirit self is an encapsulation of the Invisible Substantial World, and his physical body is an encapsulation of the Visible Substantial World. God made man as the microcosm of both the Invisible and the Visible Substantial Worlds. So man is called a microcosm.

Secondly, God created man to be the ruler of both realms of the cosmos (Gen 1:28, 1 Cor 6:3). To put it another way, God created man's physical self from the elements that make up the physical world and gave man dominion over the physical world through his five physical senses. Similarly, God created the spirit self from the elements that make up the spirit world and gave man dominion over the spirit world through his five spiritual senses. Man was originally created with two sets of five senses, one for the physical self and the other for the spirit self. As a result of the Fall, man's five spiritual senses became dulled and man became unable to perceive the spirit world, which can be perceived only by the spirit mind and spirit body. Those whose spiritual senses have been restored by God's grace and a religious life can experience this world, either partially or completely (the Book of Revelation, 2 Cor 12:2, the Transfiguration (Mt 17:2)).

Thirdly, God created man to be the medium of interaction and the center for the harmony of the Creation. The spirit world and physical world cannot communicate directly with each other. When man's physical self and spirit self become one through Give and Take Action, the physical world and the spirit world will communicate with one another through man.

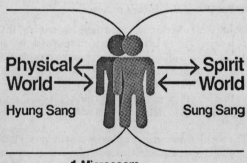

Physical ← → Spirit
World → ← World

Hyung Sang   Sung Sang

1 Microcosm
2 Ruler
3 Medium of harmony

From what has been said above, we can summarize man's position in the Creation as follows: man is the microcosm of the spirit world and the physical world; he was created to be the ruler of these two worlds; and he is the center for the harmony of these two worlds. However, because of man's Fall, the Creation lost its ruler and center of harmony. Thus,

> ... the creation waits with eager longing for the revealing of the sons of God; ... because the creation itself will be set free from its bondage to decay and obtain the glorious liberty of the children of God. We know that the whole creation has been groaning in travail together until now....
>
> (Rom 8:19-23)

C. The Relationship between the Spirit Self and the Physical Self

1. The Structure and Functioning of a Human Being

a. The physical self

The physical self consists of the *physical mind* and the *physical body*. The physical mind is the subject part of the physical self, controlling the physiological functions of existence, reproduction, and action. Thus, the physical mind is similar to an animal's instinct, manifesting such desires as the desire for nourishment and the desire for reproduction. The physical body consists of various organs, muscles, and bones. In order for man's physical self to grow in good health, it must take in air and sunlight, which are nutrients of a Positive (Yang) nature, and also take in various foods and water which are nutrients of a Negative (Um) nature. The physical self returns the *Vitality Element* to the spirit self.

b. The spirit self

The spirit self was created to be the subject of the physical self; it can be perceived through our spiritual senses. Even though a person may believe in the existence of the spirit self as a result of his life of faith, since fallen man has very poorly developed spiritual senses, he still has many questions about what happens to the spirit self after its separation from the physical self at death. When separated from the physical self, does the spirit dissipate like smoke? Is it just a spirit which leaves the physical self? Does it go to the spirit world with a substantial form? If it does go to the spirit world, does it merely merge into God, or does it occupy a separate place in the spirit world? If so, what is the spirit like?

According to The Principle, just as each person has his own physical self, he also has his own spirit entity; so the spirit entity is called a spirit self. The spirit self is identical in appearance to the physical self, and it can communicate directly with God after it is perfect. After leaving the physical body at death, the spirit self lives for eternity in the spirit world. Man desires to live forever because he has a spirit self which has an eternal nature. The spirit self consists of a *spirit mind* and a *spirit body*. The spirit mind is the core of the spirit self, controlling the eternal life, love, and ideals of man. The spirit mind functions so that man lives a life of value, seeking for truth, beauty, and love. The spirit mind is the essence of the spirit self, is the subject of the spirit body, and is the place where God can dwell. The spirit body is the body of the spirit self, just as the physical body is the body of the physical self.

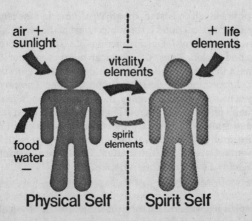

air +
sunlight

+ life
elements

vitality
elements

spirit
elements

Physical Self   **Spirit Self**

food
water
—

The spirit self needs nutrition for its growth and perfection. The positive (Yang) nutrient for the spirit self is the *Life Element* from God. The Life Element from God is the basic element that develops Heart within a person and develops him as a being of truth. On the other hand, the negative (Um) nutrient for the growth of the spirit self is the Vitality Element which comes from the physical self. When the physical self acts in accordance with God's Word, it projects good Vitality Element for the growth of the spirit self. The spirit self not only receives the Vitality Element from the physical self, but also projects in return a certain element which is called the *Spirit Element*. The Spirit Element is the element that gives joy and strength to the physical self.

c. The relationship between the spirit self and the physical self

As explained above, the relationship between the spirit self and the physical self is that of subject and object, with the spirit self growing and perfecting itself on the basis of its relationship with the physical self. The quality of a person's physical life is converted into Vitality Element and transferred to the spirit self. Thus, the quality of the spirit self is dependent upon the quality of the physical life. Accordingly, a spirit self that receives wholesome Vitality Element from the physical self becomes a being of goodness, whereas a spirit self that receives bad Vitality Element from the physical self will become evil. In order for an evil spirit self to become a good one, that person must repent while his spirit self is still in his physical self, for a person's evil spirit self is healed by receiving good Vitality Element through his repentance and faith in God's Word.

The most important aspect of the spirit self which has to be perfected through the physical self is a person's sensitivity to the love of God. It was explained earlier that God's Purpose for the Creation is fulfilled through the family (Four Position Foundation, the basic foundation in which his ideal of love can dwell. Therefore, only a spirit person who while on earth has fully perfected his sensitivity to love as a child, as a husband or wife, and as a parent, all centered on God, can go to the Kingdom of Heaven in the spirit world. The Kingdom of Heaven is ruled and harmonized by the love of God; it is the place where all are satisfied through God's love.

All created beings reach perfection through three growth stages. Based on the physical self, man's spirit self also goes through three stages of growth. A spirit self in the formation stage is called a *form spirit;* in the growth stage, a *life spirit;* and in the completion stage, a *divine spirit*.

The relationship between the physical self and the spirit self is like that between a tree and its fruit. A ripened fruit is harvested, whereas its vine returns to the earth. Likewise, because the spirit self was created to live for eternity, after separating from the physical body it remains and lives eternally in the spirit world, whereas the body returns to the earth. Many believe that man's physical body dies because he fell, but this is incorrect. God warned in Genesis 2:17 that " '. . . in the day that you eat of it you shall die.' " Adam and Eve "died" as a result of eating the *Fruit of the Tree of the Knowledge of Good and Evil*. Nevertheless, after Adam and Eve fell, they lived for several hundred years on earth and bore children. This means that the death caused by the Fall is not the death by which the physical body returns to the earth. As soon as the first ancestors fell by disobeying God's Word, their eternal spirit "died"—that is, their spirit selves, which could communicate with God, ceased to function. Ecclesiastes 12:7 says, ". . . the dust returns to the earth as it was, and the spirit returns to God who gave it." This indicates that the physical self's returning to the earth is in accordance with the natural order of the Creation. A more detailed explanation of this matter will be given later, in the chapter "Resurrection."

When a person lives in his physical body according to God's Ideal for the Creation, he will be living in the Kingdom of Heaven on earth, and the world where his perfected spirit self will go after his life on earth will be the Kingdom of Heaven in the spirit world.

However, since God's Purpose for the Creation is to be realized on earth, his first objective in the work of salvation must also be man on earth. Thus, God has over and over again sent his prophets to this faithless world and even sent the Messiah himself to earth. This crucial role of the physical life (and self) is why the Bible teaches that ". . . whatever you bind *on earth* shall be bound in heaven, and whatever you loose *on earth* shall be loosed in heaven" (emphases added) (Mt 18:18), and why it teaches us to pray that God's Ideal for the Creation should be realized on earth (Mt 6:10).

It is not God who determines whether a spirit person goes to the Kingdom of Heaven or to *hell*. It is each person himself who determines this through his daily life while in his physical body on earth. Each person goes to the place in the spirit world corresponding to the stage of development that his spirit self attained while he was on earth. God, the Messiah, and religion can only teach people how to avoid hell and show the way to the Kingdom of Heaven. Whether or not one receives the teachings of God and church is the responsibility of each individual.

In the world where the Purpose for the Creation is realized, Satan, sin, and hell cannot possibly exist. In God's Ideal for the Creation, only heaven was to exist. But, because of sin, man lost his original value and became like refuse. The place where this refuse is kept is what we call hell.

2. The Human Mind in terms of the Relationship between the Spirit Mind and Physical Mind

The relationship between the spirit mind and the physical mind is that of Sung Sang (internal character) and Hyung Sang (external form). When the spirit mind, which is subject, and physical mind, which is object, become one through Give and Take Action, a human mind is formed. In a perfect person, the spirit mind and the physical mind perform perfect Give and Take Action centered on God and unite, forming what is called the *original mind*. Man's original mind always directs him toward the Will and Purpose of God. When the physical body returns to the earth, the physical mind ceases to exist, but the original mind, which is formed through the interaction of the spirit mind and the physical mind, remains within the spirit self.

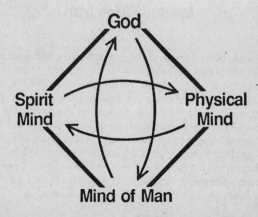

The spirit mind and the physical mind engage in Give and Take Action and unite centering on what man thinks is true. We call this union the *conscience* of man. A perfect human being always stands on the perfect truth. Therefore, the original mind and conscience should not diverge in two directions, but should be united. That is, the original mind and the conscience should relate as inner and outer aspects and always direct man toward God's Purpose and Will of goodness. Fallen man still has within him the original mind, which directs him toward goodness. However, fallen people have lost the absolute standard of goodness, and therefore their standards of conscience differ from one another according to their opinion of what is true. Wherever a different view or theology is held, a different direction of conscience will exist.

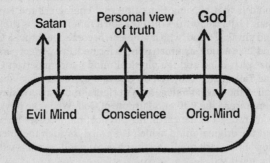

Mind of Fallen Man

Also, because man came under Satan's influence as a result of the Fall, his spirit mind cannot properly receive the Life Element from God and remains immature. Such a spirit mind is incapable of being in the subject position to the physical mind and is instead dominated by the physical mind. And when this immature spirit mind performs Give and Take Action with the physical mind which is under Satan's dominion, another mind is produced, one directed toward evil. We call this mind the *evil mind*. The original mind and conscience of man fight against this evil mind, which is against God's Will and direction, and direct man toward goodness.

CHAPTER TWO

The Fall

Every person has an original mind, which has the nature to pursue goodness and repel evil. But fallen people are unconsciously driven by an evil force to commit evil acts, contrary to the desires of their original mind. In Christianity, the one who controls this evil force is known as Satan. This chapter, "The Fall," makes clear the identity of Satan and the origin of evil.

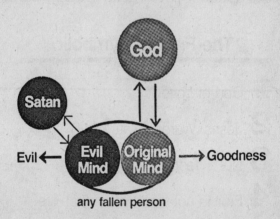

any fallen person

I. THE ROOT OF SIN

A. The Tree of Life and the Tree of the Knowledge of Good and Evil

Based on the Book of Genesis in the Bible, Christians have traditionally held the somewhat vague belief that the Original Sin and root of sin and evil was the first human ancestors' eating a piece of fruit—the Fruit of the Tree of the Knowledge of Good and Evil (for brevity, often referred to hereafter as the fruit of good and evil). However, is the fruit of good and evil a literal fruit, or is it a symbol, as are many other terms in the Bible? According to The Principle, it is a symbol.

How could a God of love, the parent of mankind, make such an attractive fruit and leave it in a place where it could be eaten by his children and cause them to fall (Gen 3:6)? Jesus said in Matthew 15:11, " '. . . not what goes into the mouth defiles a man. . . .' " How then could something edible cause man to fall? It is also inconceivable that the God of love created the fruit of good and evil to test man—so mercilessly as to ultimately cause his death—merely to see whether or not man would obey His Word. The fact that they ate the fruit, despite having been told that they would die, indicates that the fruit must represent something so extremely stimulating that their desire for it was even greater than their desire for life.

The Fruit is Symbolic

1 God of Love

2 Jesus' Words (Matt 15:11)

3 Not a Test

4 Fruit is not worth more than life

Before we can determine what the fruit of good and evil symbolizes, we must know what the Tree of the Knowledge of Good and Evil was. Yet the Tree of the Knowledge of Good and Evil is mentioned only a few times in the Bible. So, in order to determine what the Tree of the Knowledge of Good and Evil symbolizes, we will first study the Tree of Life, which, according to the Bible, stood with the Tree of the Knowledge of Good and Evil in the Garden of Eden (Gen 2:9, 2:17, 3:3) and is mentioned in numerous places throughout the Bible.

1. The Tree of Life

Proverbs 13:12 says, "Hope deferred makes the heart sick, but a desire fulfilled is a tree of life." The Tree of Life is the most fundamental hope of man. As Revelation 22:14 says, "Blessed are those who wash their robes [of sin and evil], that they may have the right to the tree of life and that they may enter the city by the gates." These passages show that attaining the Tree of Life will lead to happiness for fallen man. Then, what is this Tree of Life, such that it was the hope of the Israelites of the Old Testament Age and the hope of the Christians of the New Testament Age?

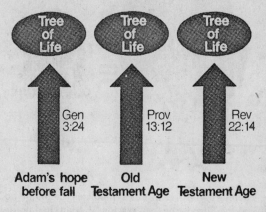

Gen 3:24 — Adam's hope before fall

Prov 13:12 — Old Testament Age

Rev 22:14 — New Testament Age

If fallen people are asked what the essence of happiness and hope is, each person will give a different answer. One person might answer that it is power, and another that it is wealth or knowledge. Then what has been the common hope of people of faith throughout the history of mankind? One thing is clear. If the innermost hope of fallen man is the Tree of Life, then the hope of Adam before the Fall also must have been the Tree of Life. The reason is that each person retains his original nature deep within himself, and thus longs for that which was originally desired before the Fall, but was lost. Genesis 3:22-24 shows that Adam desired to reach the Tree of Life, but because of his sin was not allowed to. Thus, the Tree of Life has remained as only a hope of fallen man.

Then what was this Tree of Life, the hope of the growing,

not-yet-perfected Adam? Could material possessions have
been the basic hope of Adam in the Garden of Eden, or power,
or any external concerns? Since he was to be lord of the
cosmos and to rule all things, there was no reason for Adam to
hope for more material possessions or power. If Adam had any
deep wish while he was still unperfected, it would only have
been to achieve his own perfection. In other words, his desire
would have been to become a man of perfect character—one
who has fulfilled the Ideal for the Creation.

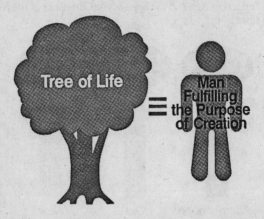

Therefore, the Tree of Life symbolizes the man who has
fulfilled the Purpose of the Creation. If Adam had not fallen
and had attained the Ideal for the Creation, then he would
have become the Tree of Life and he would have established
the Kingdom of Heaven on earth, which is the garden of the
Tree of Life. However, Adam fell, and God blocked his way to
the Tree of Life with a flaming sword (Gen 3:24).

Since Adam abandoned the Purpose of the Creation, he
became a false tree of life and bore descendants who were false
trees of life, thus establishing a garden of false trees of life,
rather than the garden of the trees of life. Therefore, in order to
establish the Kingdom of Heaven on earth, which is the garden of the trees of life, a true Tree of Life must appear in the
fallen world and engraft all mankind to himself. Knowing
that the Tree of Life represents Adam, we can then understand
that the Tree of Life in the Old Testament (Prov 13:12) repre-

sents Jesus (1 Cor 15:45), and the Tree of Life in the New Testament Book of Revelation (Rev 22:14) represents the returning Messiah. Furthermore, we can understand why the purpose of the dispensation for salvation is to restore the Tree of Life that was lost in the Garden of Eden (Gen 2:9) in the Tree of Life that is mentioned in the Book of Revelation (Rev 22:14).

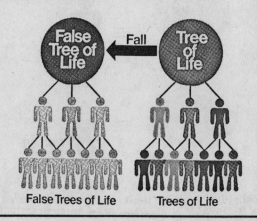

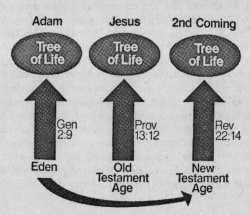

2. The Tree of the Knowledge of Good and Evil

In the Garden of Eden, God created Adam, and Eve to be his spouse. If in the midst of the garden there was a tree to

symbolize the man, isn't it likely that there would also be a
tree symbolizing the woman? Yes, and the Tree of the Knowledge of Good and Evil, which stood with the Tree of Life (Gen
2:9, 2:17, 3:3), is this tree.

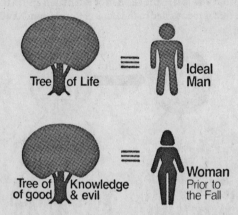

In the Bible, Jesus is at times symbolically represented as
a vine (Jn 15:5) or an olive tree (Rom 11:17). In a similar
fashion, Adam and Eve are represented by two trees, and
through this a clue has been provided concerning the secret of
man's Fall. To assert that there was a Tree of Life and a Tree of
the Knowledge of Good and Evil in the midst of the Garden of
Eden does not mean that there were two literal trees in the
geographical center of a literal garden, but rather means that
the two people, Adam and Eve, are the center and nucleus of
God's Ideal for the Creation. God's entire Ideal for the Creation
is to be fulfilled through man. When we see things in these
terms, we can see that the Tree of the Knowledge of Good and
Evil represented the woman, Eve. We must then conclude that
the fruit of this tree is somehow related to Eve. However, in
order to understand clearly what the fruit represents, we must
first determine the identity of the serpent.

B. The Identity of the Serpent

In Genesis 3 the Bible shows that it was a serpent that tempted
Eve to sin. However, the serpent referred to there cannot be a
serpent in the literal sense—it must be a symbol.

In Genesis 3 we also see that the "serpent" talked with the woman and that he understood that God had told Adam and Eve not to eat the Fruit of the Tree of the Knowledge of Good and Evil. In order for the "serpent" to be able to speak to man and know what God had instructed, the "serpent" must have been a spirit being. Revelation 12:9 says, "And the great dragon was thrown down, that ancient serpent, who is called the Devil and Satan, the deceiver of the whole world—he was thrown down to the earth, and his angels were thrown down with him," indicating that the "ancient serpent" is the Devil. This "ancient serpent" is the very "serpent" which tempted Eve. Since Revelation 12:9 says that the "serpent" was thrown down from heaven, we know that the "serpent" was in heaven prior to being thrown down, and therefore that he must have been a spiritual being.

Since we know that the "serpent" is Satan (Rev 12:9), we can learn who the "serpent" was by discovering who Satan is. In order to know who Satan is, we must discover the identity of the spirit being which was in heaven before it sinned. It can be argued that since the "serpent" was originally in Eden before being thrown down from heaven, the "serpent" must originally have been a being that God created with the nature of goodness and a being that was not yet perfect, because (1) there was no being in Eden which was not created by God; (2) God creates only good; and (3) no good being could commit a sin after becoming perfect.

Some imagine that this spirit being which is symbolized as a serpent was a being which existed even before the Creation existed and was a being whose intent was evil, contrary to that of God. However, with the exception of fallen man, everything in the cosmos exists according to one perfect order; so it is not possible that there could have been from the beginning a source of evil which was contrary to God. If there had originally been two opposing forces in the universe, their contradictory purposes would have caused the universe to be destroyed. It can only be concluded that this spirit being was originally created for the purpose of goodness, but later, while in the process of growing, fell and became Satan. This being was able to converse with man; it knew God's Will; it originally lived in heaven; it had the ability to tempt man; and this being, after falling and becoming Satan, was still able, transcendent of time and space, to influence man's mind and spirit,

THE SERPENT Gen 3:1-4

1 Able to communicate with man

2 Knew of God's commandment

3 Rev 12:9 "ancient serpent" ≡ Devil, Satan

4 Originally lived in heaven

5 Able to tempt man

6 Has dominated man's spirit since the Fall

causing man to lead a life of evil. What being is endowed with such abilities? No being other than the angel is endowed with such abilities. One might ask whether angels can commit sins, but biblical evidence for this is clear. In fact, when we read 2 Peter 2:4, which says ". . . God did not spare the angels when they sinned, but cast them into hell and committed them to pits of nether gloom. . .," we can clearly see that angels can and do sin. Taking due note that Revelation 12:7-9, in saying "his angels," indicates that the "serpent" was in fact a leader of angels, we can understand that the "serpent" was an angel.

C. The Sin of the Angel and the Sin of the First Man and Woman

Then what was the sin of this angel? Jude 6-7 says, "And the angels that did not keep their own position but left their proper dwelling have been kept by him in eternal chains in the nether gloom until the judgment of the great day; just as Sodom and Gomorrah and the surrounding cities, which like-wise [like the angels] acted immorally and indulged in un-natural lust, serve as an example by undergoing a punishment of eternal fire." The sin of the angel (in the Garden) was the sin of fornication. Since fornication cannot be committed alone, there must have been a partner. But who could it have been? The Bible tells us of only three beings that sinned in the Garden of Eden; the serpent and Adam and Eve. Let us consider what the sin of the first man and woman could have been.

In Genesis 3:7 we read that after being tempted by the serpent and committing sin, the first ancestors became ashamed of their nakedness and covered the lower parts of their bodies. However, before their fall Adam and Eve were naked but unashamed (Gen 2:25). Then when we read that they covered the lower, or sexual, parts of their bodies with fig leaves after they sinned, we must ask ourselves whether man also committed the sin of fornication.

It is in fallen man's nature to try to conceal his faults and wrongs; so if the fruit of good and evil were a fruit in the literal sense, Adam and Eve should have covered their hands or mouths if they had taken the fruit with their hands or had eaten it with their mouths. Yet we find that they covered their sexual parts, not their hands and mouths. This is an indication that Adam and Eve's transgression involved their sexual parts. Job 31:33 says, ". . . I have *concealed my transgressions . . . like Adam* by hiding my iniquity in my bosom" (emphasis added). Job's words indicate that Adam concealed his transgression, and since we know that Adam and Eve concealed their sexual parts, we can conclude that their sin involved their sexual parts.

In the Garden of Eden, the only sin that man would possibly commit at the risk of his life was a sin involving love. Adam and Eve were to grow as brother and sister, and, after perfecting themselves, were to establish the Kingdom of Heaven by becoming the first husband and wife and creating God's family, fulfilling the Purpose of the Creation. However, when Jesus says in John 8:44, " 'You are of your father the devil. . . ,' " he clearly shows that fallen people are descendants of the Devil. Adam and Eve forsook God, their true father, and became one with a false father, Satan, which is the reason that Romans 8:23 says, ". . . we ourselves, who have the first fruits of the Spirit, groan inwardly as we wait for *adoption* as sons, the redemption of our bodies" (emphasis added). The fact that we are waiting for adoption into God's lineage tells us that we are not of God's lineage. In Matthew 3:7 and Matthew 23:33, respectively, John the Baptist and Jesus called the people a "brood of vipers"—in other words, the offspring of serpents—clearly indicating that fallen man is the offspring of Satan. Thus we can clearly understand that fallen man belongs to Satan's lineage, not God's. This is the result of Eve's committing the sin of fornication with the angel. As a result of this crime, all human beings have been born as the "children" of Satan.*

D. The Fruit of Good and Evil and the Root of Sin

Since a tree reproduces itself by its fruit (which bears the seeds) and man reproduces by a sexual relationship, then the Fruit of the Tree of the Knowledge of Good and Evil symbolizes the sexual love of Eve. The fact that Eve ate the fruit which Satan persuaded her to eat means that she committed fornication with Satan. Since eating something means to make it a part of our flesh and blood, Eve's giving Adam the fruit of good and evil and his eating it mean that Eve caused Adam to fall through this same act of illicit love.

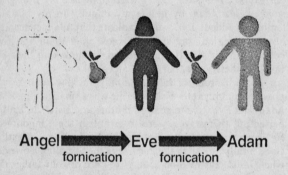

Angel ➡ Eve ➡ Adam
fornication   fornication

Therefore, the root of sin is not the first human ancestors' eating a literal fruit, but their establishing a blood relationship through fornication with the archangel, who was sym-

---

* Although Eve and the archangel united in actual fornication by means of Eve's spirit body and the archangel's body (a spirit body), no children can actually be born of a relationship between a human being and an angel. Nonetheless, Eve inherited satanic "love," so when Eve and Adam had their relationships, which could, of course, produce children, their relationships were motivated by satanic "love," and their children were born of that "love." Thus, all people are the "children" of Satan.

bolized by the serpent. This blood relationship is the cause for the Original Sin's being passed on from generation to generation. All religions which try to remove sin have branded and treated adultery as one of the greatest sins. Based on this view of Original Sin, we can understand why the Israelites had to be circumcised to be considered God's chosen people. It was required in order to make restitution for the misuse of the sexual parts, by which man had become Satan's descendants. We may be able to put a stop to all other sins through social, educational, or economic improvements, but even though civilization develops and social and economic conditions improve to the point where we can enjoy a more stable life, the increase of sexual promiscuity and of man's inclination toward moral degradation cannot be stopped by anyone.

Religion : fornication, adultery among greatest sins

Israelites : circumcision

Advanced Civilizations : Can't control sexual promiscuity and degradation

The reason that Satan is able to break down the proper order of man's love as the Last Days approach is because the first ancestors became husband and wife without the permission or blessing of God and united with Satan as their false father. Their children were thus born as children of sin, and not of God, and they established a world of faithlessness, evil, and war. Consequently, Satan has dominated man as he has seen fit (Jn 8:44).

Despite the fact that God created man and the cosmos, He has never been able to have the central role in any of the world's affairs—to rule according to his Will alone. Man cast

Satan in the starring role, and Satan has been falsely playing the part of the lord. It is for this reason that Satan is referred to as "the ruler of this world" (Jn 12:31) and "the god of this world" (2 Cor 4:4).

II. THE MOTIVES AND PROCESS OF THE FALL

A. The Creation of the Angels

Then with what motive and by what process did Adam and Eve and the angel fall in the Garden of Eden?

God first created the angels as servants to help with his creation and administration of the world (Heb 1:14). However, since man was created as the child of God and was to have dominion over the Creation, man was also to have dominion over the angels. The reason that today angels are usually considered higher than man is that because of the Fall, man

became so corrupt (Jer 17:9) that he stood in a position lower than the things of the Creation, including the angels.

God

Angels &
the rest of creation

Fallen Man
"Corrupt"
(Jeremiah 17:9)

1 Corinthians 6:3 clearly tells us that man will have the authority to judge the angels, and many spiritualists see that there are angels surrounding and protecting the faithful in Paradise. Man is to judge angels and the angels protect man because man originally has greater value than the angels.

B. The Spiritual Fall and the Physical Fall

1. The Spiritual Fall

Lucifer (Is 14:12) was in the position of *archangel* and was thus the channel for God's love to the angelic world. It seemed as if only he were in a position to receive God's love. However, since Adam and Eve were created as God's children, God loved them much more than he did Lucifer, who was created as a servant. Yet, in no way did Lucifer actually receive any less love from God after Adam and Eve's creation than he did before their creation. However, by God's giving so much more love to Adam and Eve, Lucifer felt as though there had been a reduction in the amount of love he was receiving. Because of this feeling, Lucifer then tried to supplement the love he received by coming closer to Adam and Eve.

Because God's love is the source of life and beauty, Eve, who received much love from God, was very beautiful in Lucifer's eyes. Lucifer was often very close to Eve and was strongly stimulated by an impulse of love toward her. Eve,

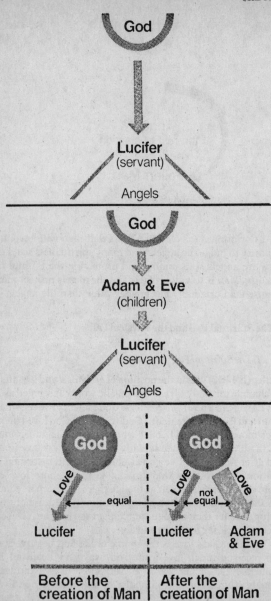

still being in a state of imperfection, was susceptible to Lucifer's temptation, and they committed the sin of fornication. This was the *spiritual fall*.

One might ask how it is possible for a sexual relationship to take place between an angel and a human being. This question arises only because man's spiritual perception fell to such a low state due to the Fall. However, in Genesis 32:25, the Bible shows that direct contact between man and angel is possible when it records that an angel wrestled with Jacob and dislocated his hip.

2. The Physical Fall

When Eve united with the archangel (through their spirit selves), she felt a sense of fear, which came from a guilty conscience, and she gained the knowledge that her intended spouse was Adam, not the angel.

Eve wanted to restore her relationship with God and she also wanted to rid herself of the fear derived from the Fall. Adam was her only hope for returning to God, and Eve thought she could accomplish this by even then becoming one with Adam, who was meant to be her spouse, and so she seduced Adam. This was the motive of the *physical fall*.

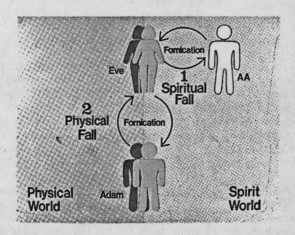

As explained in "The Principles of the Creation," Adam and Eve were to realize the Three Blessings. In order to do this they ultimately had to become husband and wife. In other words, the Ideal for the Creation was for Adam and Eve to perfect themselves individually and then become husband and wife of eternal love, centered on God. But because they acted as husband and wife prematurely and centered on Satan, their relationship resulted in the Fall and not in the realization of God's ideal. By uniting with Eve, Adam inherited the evil elements which Eve had received from Lucifer. These evil elements were then transmitted to their descendants from generation to generation.

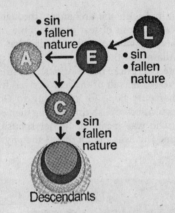

If the first ancestors had not "eaten of the fruit of good and evil," they would have perfected themselves as the son and the daughter of God, and then, blessed by God, they would have become husband and wife centered on God's love and produced children with natures of goodness, fulfilling the Ideal for the Creation. Then, after Eve fulfilled the Ideal for the Creation, her love would have been a fruit of goodness, and she would have been likened to a tree of goodness.

However, before she could become perfect, Eve committed the sin of fornication with the archangel and became a fallen person. She furthermore caused Adam to fall, thus creating the first of the fallen families, none of which God can work through. Therefore, fallen Eve was likened to a tree of the knowledge of evil and her love to a fruit of that tree.

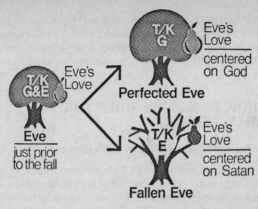

In retrospect, we can see that since just prior to the Fall, Eve was in a position to become either a tree of goodness, by accomplishing the Purpose of the Creation, or a tree of evil, by falling, she was symbolized by the Tree of the Knowledge of Good and Evil. Since prior to the Fall, Eve's love was capable of bearing either a fruit of goodness, fulfilling the Purpose of the Creation, or a fruit of evil causing the Fall, her love was symbolized by a fruit of good and evil.

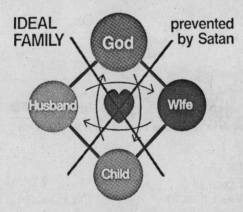

According to "The Principles of the Creation," God was to accomplish the purpose of man's creation through love. Thus, love is the source of man's joy, life, and happiness. However, because the first ancestors disobeyed the rules of heaven, and fell, love itself was corrupted, and Satan has dominated man and has made him suffer. Thus Satan, who corrupted man's love, is the ringleader behind the destruction of the ideal family.

III. HOW IT WAS POSSIBLE FOR MAN TO FALL

A. The Force of Love and the Force of *The Principle*

Man was created to grow to perfection, moved from within during the growth period, or period of indirect dominion, by *the force of The Principle* to live in accordance with *The Principle*.* Therefore, the force of *The Principle* cannot itself derail man from the track of *The Principle* and make him fall. But, prior to perfection man is liable to be derailed from the track if hit by a force stronger than that of *The Principle*, which directs man's growth. The only force stronger than that of *The Principle* is the force of love. Then while man is still imperfect, prior to experiencing the perfect love of God's direct dominion, it is possible for him to fall because of non-Principle "love," love directed toward a purpose different from God's.

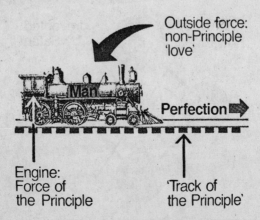

Outside force: non-Principle 'love'

Perfection ➡

Engine: Force of the Principle

'Track of the Principle'

Then why did God make the force of love stronger than the force of *The Principle*? Love is the motive and purpose for God's creating the Creation, and therefore, love is the most precious aspect of all things. To the Creation it is the source of life, happiness, and joy. Although God created all things in accordance with *The Principle*, or laws, since he ultimately desired a dominion of love, he made love the strongest force.

B. The Purpose of the Commandment and the Period Necessary for It

Because the force of love is stronger than the force of *The Principle*, there is always the possibility that during his growth period a person may fall due to non-Principle "love." What can prevent this? Once the force of non-Principle "love" comes into play during the period when a person is still imperfect and not directly in the dominion of God's love, he may fall. In order to prevent this, God gave man the commandment 'not to eat of the fruit of good and evil'. As long as the human ancestors had faithfully kept the commandment, they would not have established a reciprocal base with the archangel. Accordingly, the force of non-Principle "love" would not have come into existence. However, since they did not maintain their faith and observe the commandment, but instead established a reciprocal base and a give and take relationship with the archangel, the force of immoral "love" caused them to deviate from the track of *The Principle*.

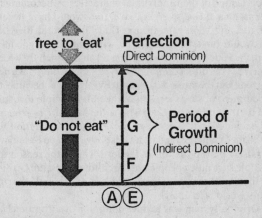

Then how long would God have required the first ancestors to keep the commandment "not to eat," which is the
condition of faith that God gave them? Once Adam and Eve
had perfected themselves and established *horizontal* love as
husband and wife centered on God, there would have been no
force that could break that love, because the love created
between them would have been absolute love. Then, after
having perfected themselves, they could never have fallen.
The force of the lower-level love of the archangel cannot
violate the love between a perfected husband and a perfected
wife. Accordingly, God's commandment 'not to eat' was required only as long as Adam and Eve were still in the period
prior to their perfection.

IV. THE RESULTS OF THE FALL

A. Satan and Fallen Man

What were the results brought about in the Creation by the
spiritual and physical falls of Adam and Eve and the
archangel? Let us consider this by comparing the results of
the Fall with what would have happened if Adam and Eve had
not fallen, but had realized the Three Blessings.

If Adam and Eve had not fallen, but instead had achieved
the perfection of their individual characters by becoming the
incarnations of God's vertical love, they would have become
husband and wife, establishing God's horizontal love, and
they would have borne children with natures of goodness.
Then, the Four Position Foundation through which they could
experience the direct dominion of God's love would have been
realized. But because Adam and Eve fell and became the
embodiment of sin as a result of the 'non-Principle love initiated by the archangel, God, who is the lord of *The Principle*,
was excluded, and a *pseudo Four Position Foundation* was
established centered on Satan's false 'love' and on Satan, who
has falsely played the role of the lord. This is the reason that
the Bible says fallen people are the children of Satan (Jn 8:44)
and that he is "the god of this world" (2 Cor 4:4) and "the ruler
of this world" (Jn 12:31).

Originally man was to have dominion over the angels, as
well as over the rest of the Creation. However, Satan reversed

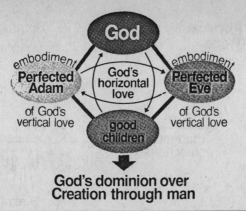

God's dominion over Creation through man

Satan's dominion over Creation through man

this and came to dominate man and the cosmos. Therefore, as Romans 8:19 says, ". . . the creation waits with eager longing for the revealing of the sons of God. . . ." Because of man's fall, all things are crying out to be freed from the dominion of Satan and to experience the dominion of true persons.

B. Satan's Actions in the Fallen World

How does Satan control the fallen world? Even Satan, who is "ruler of this world," can perform satanic actions only when

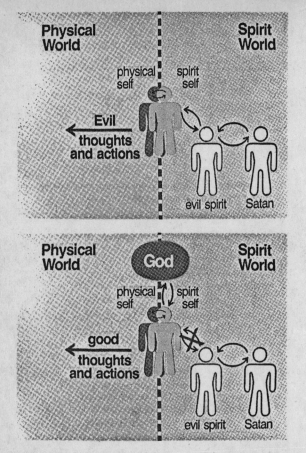

he has an object with whom he has a reciprocal base. Satan's objects are evil *spirit persons* (those who dwell in the spirit world); their objects are the spirit selves of persons on earth; and, of course, the objects responding to people's spirit selves are their own physical selves. Accordingly, Satan's power is manifested in persons on earth through the influence of evil spirits in the spirit world. Furthermore, since Satan is a spirit being, he can manifest himself transcendent of time and space, as long as he has a reciprocal base. When Luke 22:3 says that Satan entered into Judas Iscariot, it means that by establishing a reciprocal base and having a give and take relationship with Satan, Judas became the instrument of Satan. To restore the Kingdom of Heaven on earth means to realize the world in which Satan cannot act at all. To do this, every person must completely dissolve his relationship with Satan and restore a relationship with heaven, having a give and take relationship with God alone.

C. Good and Evil Seen from the Viewpoint of Purpose

If Adam and Eve had become the incarnations of goodness and established the Four Position Foundation with love centered on God, they would have realized the world of goodness. Yet, because they related through love that was directed toward a purpose other than God's, they became incarnations of evil, established a pseudo Four Position Foundation (centered on Satan), and established a world of evil.

Although in their initial stages of development good and evil actions appear to be similar to one another, as they move to accomplish their opposing goals they become separate and distinct. Good and evil are not innately decided by the parti-

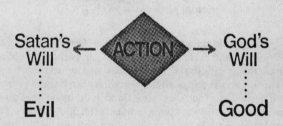

cular action or type of action and result themselves, but are decided by whether the motive, direction, and purpose are toward the Will of God or toward the will of Satan.

D. Sin

Sin is an act or thought which violates *heavenly law**, creating
the condition through which one forms a reciprocal base with
Satan and enters into a give and take relationship with him,
directly or indirectly. In the ideal world which God originally
conceived of, sin could not exist—there could not be a sinful
act in the realm of God's love, for Satan could not exist there.
As the result of Adam's and Eve's forming a reciprocal base
with Satan and sinning, man lives in the non-Principle world
and commits sin by becoming Satan's partner, directly or
indirectly.

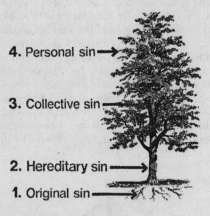

4. Personal sin →

3. Collective sin —

2. Hereditary sin →

1. Original sin —

Sin can be classified as *Original Sin, Hereditary Sin, Collective Sin,* and *Personal Sin.* Original Sin is the sin derived
from the spiritual and physical fall of the first man and
woman. It is the root of all sin. Hereditary Sin is the sin which
is inherited from one's ancestors through the blood lineage (as
mentioned in the Ten Commandments (Ex 20:5)). This sin is
analogous to the trunk of a tree. Collective Sin is neither one's
own sin nor hereditary sin, but is the sin for which everyone is
partially responsible as a member of mankind. The faithlessness of John the Baptist, the chief priests, and the scribes
toward Jesus was responsible for his crucifixion. Though a
relatively small group of people was directly responsible for

---

* Heavenly law is *The Principle* as it applies to proper human conduct.

the Crucifixion, Christianity, in particular, and mankind as a whole, have had to bear the responsibility for that sin and as a result have suffered greatly. Collective Sin is like the branches of a tree. Personal Sin is the sin committed by each individual. Such sins may be compared to the leaves of a tree. All sins originate with Original Sin, which is the root of all sin. Thus, man cannot be finally cleansed of any sin without first being cleansed of Original Sin.

E. The Fallen Nature

The angels and the first man and woman were created with the purpose of goodness and were to have only the *original nature* that they were endowed with when they were created. Prior to the Fall, the relative position of the archangel within the entire order of the Creation was not yet completely clear. The first man and woman were still in their growth period, in other words, they had not yet fully perfected themselves in accordance with their original nature. The archangel and Eve, and then fallen Eve and Adam, had illicit love relationships while they were still not perfected. At the moment of the Fall, the original nature was suddenly turned in the wrong direction, and this wrongly-directed "original nature" became man's *Fallen Nature*. This Fallen Nature was passed from the archangel to Eve, from fallen Eve to Adam, and from Adam and Eve to all their descendants. The origin of the Fallen Nature was this wrongly-directed "original nature." Ultimately, this wrongly-directed "original nature" is the fundamental nature which gives rise to all of the fallen natures of fallen man. In The Principle it is called the *original* (in the sense of fundamental) *Fallen Nature*.

The basic motive that caused the original Fallen Nature grew out of the archangel's sensing a lessening of God's love for him after God's creation of man. This feeling of being loved less was an inevitable by-product for the archangel because he was endowed with desire and wisdom in his original nature. However, it was not also inevitable that the archangel fall because of the desire that he had been endowed with. When man perfected himself and loved the archangel as the (archangel's) lord, the feeling of being loved less would have disappeared. Even in man's immature period, when a lessening of God's love was felt by the archangel, if the archangel had maintained his original direction, longing for God's love and centering on Him alone, the archangel could not have fallen. However, when the archangel's feeling of rejection causd him to alter his direction and center on himself, he developed a strong feeling of jealousy toward Adam. When Eve sympathized with the archangel's feelings and viewpoint, she then formed a reciprocal base with the archangel that led to their illicit relationship and fall.

We can separate the original Fallen Nature into four major aspects. First, the motivation of the archangel's fall lay in his failure to see Adam from God's viewpoint, his failure to love Adam as God loved him; instead he took his own direction and became jealous of Adam. We see something of this when students feel jealousy toward a teacher's favorite instead of loving him as the teacher does. This reaction has its origin in the original Fallen Nature.

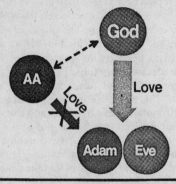

Not loving as God loves

The second major aspect of the Fallen Nature is the nature to leave one's own given position. The archangel's excessive desire to receive more love from God and to enjoy the same position of love in human society as he did in the angelic realm led to his leaving his position and falling. The actions that fallen people perform beyond the limits of their position and authority in order to fill an unrighteous desire are manifestations of this original Fallen Nature.

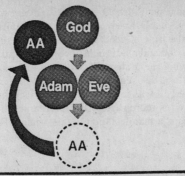

Leaving the proper position

The third major aspect of the Fallen Nature is the nature to reverse the order of dominion. The angel was ultimately supposed to be under man's dominion, yet he dominated Eve, reversing the proper order. Eve was supposed to be under Adam's dominion, yet she dominated him. These reversals of dominion resulted in the Fall. All of the various disorders in the fallen world have their origin in this aspect of the original Fallen Nature.

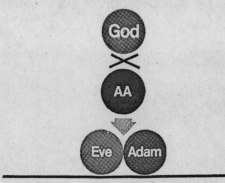

Reversing the order of rule

The fourth major aspect is the nature to multiply (or pass on) unrighteous desires and sinful actions. If Eve had not multiplied her crime by seducing Adam after her fall, Adam

would have not fallen. To restore Eve alone would have been
relatively simple. Eve took the archangel's unrighteous desire
'to eat the fruit of good and evil' and his sinful act of disobeying God and made them her own will and direction, thus
multiplying the archangel's will and actions. That unrighteous will and disobedience were then multiplied in Adam, and
thus, the Fall was brought about. The fact that in the fallen
world evil is more rapidly transferred and multiplied than
goodness is a manifestation of this original Fallen Nature.

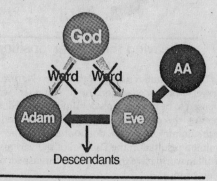

Multiplication of sin

CHAPTER THREE

The Purpose of the Messiah

I. GOD'S PURPOSE IN THE DISPENSATION FOR SALVATION

Each person is created as a child of God. When he perfects himself and becomes an embodiment of goodness, he lives in the Kingdom of God on earth and in the spirit world. God's purpose in making the Creation is to feel joy through experiencing his children living in the Kingdom of Heaven, which is the world of God's love and Heart. It is established through and based on the fulfillment of the Three Blessings. However, because of the Fall of the first ancestors, man became the embodiment of sin and evil, and ever since has lived in suffering both on earth and in the spirit world, and the Purpose of the Creation has not been realized. Would God abandon his original Ideal for the Creation and leave it unrealized? No, he would not.

As God says in Isaiah 46:11, " 'I have spoken, and I will bring it to pass; I have purposed and I will do it.' " God will surely accomplish his purpose. The God of love could not

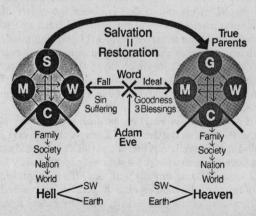

leave fallen man in such a state, for man was created as His child. Instead, God has been working for man's salvation.

Then what is salvation? Salvation is *restoration:* to save a dying person is to restore him to his normal state; to save a drowning person is to rescue him and restore him to the state he was in before he began to drown. God's salvation of man means God's restoration of fallen and sinful man to his original state of goodness—to the position where he can fulfill the Purpose of the Creation.

Thus, God's purpose in salvation is to restore an individual to the sinless state that God originally created, raise him to be an ideal individual, establish an ideal family centered on that individual, and then establish an ideal society, nation, and world, based on that ideal family.

II. THE FULFILLMENT OF THE DISPENSATION FOR SALVATION IS THE FULFILLMENT OF THE PURPOSE OF THE CREATION

If a person were to become such an ideal individual, namely a restored person who has realized the First Blessing, what would he be like? This perfect individual would have the same relation to God as the body of an individual has to his mind. The mind dwells in the body, and the body acts as the mind directs it. Similarly, a perfect person is a temple of God, and God dwells in his mind. God becomes the center of his thoughts and actions—the center of his life. Such a person of perfected character achieves the ideal of unity with God, just as our body achieves harmony with our mind. This is expressed in 1 Corinthians 3:16, which says, "Do you not know that you are God's temple and that God's Spirit dwells in you?" and John 14:20 says, " 'In that day you will know that I am in my Father, and you in me, and I in you.' "

If Adam and Eve had become such perfect individuals, then in their life in the Garden of Eden would they ever have needed prayer, a religious life, or a savior? Why would prayer have been necessary for those who were continuously living and communicating directly with God? If a religious life is a life of faith in which fallen man desperately gropes in darkness in search of the God he lost, then why should a perfect person who lives his daily life as a temple of God have need of any form of worship? Thus, if man had not fallen in the Garden of Eden, there would be no churches or Bibles, no sermons, no all-night prayer vigils, no revival meetings, nor the like. All each person would need to do is live as the embodiment of goodness, attending God in his everyday life. Just as those who are not drowning have no need of a rescuer, perfected people, who are sinless, have no need of a savior.

Ideal Individual

1. Body / Mind ≡ Ideal Ind. / God

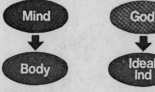

- • Dwelling
- • Direction
- • Harmony

- • Temple
- • Center
- • Unity

Ideal Individual

1 Body / Mind ≡ Ideal Ind. / God

2 No Religious Life Needed

3 No Prayer Needed

4 No Savior Needed

Then, if man had established the ideal family, fulfilling God's Second Blessing, what would such a family have become? If Adam and Eve had become husband and wife embodying goodness, giving birth to children embodying goodness, this family would have become the origin of a sinless tribe, society, nation, and world. With this family, the Kingdom of Heaven would have been established, and from that family an ideal society of one world family would have developed, with one set of *true parents* (the first man and woman) and endless generations of sinless descendants growing in prosperity. God's dispensation for salvation is to develop such heavenly individuals, people who have realized God's Three Blessings and have thus established the Kingdom of Heaven.

It is for this purpose of salvation that God sent his Son, Jesus Christ, as savior to this world. Thus, the *Messiah* must stand before God as the origin of all ideal individuals and must establish the ideal family, which is the family that fulfills the Purpose of the Creation and is the place where God's love can dwell. He must then also establish the ideal nation and world, thereby realizing the originally intended Kingdom of Heaven on earth, fulfilling the Purpose of the Creation. This is the purpose for which the Messiah comes.

III. THE DISPENSATION OF SALVATION THROUGH THE CROSS

A. The Crucifixion of Jesus

God truly loved his chosen people, the Israelites, who were to be the foundation for the coming of the Messiah. Many times God prophesied the coming of the Messiah, and he even warned the people to remain alert and wait for him. God even prepared a great witness, John the Baptist, to testify to the Messiah. In fact, the nation of Israel was passionately longing for the Messiah to arrive.

Tragically, however, the much-prepared chosen people failed to recognize the Messiah when he came. The Son of God cried out that he was the Son of God, but his words fell on deaf ears. He was never understood; he was branded a blasphemer and ultimately crucified. Ironically, the pagan rulers of that age knew of Jesus' innocence (Lk 23:14-16; Jn 18:38; Mt 27:19,23; Mk 15:10-14), while those who judged him guilty were his own people and the leaders of Judaism, whom God himself had nurtured and prepared for so long. They were even anxious to send Jesus to the cross. Why?

Christians have traditionally believed that Jesus' death on the cross was predestined as the original plan of God. No, it was not! It was a grievous error to crucify Jesus Christ. The crucifixion of Jesus was the consequence of the sheer ignorance of the people of Israel concerning God's dispensation. God's will was clearly for the chosen people to accept and believe in Jesus (Jn 6:29, 10:37,38) and receive salvation. The people of Israel did not understand who Jesus of Nazareth was, for even as he hung dying on the cross they mocked him, shouting that they would believe in him as savior only if he came down from the cross. The Bible points out that "he came to his own home, and his own people received him not" (Jn 1:11); and the Apostle Paul testified that "none of the rulers of this age understood this; for if they had, they would not have crucified the Lord of glory" (1 Cor 2:8).

Christians today do not have a clear understanding of the truth behind the historic events that took place in Jesus' time. If God's will for man's salvation could be accomplished only by the Crucifixion, why did he spend so much time preparing a chosen people? Was it not because he did not want to hand his Son over to faithless people?

In the garden at Gethsemane, Jesus prayed, " '. . . My soul is very sorrowful, even to death; remain here, and watch with me. . . . My Father, if it be possible, let this cup pass from me. . . .' " (Mt 26:38,39). Jesus uttered this prayer, not once, but three times. Many Christians, who believe that Jesus' mission was to bring salvation by dying on the cross, explain that Jesus uttered this prayer out of human weakness or frailty. But could Jesus Christ, the savior of mankind, utter any prayer out of weakness?

The first Christian martyr, Stephen, and many of the martyrs who followed, never prayed from such weakness. Did they ever ask, "Let this cup pass from me," as they were dying? How can we say that Jesus was weaker than these martyrs? Especially if the purpose of his coming was to save all mankind by dying on the cross, could there be any reason that he would pray to escape from it?

This prayer of Jesus was not a selfish or timid prayer, uttered out of fear of dying. If the crucifixion had been the very way for Jesus to save mankind, he would gladly have died on the cross thousands of times over. Jesus was beset with anxiety when he thought about his mission as the Messiah, which was to realize God's Purpose for the Creation on earth. His heart was so troubled because he knew how sorrowful God would feel if the completion of the dispensation for salvation were delayed. Jesus also foresaw the sufferings and bloodshed of his disciples and followers, the Christians, who would have to follow his path of suffering and the cross. He also anguished over the troubled future that would come to the people of Israel if they rejected him. With all of this in mind, in the

The Reasons Jesus Prayed not to be Crucified

(Matthew 26: 38-39)

1 Concern for God

2 Concern for his followers

3 Concern for Israel

garden of Gethsemane, Jesus uttered a last desperate prayer
to God, repeatedly pleading that God let him remain on earth,
even in those hopeless circumstances, so that he could continue his mission and change the hearts of the people to the
point where they would accept him.

If Jesus' death on the cross was predestined by God, then
why did Jesus say to Judas Iscariot, his betrayer, " '. . . woe to
that man by whom the Son of man is betrayed! It would have
been better for that man if he had not been born' " (Mt 26:24);
and how can we explain Jesus' crying out on the cross, " '. . .
My God, my God, why hast Thou forsaken me?' " (Mt 27:46). If
the crucifixion were truly God's original will for Jesus, then
Jesus should have felt resounding joy on the cross, having
successfully completed his mission.

B. The Extent of Salvation Available through the Cross and the Purpose of the Second Coming of Christ

Death on the cross was not the mission that God had originally intended for Jesus, his Son. Rather, it became God's painful
secondary dispensation necessitated by the faithlessness of
the people of Israel. What would have happened if all the
people of Israel had believed in Jesus and had welcomed him,
loved him, and united with him? Most certainly, complete
salvation would have been realized. In other words, Jesus
would have completely established the Kingdom of Heaven
on earth, the place where the Purpose of the Creation has been
realized. God's world would have been realized—the world in
which all people believe in and follow the Son of God. The
people of Israel would have become the glorious core of
heaven. The Jewish and Christian worlds would never have
been divided, nor would the early Christians have had to
endure any of their terrible sufferings. Furthermore, because
the Messiah would have completed his mission, there would
be no reason for a Second Coming.

Understanding the question of salvation in this light, we
can see that Jesus' crucifixion was a secondary course of salvation and provided only *spiritual salvation*. When the people
came to the point of completely disbelieving Jesus and aban-
doning him, God had to pay the price for the sinful lack of faith
of the Israelites and all mankind by giving the life of his only
Son to Satan as a ransom. As a result, Satan destroyed Jesus'

physical body by nailing him to the cross, and Jesus' blood on the cross became the price for the redemption of mankind.

By resurrecting the crucified Jesus, God opened up a way of spiritual salvation, a way to a realm free from satanic invasion. God's victory was not the crucifixion, but Jesus' resurrection. As a result of the crucifixion, the physical selves of mankind are still subject to satanic invasion, even though they were meant to be saved by man's believing in Jesus and being engrafted to him (Rom 11:17). Only man's spirit can attain salvation, by the condition of participating in the resurrection through man's belief in the victorious Christ. Our body still awaits redemption (Rom 8:23).

If the People of Israel Had Followed Jesus

1 Kingdom of Heaven Established on Earth

2 No Jewish—Christian Split

3 No Persecution of Christians

4 No Second Coming

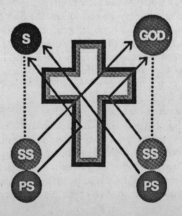

Thus, even after Jesus' appearance on earth, the world continues to suffer under the power of Satan, and sin mercilessly persists in the bodies of people everywhere. The Apostle Paul lamented, "Wretched man that I am! Who will deliver me from this body of death? . . . I of myself serve the law of God with my mind, but with my flesh I serve the law of sin" (Rom 7:24,25). As a saint, Paul was devout and in the full grace of the Lord, but his flesh continued to be oppressed by sin. This confession is not limited to Paul alone, but applies to every person alive. This is the reason that the Bible teaches us to "pray constantly" (1 Thess 5:17)—to protect us from satanic invasion. Also, 1 John 1:10 says, "If we say we have not sinned, we make him a liar . . .," telling us that mankind is still under the bondage of original sin. There is no one who has been cleansed of original sin. It is for this reason that the Messiah must appear again on earth, to liquidate our sins completely and establish the Kingdom of Heaven on earth, fulfilling God's Purpose for the Creation.

C. Two Kinds of Prophecy Concerning the Messiah

If Jesus' death on the cross was not essential for the fulfillment of his messianic purpose, then why did Isaiah 53 predict the Messiah's suffering and death? Here we must remind ourselves that there are also verses in the Bible which prophesy that the Messiah will come as the Son of God and the King of kings and bring about the Kingdom of Heaven on earth. These prophecies appear in Isaiah 9, 11, and 60, in other verses in the Old Testament, and in Luke 1:31-33.

When God first created man, he created him to grow to perfection only by man's completing a share of responsibility. Man can either accomplish his responsibility, as God wants him to do, or to the contrary, he can fail to accomplish it. Accordingly, it was necessary that God give two kinds of prophecies regarding the fulfillment of His Will.

It is God's responsibility to send the Messiah, but it is man's responsibility to believe in him. Unfortunately, by not accepting Jesus, the Israelites failed to fulfill their responsibility; they did not fulfill God's primary prophecies for the Messiah's coming, which are in Isaiah 9, 11, and 60 and Luke 1:31-33, but, to the contrary, carried out the alternative or secondary prophecy of the suffering Messiah, in Isaiah 53.

Two Kinds of Prophecy Concerning the Messiah

IV. JOHN THE BAPTIST AND THE RETURN OF ELIJAH

A. The Messiah and Elijah

At this point, there is one matter which we must look into regarding God's dispensation of having Jesus go the way of the cross. God had repeatedly prophesied to the chosen people about the coming of the Messiah, and the chosen people themselves longed for him and cherished the promise of his coming. How could God send the Messiah in such a way that the chosen people were unable to recognize him? Was it God's will that they not recognize and receive the Messiah? Or did the people fail to recognize him despite God's clearly showing them how he was to come?

In order to find the answers to these questions, let us first examine the second coming of Elijah. In Malachi, the last book of prophecy in the Old Testament, it says, " 'Behold, I will send you Elijah the prophet before the great and terrible day of the Lord comes. . . .' " (Mal 4:5,6). The "great and terrible day" that is referred to is the time when the Messiah comes, and thus this prophecy shows that before the Messiah comes, Elijah must first return.

Elijah was a great prophet of Israel who lived nine hundred years before Jesus. There is record of his having ascended into heaven on a chariot of fire (2 Kings 2:11). The Israelites' longing for the Messiah was actually intensely focused on the arrival of the historical prophet, Elijah. This was because the Old Testament did not clearly foretell when the Messiah would come, but did clearly indicate that Elijah would precede him.

It was under these circumstances that Jesus appeared, proclaiming himself the Messiah. He told the Jewish people that he was the Son of God—this to the very people who thought that he was simply a young man from Nazareth. They had not yet heard any news of Elijah's coming, so they asked, "How could Jesus of Nazareth be the Son of God?"

Thus, when Jesus' disciples went out among the people of Israel, testifying to Jesus, the people doubted that Jesus was the Messiah and challenged the disciples by asking where Elijah was, since Elijah was to precede the Messiah. So Jesus' disciples turned around and asked Jesus, " '. . . then why do the scribes say that first Elijah must come?' " (Mt 17:10). Jesus replied, " '. . . Elijah does come, and he is to restore all things; but I tell you that Elijah has already come, and they did not know him, but did to him whatever they pleased. . . .' Then the disciples understood that he was speaking to them of John the Baptist" (Mt 17:10-13).

Jesus understood the meaning of the scribes' important question and indicated that John the Baptist was the second coming of Elijah. Jesus' own disciples could easily believe this, but could the Israelites bring themselves to believe it? John the Baptist did not come directly from heaven, and he himself even denied he was Elijah (Jn 1:21). Jesus himself knew that the people would not easily accept it, saying, " '. . .

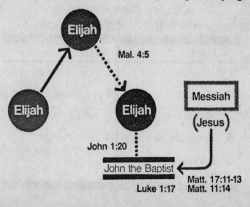

if you are willing to accept it, he is Elijah who is to come' " (Mt
11:14).

Jesus said that John the Baptist was the Elijah whom the
people had been long awaiting, but since John himself denied
it, whom would the people of Israel believe? Naturally, it
would depend on how these two men were viewed by the
people of that time.

First, how did Jesus appear to the Israelites of the time?
Jesus was an obscure young man raised in a humble carpen-
ter's home and was not known to be experienced in spiritual
disciplines. Yet Jesus proclaimed himself "lord of the sabbath" (Mt 12:8), was known as one who was abolishing the law
(Mt 5:17), was the friend of tax collectors and sinners, and was
known as a glutton and a drunkard (Mt 11:19). He put himself
on an equal footing with God (Jn 14:9-11) and told the people
that they had to love him more than anyone else (Mt 10:37).
Because of this, the Jewish leaders went so far as to claim that
Jesus was working by the power of Beelzebub, the prince of
demons (Mt 12:24).

On the other hand, how did the Israelites of that time see
John the Baptist? He was the son of a prominent family, and
the miracles surrounding his conception and birth were
known throughout the country Lk 1:5-66). When he was older,
he lived on locusts and honey in the wilderness, and thus, in
their eyes, he led an exemplary life as a man of faith. In fact,
John was held in such high regard that high priests, as well as
the common people, even asked if he were the Messiah (Lk
3:15, Jn 1:20).

Jesus' Image versus
John the Baptist's Image

Jesus	John
1 From humble family	1 From prominent family
2 Not ascetic	2 Miracles at birth
3 Startling proclamations	3 Ascetic
4 Lower-class associates	4 Supported by Jewish leaders
5 Denounced by Jewish leaders	

Under these circumstances, the people of Israel tended to believe more in John the Baptist, who asserted he was not Elijah, than in Jesus, who told them that John the Baptist was Elijah. The people decided that Jesus' view of John as Elijah was untrustworthy, thinking that Jesus said this only to make believable his claims about himself.

B. The Mission of John the Baptist

Then why did Jesus say that John the Baptist was Elijah? As Luke 1:17 indicates, John the Baptist came with the mission of Elijah. The people of Israel, who believed the words of the Old Testament literally, assumed that the original Elijah would actually come down from heaven. But God chose John and sent him with the mission of Elijah.

John the Baptist himself declared that he was "sent before" the Messiah (Jn 3:28), to "make straight the way of the Lord" (Jn 1:23). Being a man with such a unique and important mission, John, by his own wisdom, should have known that he himself was Elijah.

Many of the chief priests and of the people of Israel who respected John the Baptist thought that he might even be the Messiah. Therefore, if John had proclaimed that he was Elijah and had testified that Jesus was the Messiah, the Jewish people of that time would have been able to recognize and receive Jesus, thereby obtaining salvation. Then Jesus' family background and seeming lack of experience in spiritual disciplines would not have mattered. However, because of his ignorance of God's dispensation, John insisted that he was *not* Elijah. This was the main factor that prevented the people of Israel from coming to Jesus.

In Matthew 3:11, John the Baptist said that he baptized with water, but that the one who would come after him (the Messiah) would baptize with the Holy Spirit and with fire; he said that he was not even worthy to untie the thong of his sandal (Jn 1:27). In John 1:33, John said, " 'I myself did not know him; but he [God] who sent me to baptize with water said to me, "He on whom you see the Spirit descend and remain, this is he who baptizes with the Holy Spirit [Christ]." And I have seen and have borne witness that this is the Son of God.' " Thus God gave John the Baptist a direct revelation that Jesus was the Son of God. Although John did initially fulfill his mission to testify to Jesus Christ, regretfully he did not testify to Jesus throughout his life.

After meeting the Messiah, everyone should believe in him and serve him throughout their lives. This was especially true for John the Baptist, who came with the mission of Elijah, which was to prepare the Messiah's way (Lk 1:76). Therefore, John should have served and attended Jesus as one of his disciples. John's father was told of his son's mission when he was born and he prophesied, saying, ". . . 'And you, child, will be called the prophet of the Most High, for you will go before the Lord to prepare his ways, to give knowledge of salvation to his people . . . ' " (Lk 1:76,77). However, we cannot find any instance in the Bible where John the Baptist actually served Jesus.

Just before John the Baptist died in prison, having lived without fulfilling his mission to serve Jesus, he began to have doubts concerning his life and Jesus and sent his disciples to Jesus to ask, ". . . 'Are you he who is to come, or shall we look for another?' " (Mt 11:3). This verse proves beyond any shadow of a doubt that John did not believe in Jesus and failed to serve him.

Jesus was indignant at such a question and answered quite judgmentally, " '. . . blessed is he who takes no offense at me' " (Mt 11:6), indicating that despite Israel's great respect for John, John had already failed his mission.

Jesus also said, " '. . . among those born of women there has risen no one greater than John the Baptist; yet he who is least in the kingdom of heaven is greater than he' " (Mt 11:11). If one were the greatest born of women, surely he should be equally great in the Kingdom of Heaven. Then how could John the Baptist, who was born as the greatest in history, be less than the least in heaven?

God sent John the Baptist as the greatest of prophets, for he was to serve the Messiah and testify to him before all the people. But he was a dismal failure in fulfilling his responsibility. Matthew 11:12 also explains this, saying, " 'From the days of John the Baptist until now the kingdom of heaven has suffered violence, and men of violence take it by force.' " If John the Baptist had served Jesus well, fulfilling his responsibility, he would have become Jesus' chief disciple; but because he failed, Peter, who made the greatest effort among Jesus' disciples, became the leader of the Twelve.

In order to prepare the people of Israel to have faith in Jesus, God gave many testimonies to John's parents, Zechariah and Elizabeth, who were representatives of the Judaism of that time. God continually worked miracles so that the people would accept that he was directly working in the conception and birth of John the Baptist. Undoubtedly, John was told by his parents about his being related to Jesus, and, as mentioned above, he must have received many revelations directly from God.

Yet, despite all of this preparation, John the Baptist failed because of his disbelief and ignorance. Moreover, his personal ignorance and disbelief led not only to his individual loss, but also to the disbelief of most of the people and ultimately to Jesus' crucifixion.

CHAPTER FOUR

The Consummation of Human History

Let us discuss the biblical concept of the *Last Days*. The Bible tells us that in the Last Days the heavens will pass away and the elements will be dissolved by fire (2 Pet 3:10); and it tells us that the sun will be darkened, the moon will not give its light, and the stars will fall from heaven (Mt 24:29). It further predicts that with the trumpet call of God, Christ will return, and the deceased believers in Christ will rise up to meet him in the air, followed by those believers who are living when Christ returns (1 Thess 4:16,17).

Are these predictions to be taken literally, or are they to be taken symbolically, like many other crucial passages in the Bible? Let us answer these questions through understanding human history. How did it begin? Where is it going? What is its ultimate goal?

I. THE MEANING OF THE LAST DAYS

What kind of world would have come about if Adam and Eve had obeyed the command that God gave them in the Garden of Eden? Adam and Eve would have become perfect as individuals, and on that basis they would have established an ideal family and borne sons and daughters with natures of goodness. Their thoughts and actions would have been centered on God, and they would have thus built a family, society, nation, and world in which God alone is sovereign. Such a world would have been the Kingdom of Heaven on earth. If this had come to pass, their lives would have been lives of goodness, and the histories of their family and the world would also have been histories of goodness. The history that God originally purposed was to be one of only goodness.

However, because the first man and woman fell, they did not become true persons embodying divine nature, but rather became persons embodying evil nature. Fallen Adam and Eve gave birth to children with original sin and thus formed evil families and societies and an evil world. The thoughts and actions of fallen man have always been dominated by Satan, and this world thus became Hell on earth, full of sin and suffering. Man's individual, family, national, and world histories, without exception, have been histories composed primarily of conflict, sin, and evil.

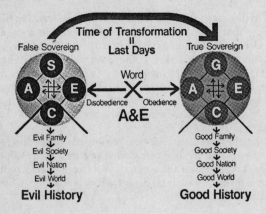

According to God's original plan, the content of human history was to have been only goodness, but because of the Fall, human history began with evil. Could God simply be indifferent and leave mankind in that state? No. Through His work for salvation, God will definitely fulfill what he originally purposed (Is 46:11). Although human history began as a history of sin and evil, because of God's dispensation to realize the Purpose of the Creation, human history has been the history of the dispensation to "restore" the lost Purpose of the Creation. The ultimate goal of human history has been to supplant the evil history with the good history that God had originally planned. The Last Days is the period when the evil world of Satan's sovereignty is finally transformed into the ideal world of God's sovereignty. The Last Days is the time when the fallen world, or Hell on earth, is transformed into the Kingdom of Heaven on earth, the place where the Purpose of the Creation has been realized.

Many have lived in fear of the Last Days because they

thought it would be a time of supernatural calamities. However, contrary to what they have believed, it will not be a time of such calamities. Rather it will be a time of joy, because it is the time when the ideal world which man's original nature has longed for will be established. The Last Days is the time when the evil history will end, but it is also a time of hope because it signals the beginning of the age of goodness. However, God cannot establish goodness and build the Kingdom of Heaven without destroying evil and hell. This judgment will be brought about by the *Word* of God (as explained in Section IIB). So those who live a life of evil should look to the Last Days with dread while those who are obeying the Will of God should look forward to the Last Days with hope and joyous anticipation.

Investing all of his heart and love, God has constantly worked to realize the ideal world; thus, he has constantly worked to bring about the Last Days. But unfortunately, each time that God has tried to bring about the Last Days, man has not fully carried out his responsibility, and God's Will has been left unfulfilled. According to "The Principle of the Creation," God's purpose cannot be fulfilled by God alone; man's cooperation is also absolutely necessary. Then, according to this principle, the dispensation for the Last Days, which is to fulfill the Purpose of the Creation, also cannot be fulfilled by God alone.

**Fullfillment of the
Dispensation for
the Last Days**

Man's Cooperation

God's Work to bring about
the Last Days

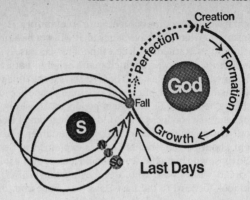

It is for this reason that the Bible indicates there have been a number of attempts to bring about the Last Days. For example, at the time of Noah, God said, " 'I have determined to make an end of all flesh; for the earth is filled with violence through them; behold, I will destroy them with the earth' " (Gen 6:13), indicating that Noah's time was to have been the Last Days. God intended to put an end to the sixteen hundred years (biblical record) of the history of sin and evil by means of the *Flood Judgment*. God intended to destroy evil and then establish the ideal world of his sovereignty and begin a new history of goodness centered on Noah's family. Noah's time was to have been the Last Days, but because of Ham's failure, Noah's family could not fulfill its responsibility (refer to "Noah's Family in the Dispensation for Restoration"), and God's intention to bring about the Last Days could not be fulfilled at that time. Though Noah's family could not accomplish God's Will, since his Will itself is absolute, God continued his dispensation. Centered on the prophets, God has continued the dispensation toward the Last Days—that is, toward the judgment of sin and evil and the preparation for establishing the ideal world.

On this foundation Jesus came to end the history of evil and to realize the *Ideal for the Creation*. Thus, his coming marked another attempt to bring about the Last Days. This is why Jesus referred to himself as coming to judge (Jn 5:22) and why Malachi prophesied, " 'For behold, the day comes, burning like an oven, when all the arrogant and all evildoers will be stubble; the day that comes shall burn them up, . . . so that it will leave them neither root nor branch' " (Mal 4:1).

But by not believing in Jesus, the people of Israel failed ir their responsibility. This delayed the fulfillment of God's Wil until the Second Coming. Therefore, the Last Days will be at the time of the Second Coming. This is why Jesus said, " 'As it was in the days of Noah, so will it be in the days of the Son of man' " (Lk 17:26). It is also why Matthew 24:29 predicts that at the Second Coming wonders and changes in the heavens similar to those predicted for Noah's time and Jesus' time will take place (Gen 6:6,7,13 and Is 24:19, respectively).

II. PHENOMENA PROPHESIED FOR THE LAST DAYS

To understand the Bible passages which describe the various phenomena prophesied for the Last Days, it is necessary to understand the nature of God's will for the Purpose of the Creation, which underlies the dispensation for the Last Days. Since God cannot fulfill the Purpose of the Creation until he ends the world of evil, in the Last Days evil will be destroyed. More importantly, however, the Last Days is the time for the fulfillment of the Purpose of the Creation. Once we understand that the history of mankind is a history of the dispensation to fulfill the Purpose of the Creation, it is easy to see that the passages in the Bible that predict terrifying calamities for the Last Days, such as the destruction of heaven and earth,

Bible Predictions for the Last Days

Destruction of Heaven and Earth	II Pet 3:12 Gen 6:13
New Heaven and New Earth	Isa 66:22 Rev 22:1
Judgment by Fire	II Pet 3:12
Meeting the Lord in the Air	I Thess 4:17
Sun and Moon Darken	Matt 24:29
Stars Fall from Heaven	

cannot be taken literally. If these passages are not to be taken literally, what do they signify?

A. The Heavens and the Earth Destroyed and a New Heaven and New Earth Established
(2 Pet 3:12, Gen 6:13, Is 66:22, Rev 21:1)

Though Genesis 6:13 says that God intended to destroy the earth at Noah's time, God did not actually do so. Elsewhere, the Bible assures us that the earth is eternal: "A generation goes, and a generation comes, but the earth remains for ever" (Eccles 1:4) and "He built his sanctuary like the high heavens, like the earth, which he has founded for ever" (Ps 78:69). God would never have made any plan for the Garden of Eden, the eternal Kingdom of Heaven on earth, if it could not be realized. Since God's Kingdom is to be eternal, and the earth is the place where he will establish his Kingdom, then the earth must also be eternal. By all means God will fulfill the Purpose of the Creation on this earth.

Then what is the meaning of the Bible verses 2 Peter 3:12 and Isaiah 24:19, which refer to the destruction of the heavens and the earth? The destruction of the heavens and the earth that are described in the Bible mean the destruction of the satanic sovereignty that has controlled heaven and earth since man's fall. The appearance of a new heaven and earth means the establishment of the Kingdom of Heaven, centered on the Messiah, under the sovereignty of God.

B. Heaven and Earth Judged by Fire
(2 Pet 3:12)

2 Peter 3:12 tells us, ". . . the heavens will be kindled and dissolved, and the elements will melt with fire!" If this were to happen literally, then God's Purpose for the Creation could not be realized. Malachi 4:1 prophesied that Jesus' day would be a day of destruction by fire; in John 5:22 and John 9:39, Jesus is the master of Judgment; and in Luke 12:49, Jesus said he came to cast fire upon the earth. But Jesus never brought about a judgment by literal fire.

So what do these verses mean? They must have a symbolic meaning. In Jeremiah 23:29, God says that His Word may be likened to fire. Judgment by fire is really judgment by the Word, or Truth. In John 12:48, Jesus says, " 'He who rejects me and does not receive my saying has a judge; the word that I have spoken will be his judge on the last day.' " 2 Thessalonians 2:8 says that ". . . the lawless one will be revealed, and the Lord Jesus will slay him with the *breath of his mouth*," which actually means by the Word. Similarly, Isaiah 11:4 says, ". . . and he shall smite the earth with the *rod of his mouth*, and with the *breath of his lips* [the Word] he shall slay the wicked" (emphases added). John 5:24 says, " '. . . He who hears my word and believes him who sent me, has eternal life; he does not come into judgment, but has passed from death to life.' " From these verses, it is clear that judgment by fire means judgment by the Word.

C. Meeting the Lord in the Air
(1 Thess 4:17)

1 Thessalonians 4:17 says, "Then we who are alive, who are left, shall be caught up together with them in the clouds to meet the Lord in the air; and so we shall always be with the Lord." The Last Days is the time of the fulfillment of the Purpose of the Creation. Therefore the prophecy that believers will meet the Lord in the air in the Last Days cannot be a literal one, because the air is not the place where the Purpose of the Creation is to be fulfilled.

In the Bible 'heaven' usually means the holy, exalted, and sinless realm which is under the sovereignty of good, while 'earth', its opposite, means the unholy, base, and sinful realm under the sovereignty of evil. For example, when we say, " '. . . Our Father who art in heaven . . . .' " (Mt 6:9), we do not mean that God is located in the sky, but are referring to the holy and exalted realm of God's existence. Thus, to "meet the Lord in the air" does not mean the physical elevation of Christians to meet Christ in the sky, but rather refers to the development of their inner spiritual qualities and their serving Christ in the world of good sovereignty when he returns and establishes the Kingdom of Heaven on earth.

D. Sun and Moon Darkened; the Stars Fall from Heaven
(Mt 24:29)

Matthew 24:29 says, " 'Immediately after the tribulation of those days the sun will be darkened, and the moon will not

give its light, and the stars will fall from heaven . . . .' " Should
these calamities come to pass, then the Purpose of the Creation could not be fulfilled. Then, what is the meaning of these
predictions? Genesis 37:9,10 gives us an insight. There we find
the interpretation of one of Joseph's dreams, in which the sun
symbolizes the father, the moon symbolizes the mother, and
the stars, their children. Jesus and the Holy Spirit give rebirth
to fallen man and thus stand in the position of father and
mother (refer to "Christology"). Therefore, in the New Testament (Mt 24:29), the sun and the moon represent Jesus and the
Holy Spirit, who are the source of the light of truth which
illuminates the spirit and heart of mankind, and the stars
represent the believers (Christians), who are the "children" of
Jesus and the Holy Spirit.

Viewed in this manner, the sunlight symbolizes the light
of truth of Jesus' words, and the moonlight symbolizes the
light of the Holy Spirit. To say that the sun and the moon will
be darkened is to say that the light of a new expression of the
truth will outshine that of Jesus and the Holy Spirit (i.e., the
New Testament). How is this possible? Just as the Old Testament was outshone when Jesus and the Holy Spirit came with
new words that were to fulfill the Old Testament, when Christ
comes again with a new expression of the truth, the words of
Jesus and the Holy Spirit will be outshone. For truth to lose its
light means that the period of its mission has ended with the
coming of an age for a new expression of the truth. The "stars"
falling from heaven represent those Christians in the Last
Days who do not accept the truth from the Lord and thus lose
their position as the children of God.

In Luke 18:8 Jesus asked, " '. . . when the Son of man
comes, will he find faith on earth?' " On another occasion he
said that at the Second Coming he would declare to many
believers, " ' ". . . I never knew you; depart from me, you
evildoers" ' " (Mt 7:23). Though the leaders of Israel had been
eagerly waiting for the Messiah, all "fell" by rejecting the new
teachings which Jesus brought. Jesus foresaw the possibility
that the religious leaders at the time of the Last Days would do
the same thing, and so he said these things as a warning.

III. THE PRESENT DAYS ARE THE LAST DAYS

Jesus promised that he would return soon (Rev 22:20; Mt
10:23, 16:28; Jn 21:22). As a result, Christians of every age have

believed that their time was the Last Days and the time for
Christ's return. Based on an overall view of the history of God's
Dispensation for Restoration, we can know that we are now
living in the actual age of the Second Coming. This will be
explained more fully in the chapter "The Second Coming."
However, we can also know that our time is the Last Days by
observing events in the world around us. As Jesus said,

> From the fig tree learn its lesson: as soon as its
> branch becomes tender and puts forth its leaves,
> you know that summer is near. So also, when you
> see all these things, you know that he is near, at the
> very gates.   (Mt 24:32,33)

What kinds of signs would indicate that we are in the Last
Days? The goal of human history is the establishment of God's
ideal world, which is the world based on the realization of the
Three Blessings. The Last Days is when the evil world is
destroyed, but it is also the time just prior to the establishment of the ideal world. Therefore, if our era is the Last Days,
we should be able to see signs in the world that the Three
Blessings are being realized. Based on this understanding, we
will show that we are now living in the Last Days. Let us
examine our era in light of the Three Blessings.

The Ideal World is Based on the Three Blessings

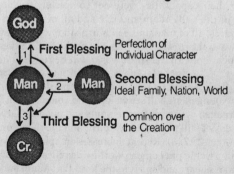

God

↓1↑ First Blessing   Perfection of
                       Individual Character

Man →2→ Man   Second Blessing
                Ideal Family, Nation, World

↓3↑ Third Blessing   Dominion over
                      the Creation

Cr.

The First Blessing is that each person can perfect his
character and become one in heart with God. In God's ideal,
such a person is to enjoy complete freedom of thought and

action and is to embody original love and have the character
and value of a child of God and of a lord of the Creation. Thus
he would live the life that is lived in the Kingdom of Heaven.
However, because of the Fall, man could not realize the First
Blessing. The Last Days is the last stage in God's dispensation
to restore each fallen person as a person of perfected character.

In the present era, fallen man is developing a deep inner
thirst for restoring the contents of the First Blessing as a
reality in his life. This inclination is evident in the recent
worldwide interest in new faiths and in movements toward
universal love, liberty, equality, and human rights and digni-
ty. The real purpose underlying these trends is not the restoration of man's external and superficial freedoms or values. It is
for man to restore the original love, original value, and original freedom which were endowed at his creation, but then lost.
The conclusion of God's dispensation in the Last Days will
bring about the realization of the First Blessing.

We can also know that the present days are the Last Days
when we see the restoration of the First Blessing in the restoration of man's spiritual state. We have already explained that
each person is created to become one in heart with God and to
be able to fully communicate with the spirit world when he
has perfected himself. However, before the Fall, Adam and
Eve were able to communicate with God and the spirit world,
although their capabilities were not completely developed.
Because of the Fall, Adam and Eve and all of their descendants, that is, all of mankind, fell into a state where they are
insensitive to the presence of God. But as the Bible indicates,
communication with the spirit world will be restored in the
Last Days: " ' ". . . in the last days . . . I will pour out my Spirit
upon all flesh, and your sons and daughters shall prophesy,
and your young men shall see visions, and your old men shall
dream dreams; . . . on my menservants and my maidservants
in those days I will pour out my Spirit; and they shall prophesy" ' " (Acts 2:17,18). Recent increases in spiritual experiences and psychic phenomena worldwide reflect the restoration of man's heart and spirit to the level that Adam and Eve
enjoyed just prior to the Fall and indicate that man is on the
verge of restoring the First Blessing.

God's Second Blessing to man was the ability for Adam
and Eve to perfect themselves as the True Parents and create

an ideal family, and then one society and one world centered on that family—in other words, the ability to create the model family and to make the world one family. The basic unit of that world is the ideal family. Through it God's dominion of love will transform the world into one of a unified culture centered on true love.

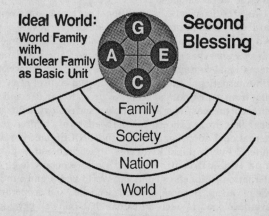

Ideal World:
World Family with Nuclear Family as Basic Unit

Second Blessing

Family

Society

Nation

World

However, Adam and Eve fell and became parents with Original Sin, and thus all of mankind became children with natures of evil and realized a world under an evil sovereignty. Therefore, God has worked through religion and through developing the external aspects of civilization to guide man toward the establishment of this unified culture and one world family.

Historically, many different cultures have come into existence. Through time, however, higher cultures have emerged centered on rising new religions. Through a process of absorption of the varied and numerous lower cultures by the higher and more universal ones, a consolidation of cultures has taken place. As a result, there are only four major cultures remaining: Christian, Moslem, Far Eastern (based on Buddhism, Confucianism, and Taoism), and Hindu. This convergent flow of history shows the trend toward man's establishing one world culture—and that God's Second Blessing is being restored.

The world of one culture centered on God's true love will

be realized when all people become brothers and sisters, with God as their parent. Based on this viewpoint, Christianity is the central religion in the work to fulfill God's Dispensation for Restoration because Christianity introduced God as the parent of all mankind, because it awaits the Messiah, who comes to establish one culture, and because it has worked to unite the world as one family.

As a result of God's dispensational work, man since World War II has, to an unprecedented extent, become aware of the need for international cooperation and world government. This awareness has given rise to the United Nations and many international commissions and organizations, all concerned with international standards and internal control of everything from nutrition and food resources to the use and resources of the seas, from atomic power and ecology to international law, from concern for the welfare of children (e.g., international adoption agencies and UNICEF) and disaster aid (e.g., International Red Cross) to world health (e.g., the World Health Organization) and world economy (e.g., the International Monetary Fund and World Bank), and a multitude of others. Economic interdependence and cooperation have developed to such an extent that the well-developed nations are to a great degree the marketplaces for the people of the world. Thus we find ourselves living in a world community, where the races, nationalities, languages, customs, cultures, and products of the world intermingle and harmonize as never before.

Because of the tremendous advances in transportation and communications, the world has "shrunk" to such an extent that we can travel to almost any part of the world in a few hours. (Just fifty or sixty years earlier, in the scope of that same few hours, our "world" was perhaps a hundred miles in radius.) With this ease of travel, travel to other countries has increased tremendously, bringing about unprecedented interaction and mutual understanding and harmony among different peoples and their customs, bringing us to the threshold of a unified world.

In this century there has been unprecedented development among many peoples worldwide of tolerance and understanding of other people and of a spirit of love. It is God's dispensation to restore the Second Blessing that has given rise to such attitudes. It also led to the benevolent treatment of the

defeated nations by the democratic victors after World War II
and the granting of independence to colonies and territories;
it has led to foreign aid programs, to increasing ecumenism, to
inter-cultural exchange, and to interracial and international
marriages and adoption of children. All of these show the
trend toward the restoration of God's Second Blessing to
man—the blessing of true love among people and the establishment of one world family.

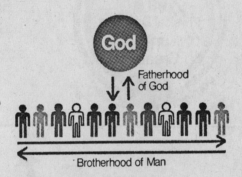

A Home is not a Home without Parents

All of these hopes and trends will reach fruition when the
final gifts of history arrive, the Lord of the Second Coming and
the new universal ideology that he brings, in other words the
gifts of God's Heart and the God-centered ideology. No home
can be truly a home without parents; so man's desires for
harmony and love will only be fulfilled when God and the
Messiah can stand in the position of man's parents.

God's Third Blessing to man is the right and ability of a
perfect person to have spiritual and physical dominion over
the Creation, that is, both internal and external dominion.
Internal dominion over the Creation means dominion
through love. External dominion is man's use and development of the Creation for his life through the means of science
and technology.

Evidence that the present time is the Last Days, and
therefore the stage just prior to the restoration of God's Third
Blessing, can be seen in the developing concern and love for

nature and also in the tremendous development of science and technology.

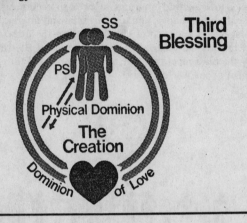

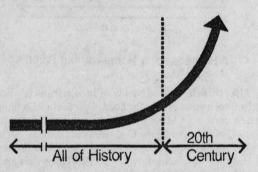

The Amazing Rise of Science and Technology in Recent Times

Originally, man's appreciation and love for the Creation are proportional to the growth of his spirit. Evidence of the restoration of man's love for the Creation can be seen in the ecology and conservation movements, in societies for the prevention of cruelty to animals, in drives to restore polluted areas, and in organizations and clubs formed for the appreciation of nature.

Through science and technology, man is restoring his external dominion over the Creation. Tremendous scientific progress has taken place in this century. Through this man has been gaining control over disease and over the sea, land, air, and even outer space. Man is also on the verge of being able to create an ideal standard of living for all people through such things as mass production, high yield crops, transformation of deserts to farmlands, and environmental control. Use of the ocean floor and even both polar caps are also examples of man's ability to turn the Creation into an ideal home.

We can see that the Three Blessings are in the process of being restored to mankind. Thus we can see that the establishment of God's ideal world is upon us—that we are in the Last Days.

CHAPTER FIVE

Resurrection

If we were to take everything in the Bible literally, then we would have to believe that at the Second Coming the buried and decomposed physical bodies of all the past believers will be restored to their original state of life in the flesh (1 Thes 4:16, Mt 27:52). But can we believe this? To resolve this question let us first look into the meaning of resurrection.

I. THE MEANING OF RESURRECTION

The word 'resurrection' means passing from death to life. To understand the meaning of 'passing from death to life', let us consider the meaning of the words 'life' and 'death'.

In Luke 9:60 we read that to the disciple who wanted to go home for his father's funeral, Jesus said, " '. . . Leave the *dead* to bury their own *dead* . . .' " (emphases added). In these words of Jesus we find two different concepts of life and death. One concept is concerned with the physiological functioning of the physical body. The other is concerned with the people who would gather for the burial of the disciple's father. Why did Jesus indicate that those people who would attend the funeral were dead when they were actually alive? It was because, being under Satan's dominion, they were ignorant of the purpose of life and did not know God, who is the source of life. Revelation 3:1 says, " '. . . you have the name of being alive and you are dead.' " From this verse we can see that even though a person is physically alive, if he is under Satan's dominion, then from Jesus' point of view he is dead. With this view of death, life would then mean to be within God's dominion, fulfilling the God-given purpose of life. In John 11:25,26 Jesus says, " '. . . he who believes in me, though he die, yet shall he live, and whoever lives and believes in me shall never die.' " This tells us that whoever is connected to God's dominion through Christ is alive, regardless of whether his physical

body is dead or alive and regardless of whether he is on earth
or in the spirit world.

1 Spiritual Death   **2** Physical Death

1   2

"Leave the dead to bury their own dead." —Luke 9:60

A. The Death Caused by the Fall

The need for resurrection is a result of the death caused by the
Fall. Let us consider which of the two kinds of death mentioned above is the death resulting from the fall of the first
human ancestors. Man's physical body is destined to return to
the earth after it becomes old and dies. If God had intended
human beings to live eternally on earth in their physical
bodies, there would have been no need to create the spirit
world for spirit selves to go to. God created the spirit world
before man fell; he did not create it after the Fall simply to
provide a dwelling for the spirit selves of fallen people. It was
always God's plan that man's physical self return to the earth
and that his spirit self dwell eternally with God in the spirit
world (Eccles 12:7). Physical death is not the death caused by
the Fall.

When God told Adam and Eve that they would surely die
on the day that they ate of the Fruit of the Tree of the Knowledge of Good and Evil (Gen 2:17), the death referred to was
not physical death. We see in Genesis that Adam and Eve
continued to be active and alive and to have children for more
than nine hundred years after they ate the Fruit of the Tree of
the Knowledge of Good and Evil. Yet, if we are to believe God's

Word, then in some sense they must have died the moment they broke God's commandment.

God's love is the source of life. Therefore leaving the realm of God's love and entering into Satan's realm, where there is no true love, is death. In 1 John 3:14 we learn that "He who does not love abides in death." Also, Romans 8:6 and Romans 6:23 respectively tell us, "To set the mind on the flesh [to be carnally minded] is death, but to set the mind on the Spirit is life and peace," and ". . . the wages of sin is death, but the free gift of God is eternal life in Christ Jesus. . . ." So from the Bible's viewpoint, the death which was causd by the Fall is the state resulting from sin—the state of being separated from God's love.

B. The True Meaning of Resurrection

Let us draw our conclusion as to the meaning of resurrection. If the physical body's return to the earth is *not* the death caused by the Fall, then it is obvious that the meaning of 'passing from death to life'—that is, resurrection—cannot be revival of a decomposed body. According to "The Principles of the Creation," it was God's original intention that man's physical body die and return to the earth when it becomes old (Eccles 12:7). So once the physical body decomposes, it will not be resurrected to its original state.

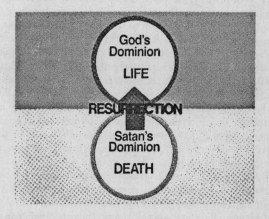

God's
Dominion
LIFE

RESURRECTION

Satan's
Dominion
DEATH

Since resurrection does not refer to physical life and death, it must refer to the life and death of man's spirit. Therefore resurrection is the process of man's being restored from Satan's dominion to God's direct dominion through the Dispensation for Restoration. If a person repents of his sins and becomes a better person today than he was yesterday, then he is resurrected to that extent. Jesus said, " '. . . he who hears my word and believes him who sent me, has eternal life; he does not come into judgment, but has passed from death to life' " (Jn 5:24). This shows that resurrection, or passing from death to life, begins from the point of hearing Jesus' words and believing in God. The Bible says, ". . . as in Adam all die, so also in Christ shall all be made alive" (1 Cor 15:22). Because of the fall of Adam, his entire lineage has been a satanic one, and therefore dead. So, to be resurrected means to become one of God's lineage, through Christ.

Based on this understanding of resurrection, we should not expect a major external change to result from resurrection. Although Adam and Eve were different after the Fall in that they were spiritually dead, no significant physical change took place. Thus there is no external difference between a man who possesses eternal life because of rebirth through the Holy Spirit and a thief who is still under the dominion of death.

However, Matthew 27:52 seems to support belief in resurrection of the physical body. Let us examine this passage. It says, ". . . the tombs also were opened, and many bodies of the saints who had fallen asleep were raised, and coming out of the tombs after his [Jesus'] resurrection they went into the holy city and appeared to many." However, if this had taken place literally, then the history of persecution in early Christianity would not have taken place. Even though the Israelites had become faithless and had crucified Jesus, they had done so believing that he was *not* the Lord. However, if they had witnessed the prophets rising from their tombs and had heard them testifying that Jesus was the Messiah, wouldn't they have believed in Jesus? Then why would they have persecuted the disciples of Jesus?

Also, since resurrection is said to result in eternal life, then shouldn't we be able to see many of those resurrected Old Testament prophets alive today? And wouldn't those brought to life through the grace of resurrection have testified to many

‘ about God and Jesus? Then certainly there would have been some record of this in the Book of Acts. However, there is only one passage in the Bible that mentions them—the one in Matthew which tells of their rising from their tombs and appearing to many (Mt 27:52).

An understanding of the true meaning of resurrection will easily solve this problem. Since resurrection does not mean bringing corpses back to life, it could not have been physical bodies that "arose from the grave" and "came back to life." Through the grace of God, the inner selves, or spirit selves, of the passed-away saints had grown closer to perfection. Matthew and other disciples, inspired by the Holy Spirit, had their spiritual sight temporarily restored, and were thus able to see those spirit people. Those who remained untouched by the Holy Spirit had only their normal physical sight, and thus could not see the spirit selves of the Old Testament prophets.

II. THE PRINCIPLES OF RESURRECTION

Since resurrection means the phenomena occurring in the course of restoring fallen man's nature to the standard originally created by God, the dispensation for resurrection is actually the Dispensation for Restoration. The Dispensation for Restoration is also the dispensation for re-creation. Consequently the dispensation for resurrection is carried out according to what is explained in "The Principles of the Creation."

First of all, according to "The Principles of the Creation," the Purpose of the Creation is fulfilled when man accomplishes his responsibility, by believing in and living God's Word. Therefore in resurrection, which is re-creation, God gives man His Word—he gave the Old Testament and the New Testament, and he promised to give the complete testament when Christ returns. In order to be resurrected, man must fulfill his responsibility—to believe in and live the Word. Thus, resurrection is accomplished by God's giving His Word (truth) to man together with man's fulfilling his responsibility to believe in and live the truth.

Secondly, according to "The Principles of the Creation," each person's spirit self is created to grow and become perfect only on the basis of a relationship with the physical self. In

Principles of Resurrection

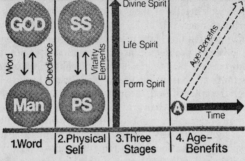

| 1. Word | 2. Physical Self | 3. Three Stages | 4. Age-Benefits |

accordance with this principle, the resurrection (purification, growth, and perfection) of a person's spirit self must also be realized based on his physical self, and thus, while he is living on earth. Actually, until today, resurrection has usually been conceived of as the reviving of the physically dead at Christ's return. But this is incorrect; God's dispensation for resurrection is an ongoing process that has focused on the people who are alive on earth. It is to them that he has sent prophets with the Truth.

Thirdly, according to "The Principles of the Creation," man is created to become perfect by growing through the three stages of the growing period. Therefore, the dispensation for the resurrection of fallen man is to be accomplished through three dispensational stages.

Fourthly, although the various central persons in God's Dispensation for Restoration could not fully carry out their responsibilities, they did their best with the deepest loyalty to God. Their loyalty and devotion has accumulated as merit on earth. Based on this foundation of heart laid by faithful people of earlier ages, people of later generations have been able to receive certain merits in each age *(merits of the age)* in the dispensation for resurrection. The dispensation for resurrection is carried out according to the merits of the age. In other words, the degree of resurrection possible in a given age is based on the historical foundation of heart established by the faithful of earlier ages.

III. THE DISPENSATION FOR THE RESURRECTION OF THE PEOPLE ON EARTH

A. God's Dispensation for Resurrection is Based on the People on Earth

Until today, when Christians thought of resurrection, they usually thought of the physically dead receiving new life at Christ's return. Yet once we understand the true meaning of resurrection and the principles of God's dispensation for resurrection, we understand that God works his dispensation for resurrection primarily based on the people on earth. From the viewpoint of man, history may seem to be merely the repetition of one generation after another. From the viewpoint of God, who is carrying out the dispensation, the succession of generations is not significant. From God's viewpoint the whole of history is nothing but the work to resurrect one dead person, Adam. If the first human ancestor, Adam, had not fallen but had grown through the three stages of the growing period, his spirit self would have grown through the stages of form spirit and life spirit to finally become a divine spirit, the spirit of one who is fulfilling the Purpose of the Creation.

However, as a result of the Fall, man's spirit self plummeted from the perfection level of the growth stage to a very base state—that is, he fell below the level at which he was originally created. Adam and Eve fell into the non-Principle realm and inherited the Fallen Nature from the fallen archangel.

B. The Three Stages in the Dispensation for Resurrection

God began his dispensation for resurrection with Adam's family, which had fallen into the non-Principle realm. However, since persons in Adam's and Noah's families failed to carry out their responsibilities, resurrection itself did not begin until Abraham's family. So in retrospect the two thousand year period from Adam to Abraham ended up being the period during which only the foundation for God's dispensation for resurrection was established. Thus, this period is called the *Dispensational Age of the Foundation for Resurrection.*

On this foundation, God carried out the formation stage

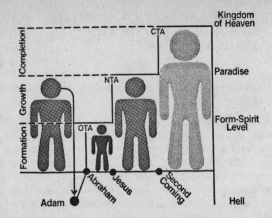

of the dispensation for resurrection, which again, because of
man's repeated failures, ended up taking two thousand years,
from Abraham to Jesus. People on earth who received the
merits of the age of formation stage resurrection were to fulfill
their responsibility by keeping and living the Old Testament
Law, the formation stage Word of re-creation. Since people
were to be justified by their practice of the Law (Word), this
age is called the *age of justification by keeping the law.* If a
person fulfilled that responsibility, based on his physical self,
his spirit self would grow through the formation stage of
resurrection and become a form spirit. When a person who
has attained the form spirit level on earth leaves his physical
self, his spirit self goes to live at the *form spirit level of the spirit
world.*

Complete resurrection should have taken place through
Jesus, the Messiah; however, because of man's failure to
accept Jesus, the period after his death has been the period for
only growth stage resurrection. Because of the Israelites'
faithlessness toward Jesus, Jesus was crucified and the completion of the dispensation for resurrection was delayed until
the Second Coming. In retrospect, we can see that the period
from Jesus' time up to the time of his Second Coming has been
the *age for* only *growth stage resurrection.* During this age,
people on earth could receive the merits of the age of growth
stage resurrection and carry out their responsibility by believing and living the New Testament, God's growth stage Word of

re-creation. Therefore, this age is called the *age of justification by faith*. People of that age could pass through the growth stage of resurrection and attain the life spirit level by believing and living the New Testament Word. When a person who has attained the life spirit level leaves his physical self, he goes to live in Paradise, which is the *life spirit level of the spirit world*.

The *Dispensational Age of Completion Stage Resurrection* will be completed with the resurrection of both spirit and body* (spirit self and physical self) by the Messiah at the Second Coming. The Messiah will bring the Completed Testament, which is to bring about the fulfillment of the Old Testament and the New Testament. People on earth can receive the merits of the age of completion stage resurrection by accomplishing their responsibility to believe in and incarnate the new Word and directly attend the Messiah with full sincerity of heart. Therefore, the age is called the *age of justification by attendance*. When a person belives in and attends the Messiah at the Second Coming, his spirit self reaches the perfection level of resurrection and becomes a divine spirit. The place on earth where the people of this divine spirit stage live is called the Kingdom of Heaven on earth. When a perfected person living in the Kingdom of Heaven on earth leaves his physical self, he goes to live in the *Kingdom of Heaven in the spirit world*, which is the region of the spirit world belonging to divine spirits.

C. Heaven and Paradise

Traditionally, Christians have understood Heaven and Paradise to be the same. However, as was already explained, the Kingdom of Heaven is the spirit world dwelling place of spirit persons who have attained the divine spirit level while in their physical selves on earth. Although Jesus, the Messiah, came to complete the salvation of man, because of his death on the cross the Purpose of the Creation, which is fulfilled in the Kingdom of Heaven in the spirit world *and* on earth, was not fulfilled at that time. There has never been a person who achieved the divine spirit level while on earth, and therefore,

---

* Though Jesus brought spiritual salvation to man, as can be seen in Romans 7:14-25, the Original Sin remains within man. The actual elimination of Original Sin will take place at the Second Coming.

the Kingdom of Heaven in the spirit world remains vacant—
not one person has entered it, since it is the divine spirit level
of the spirit world. Why then did Jesus say that whoever
believed in him would enter the Kingdom of Heaven? He said
that because his original purpose was to bring about the
Kingdom of Heaven. However, because of the faithlessness of
the people of Israel, he died on the cross without realizing the
Kingdom of Heaven.

At the time Jesus was crucified, two thieves were crucified with him, one on his right and one on his left. When the
thief on the right showed that he believed in Jesus, Jesus told
him that he would be with him in Paradise (Lk 23:43). Paradise is the life spirit level of the spirit world—the level which
people believing in Jesus reach after leaving their physical
selves. Those in Paradise must pray for the goal of perfection
and wait for the opening of the gates to the Kingdom of
Heaven.

D. Spiritual Phenomena Occurring in the Last Days

Man fell from the perfection level of the growth stage. As man
enters the Last Days, he enters the age in which he can restore
himself to the perfection level of the growth stage. By believing and living the Word of the New Testament Age, a person's
spirit self can attain the perfection level of the growth stage,
the position of man immediately prior to the Fall.

The Last Days is when man restores on a world-wide scale
the level just prior to the Fall—the life spirit level, which is the
level at which Adam attained the ability to deeply communicate with God. For this reason, in the Last Days, as the top of
the growth stage is approached there will be many people who
develop the ability to communicate with the spirit world.
Seeing things from this viewpoint we can understand God's
promise to pour out his spirit on all flesh in the Last Days (Acts
2:17).

In the Last Days, there will be many people who receive
the revelation, "You are the Lord." This does not mean that
they are the Lord of the Second Coming, but means that they
are being re-established in the position of lord of the Creation,
that position having been lost because of the Fall of Adam. In
other words, they are restoring the level of spiritual development that Adam had reached just prior to the Fall.

Just as John the Baptist was to prepare the way for Jesus,

there will be many people with various missions who are to prepare the way for the Lord of the Second Coming. Since these persons responsible for certain missions represent the Lord of the Second Coming, they each receive the revelation, "You are the Lord," though they may be working in an age or in a field different from that of the Lord. If at such a time a person receiving the spiritual communication does not understand the principle behind it and mistakenly thinks that he is the Lord of the Second Coming and acts as if he is the Lord, he becomes an antichrist. This is the reason for the biblical prophecy that many antichrists will appear in the Last Days.

Also, although people capable of spiritual communication communicate with the same spirit world, since the spiritual level, circumstances, and individual character are different in each spiritually open person, the level of the spirit world with which they communicate and the contents of the revelations they receive differ from one another (1 Cor 15:41, 12:8-10). Because of this there is often disagreement and conflict among spiritualists. Especially since they have only a vertical relationship with God and are responsible for only one part of the entire Dispensation for Restoration, they are often ignorant of their horizontal relationship with others who have spiritual communication. Since each is the best in his particular area of responsibility, God gives each the revelation "You are the best" to encourage him to do his best. Yet, because they do not know the whole picture of what God is doing, they often conflict with one another. The confusion among those who can communicate spiritually will be cleared up by the new expression of truth, which will explain the overall purpose of the Dispensation for Restoration. Based on this complete understanding, spiritualists will be able to achieve reciprocal, horizontal harmony, in addition to vertical harmony with God. Their abilities should fit in with the purpose of the whole.

IV. THE DISPENSATION FOR THE RESURRECTION OF SPIRIT PERSONS

A. Returning Resurrection of Spirit Persons

Countless people have already passed on to the spirit world, and not one has ever perfected himself while on earth in his

physical self. How can these spirit persons be resurrected? A
person's spirit self can neither grow nor be resurrected apart
from the physical self. So for those in the spirit world to be
resurrected, they must return to earth and fulfill the responsibility that they left unaccomplished during their physical life.
They accomplish this by cooperating with people on earth and
working through others' physical selves to help them to fulfill
their mission. This is the reason that Jude 1:14 says that in the
Last Days "... the Lord came with his holy myriads...." In
what manner do the spirit persons cooperate with persons on
earth to accomplish God's Will? When a person on earth,
through prayer or spiritual activities, happens to form a base
conducive to spiritual communication and partnership, then
a spirit person will return and begin to cooperate with that
person on earth by Give and Take Action with his spirit self.

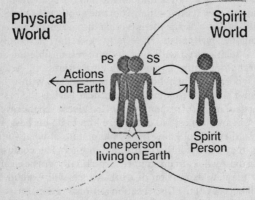

The spirit person helps the person on earth to receive revelations or to have deep experiences of truth, and sometimes
helps him to experience other spiritual phenomena such as
the power to cure diseases, the ability to prophesy, or spiritual
fire.

B. Returning Resurrection of Spirit Persons Who Believed in God

Jesus' age two thousand years ago and the time when Christ
returns in the Last Days are both special times when all the
faithful on earth can be spiritually elevated (in accordance

with the Dispensation for Restoration). Especially since these are the times when God's Word of re-creation appears anew (as the Gospel and the new words respectively), then according to the principles of resurrection these times are the most significant opportunities—opportunities when man's spirit self can be resurrected at an accelerated rate. Therefore, in Jesus' time the form spirits of the Old Testament Age, who had dealt only with the Law, all longed to return and meet the condition of cooperating with the faithful on earth.

Since Elijah appeared as a spirit person to Jesus and his disciples on the mount of the Transfiguration (Mt 17:3), it is clear that Elijah is in the spirit world. Yet, Jesus indicated that John the Baptist, who was on earth, was Elijah (Mt 17:12,13; 11:14). In light of the principles of resurrection we can understand that Elijah had returned in order to complete the mission that he had left unaccomplished while on earth by cooperating with John the Baptist. According to the principles governing returning resurrection, the physical self of John the Baptist was a substitute for that of Elijah.

Matthew 27:52 says that when Jesus died on the cross many saints rose from their tombs. This is also a phenomenon of the resurrection of spirit persons—resurrection of those who had developed a form spirit while on earth. By cooperating with those on earth who believe in and attend the Lord of the Second Coming and by helping them to become divine spirit selves, spirit persons of the life spirit level (Paradise) can receive the same benefits and themselves become divine spirits.

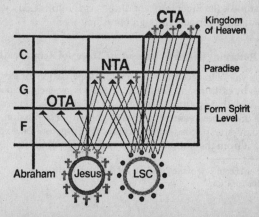

Hebrews 11:39-41 says, "And all these [saints of the Old Testament age], though well attested by their faith, did not receive what was promised [admission to the Kingdom of Heaven], since God had foreseen something better [the Kingdom of Heaven] for us [persons on earth], that apart from us they [spirit persons] should not be made perfect." These words demonstrate the principles of returning resurrection.

C. The Returning Resurrection of All Other Spirit Persons

The spirit persons who believed in religions other than Judaism and Christianity when they passed away also must return and cooperate with people on earth—with those who are of their respective religions. It is with them that they can easily form a reciprocal base.

Good spirit people who lived conscientiously while on earth, though not religiously, return and cooperate with good people on earth who have similar spiritual levels and circumstances.

Matthew 25:41 mentions the devil and his angels. In this passage, 'His [the devil's] angels' includes evil spirit persons. For evil spirit persons also, there is no way to be resurrected except through returning resurrection, which is possible only in certain ages. But evil spirit persons cannot descend to earth simply as they wish, and even if they do descend, they do not necessarily receive the benefits of returning resurrection. Before evil spirit persons can obtain the benefits of returning resurrection through the Second Coming, their work must first meet the indemnity condition* that fulfills God's will to eradicate their sins through punishing them.

D. Returning Resurrection and the Theory of Reincarnation

God works to accomplish the total Dispensation for Restoration by calling many individuals and giving each the portion of work that is suitable for him. As the Dispensation progresses and a new central person is chosen for a mission, God progressively broadens the scale of the Dispensation, expanding it from the individual level to the levels of the family, the

---

* See "Overview of the Principles of the Dispensation for
  Restoration."

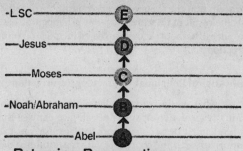

Returning-Resurrection
and the Theory of Reincarnation

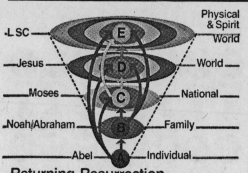

Returning-Resurrection
and the Theory of Reincarnation

nation, and the world. A person who dies without completing his mission must return and cooperate with a person on earth who has the same type of mission and the same spiritual disposition. From this mission-oriented viewpoint, the physical self of the person on earth becomes the physical self for the returning spirit person as well. In this sense, the person on earth becomes the "second coming" of the returning spirit person. When viewed with spiritual eyes, the person on earth could seem to be the reincarnation of the spirit person who is cooperating with him.

For this reason in the Last Days many people will appear claiming to be Elijah, Buddha, Confucius, or the Olive Tree. It would seem that the theory of trans-migration, or reincarnation, is the result of interpreting what is happening based on appearances, without knowing the principles of returning resurrection.

E. Unification of Religions by Returning Resurrection

Based on what was already explained in the section on the returning resurrection of spirit people, we can see that life spirit level spirit persons, who are in Paradise, must inevitably return to earth and cooperate with the faithful at the time of the Second Coming. The time and type of help that a person on earth receives from a spirit person vary depending on the person's attitude, faith, and disposition and the merits of his

ancestors. Yet those who have strong faith will ultimately be led by spirit persons to the Lord at the Second Coming, where they can devote themselves to the Will of God. Since all of the most faithful will gather around the Lord through the influence of spirit people, the unification of Christianity will be naturally realized at the time of the Second Coming.

As will be discussed in the section on central and peripheral histories (in "Second Coming"), Christianity is not a religion for Christians alone; it is the central religion with the mission of accomplishing the ultimate purpose of all religions which pursue goodness. Accordingly, those believers of various religions who have passed on to the spirit world will return to those of their own faith who are on earth and lead them to the Lord of the Second Coming. Yet, the time when each person is connected with the central religion will vary according to the spiritual level of the spirit person and the beliefs and degree of faith of the person on earth. Even though believers of the various religions may have had no communication with each other up until now, through the influence of spirit people, all the faithful of the various religions are destined to unite centered on the Lord of the Second Coming.

CHAPTER SIX

Predestination

The shortcomings of traditional teachings concerning Predestination have been the cause of confusion among theologians as well as among many religious and conscientious people. Predestination, in its broader sense, is a teaching that all things and events are predetermined by God toward the fulfillment of his eternal purpose. In its narrower sense, the doctrine of Predestination teaches that man's salvation or damnation is preordained solely by God and is not determined by man's own efforts.

The various theories of Predestination find their primary basis in the New Testament, especially in Chapters 8, 9, and 11 of St. Paul's letter to the Romans. In those chapters, Paul puts great emphasis on grace as the sole basis of salvation and election by God. Other passages in the Bible can also be interpreted as showing that all aspects of man's life are predestined by God, that man's personal happiness and misery and fortune and misfortune, as well as the rise and fall of nations, are all predestined by God.

Bible Passages Which Appear to Support the Theory of Absolute Predestination

Romans 8: 29-30   Romans 9:15-16

Romans 9:10-13   Romans 9:21

Bible Passages which Contradict the Theory of Absolute Predestination

Genesis 2:17	Ezekial 33:11
John 3:16	Jonah 3:10
Matthew 7:7-8	Mark 5:34
Genesis 6:5-7	James 5:14-15
I Samuel 15:11	

On the other hand, there are many passages that contradict this view. For example, when we see that God commanded the first man and woman not to eat of the Fruit of the Tree of Knowledge of Good and Evil (Gen 2:17), it is evident that man's fall was not predestined by God, but rather was the result of man's disobedience. Jesus said " '. . . God so loved the world he gave his only Son, that whoever believes in him should not perish but have eternal life' " (Jn 3:16). By using the word 'whoever', Jesus shows that salvation is open to everyone, and therefore no one could be predestined for damnation. In Matthew 7:7 Jesus says, " 'Ask, and it will be given you; seek, and you will find; knock, and it will be opened to you. For *everyone* who asks receives, and he who seeks finds, and to him who knocks it will be opened' " (emphasis added), clearly showing that human effort plays a decisive role in shaping events, that life is not determined solely by divine predestination.

If we were to accept unconditionally the traditional teachings of absolute predestination, then prayer, evangelism, charity, and all other human effort would be of no value in God's Dispensation for Restoration. After all, if everything is absolutely predestined by God, then human effort cannot possibly alter the preordained course of life. Now let us answer these questions concerning predestination based on The Principle.

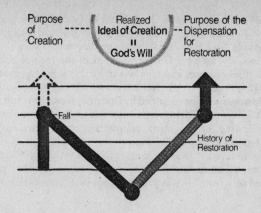

Purpose of Creation - - - Realized **Ideal of Creation** = God's Will - - Purpose of the Dispensation for Restoration

Fall

History of Restoration

I. THE PREDESTINATION OF GOD'S WILL

God's Will is to fulfill his Ideal for the Creation. As a result of man's fall, God's Will has remained unfulfilled, and God has had to work to accomplish this same Will by an alternate means: the Dispensation for Restoration. Since God is good, his original Purpose for the Creation is good. God could not possibly have predestined anything that would contradict his own Will. In this light, we can see that God could not have predestined such things as the Fall of man, sin, and the judgment and punishment of man.

God **:** Good

God's Purpose of Creation **:** Good

Purpose of the Dispensation for Restoration **:** Good

Predestination **:** Only Good

If God had predestined man's fall, then why would he look at fallen man and say that he was sorry he had made man (Gen 6:5,6)? If all of man's actions are predestined by God, then

whenever man sins or is disobedient to God, these actions
must also be the result of God's predestination. And if all sins
and acts of disobedience to God are predestined by God, then
why would God have been displeased in the case of King
Saul's disobedience, and why would he regret having made
Saul king (I Sam 15:11)? Neither man's fall nor King Saul's
faithlessness were predestined by God; they were the result of
man's failure to fulfill his responsibility. Nor did God originally predestine the judgment and punishment of fallen man.
God has no desire to see man suffer, as evidenced in the
following verses: " 'Say to them, As I live, says the Lord God, I
have no pleasure in the death of the wicked, but that the
wicked turn from his way and live; turn back, turn back from

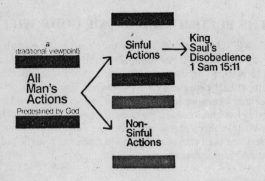

your evil ways; for why will you die, O House of Israel?' "
(Ezek 33:11). Thus, when the people of Nineveh turned from
their path of evil and repented of their sins, God did not fulfill
his prophecy that their city would be overthrown (Jon 3:10),
for as God said in Ezekiel 33:14,15, " '. . . though I say to the
wicked, "You shall surely die," yet if he turns from his sin and
does what is lawful and right, if the wicked restores the
pledge, gives back what he has taken by robbery, and walks in
the statutes of life, committing no iniquity; he shall surely
live, he shall not die.' "

Then, to what extent has God predestined his Will, namely, his Purpose for the Creation and the purpose of the Dispen-

God ●	Eternal, Unchanging,	
●	Absolute	

God's ●	Eternal, Unchanging,
Purpose ●	Absolute

God's ●	To Fulfill the Purpose of
Will ●	Creation and the Purpose of
	the Dispensation for
	Restoration

●	God's ●	Eternal, Unchanging,
● ●	Will ●	Absolute

sation for Restoration? God is absolute, eternal, and unchanging; God's Purpose must also be absolute, eternal, and unchanging. Therefore his Will, which is to fulfill the Purpose of the Creation and the purpose of the Dispensation for Restoration, must also be absolute, eternal, and unchanging (Is 46:11). Since God's Will is absolute and unchanging, if a person chosen by God fails to fulfill his responsibility, God goes on to fulfill His Will by selecting another person as his replacement.

II. GOD'S PREDESTINATION OF THE ACCOMPLISHMENT OF HIS WILL

As explained in "The Principle of the Creation," the Purpose of the Creation is fulfilled only when man fulfills his responsibility, which is to live in accordance with God's commandments. God's will for the Dispensation for Restoration, which is to fulfill his Purpose for the Creation, is absolute, and is therefore beyond human influence. Nevertheless, the fulfillment of his Will depends on man's fulfilling his responsibility. Then to what degree does God predestine the fulfillment of his Will? God's Will is absolute, but the realization of his Will depends upon man's fulfilling his responsibility. God predestines that his Will is to be accomplished—but only through the accomplishment of both God's responsibility *and* that of the *central person.* We can say that man's responsibility is "5 percent" and

God's is "95 percent" as a means of indicating that man's
responsibility in fulfilling God's Will is very small compared
with God's. However, in order to accomplish this "5 percent,"
man must put forth his 100 percent effort.

Accomplishment of
God's Will

Accomplishment of
Man's Responsibility

Accomplishment of
God's Responsibility

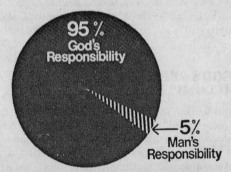

**Man's Part of the Total Responsibility
for the Fulfillment of God's Will**

Thus, God predestined that his Will was to be fulfilled
when Adam and Eve fulfilled their responsibility not to eat of
the Fruit of the Tree of Knowledge of Good and Evil (Gen 2:17).
In the dispensation for salvation through Jesus, God predestined that fallen man would fulfill his responsibility when he

believed in Jesus as the Messiah and followed him (Jn 3:16, Mt 19:21). Yet man has rarely carried out his small portion of responsibility, and this has caused the fulfillment of God's Dispensation for Restoration to be delayed again and again.

As the following Bible passages show, even in our day-to-day life we receive God's saving grace only when we do our part: ". . . the prayer of faith will save the sick man. . . . " (Jas 5:15); " '. . . your faith has made you well. . . .' " (Mk 5:34); " 'For everyone who asks receives, and he who seeks finds, and to him who knocks it will be opened' " (Mt 7:8). Clearly, God predestines that his grace can be received only when man accomplishes his responsibility.

III. GOD'S PREDESTINATION OF THE CENTRAL PERSON

In order for God's Will to be fulfilled, God must select someone to fulfill man's responsibility (as will be explained in "Overview of the Principles of the Dispensation for Restoration"). However, the person chosen by God may either fulfill his responsibility or fail to fulfill it. Thus, God does not predestine that a person will fulfill the role (mission) that God desires him to have. Then, does God predestine man at all, and if so, to what degree?

Yes, God does predestine man. When God predestines someone for a mission, he predestines that person "95 percent." In other words, he predestines a person to the extent that when that person carries out his "5 percent" portion of responsibility, he is fully able to carry out the mission for which he was chosen. Should a person fail to fulfill his responsibility, he cannot become the person that God wanted him to be, nor can God's will to fulfill things through him be realized.

For example, on the foundation of God's "95 percent preparation," God predestined that Adam and Eve become the True Ancestors on the condition that they fully carry out their responsibility. However, because of their failure to do so, God's Will was not fulfilled. As a result of this failure, it became necessary for God to send the Messiah as the True Father for mankind. God also predestined that Judas Iscariot be Jesus' apostle on the condition that he carry out his responsibility by being loyal to Jesus. However, when Judas betrayed Jesus, God's will remained unfulfilled, and God replaced Judas with Matthias (Acts 1:15-26).

Next, let us examine the factors which qualify a person to be chosen by God as the central person in the Dispensation for Restoration.

First, the person must have been born of the central nation, the nation chosen to carry out the Dispensation for Restoration. This is because the chosen people are closest to God in heart.

Second, that person must be descended from ancestors who have a history of righteousness. It is natural that for the fulfillment of the Dispensation for Restoration God would choose those who have a long line of distinguished ancestors who have accumulated merit through their sacrifice and service for the good of their fellow men.

Third, that person must be endowed with a natural disposition suited to the mission in question.

Fourth, that person must have acquired the proper education, training, and experience necessary to accomplish the mission.

Fifth, that person must have been born at the right time and place to carry out God's Will.

Qualifications for Being a Central Person in God's Dispensation for Restoration

1	Chosen Nation
2	Good Ancestors
3	Appropriate Disposition
4	Necessary Experience
5	Right Time and Place

However, even though a person may have all of these qualifications *and* be predestined by God for a particular mission, whether or not he fulfills that mission is not predestined by God. Attaining and maintaining his role is determined by his fulfilling his responsibility.

IV. CLARIFICATION OF BIBLICAL PASSAGES WHICH APPEAR TO SUPPORT THE DOCTRINE OF ABSOLUTE PREDESTINATION

How are we to interpret those Bible passages which appear to show that man's election and salvation are strictly predestined? For instance, how are we to understand Romans 8:29,30: "For those whom he foreknew he also predestined. . . . and those whom he predestined he also called; and those whom he called he also justified; and those whom he justified he also glorified."?

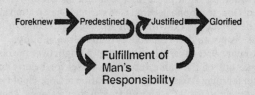

Foreknew ➡ Predestined ➡ Justified ➡ Glorified

Fulfillment of Man's Responsibility

Romans 8:29-30

Since God is omniscient, he knows who is qualified to be chosen as the central person in the Dispensation for Restoration. For the fulfillment of the Dispensation for Restoration, God predestines and calls a person. However, the person called is not predestined to be justified and glorified automatically. In order to be justified, he must fulfill his responsibility. Only after he is thus justified can he enjoy glory from God. This passage from Romans appears to support the view of absolute predestination only because in this case the Bible does not specifically mention man's responsibility.

Romans 9:15,16 says, " 'I will have mercy on whom I have mercy, and I will have compassion on whom I have compassion.' So it depends not upon man's will or exertion, but upon

God's mercy." This passage seems to show that man's desires, hopes, prayers, and efforts are to no avail and that man must depend solely upon God's grace. However, let us look more deeply into this.

Based on his foreknowledge, God alone chooses the person best suited for the fulfillment of the Dispensation for Restoration, and man's will or exertion cannot affect those decisions by God. For example, no one can decide to be born of a particular nation, or as a descendant of a particular family; no one can decide where or when he will be born; no one can decide that he will be born with particular abilities; nor can anyone decide any other matters of this nature. However, once a person is chosen, that person's desires, hopes, prayers, and efforts determine whether God can actually use him. The purpose of these Bible passages is to emphasize the power and grace of God, to emphasize that God's criteria for election and what he decides to do with man are not man's concern; its purpose is not to deny the role of man's responsibility.

Romans 9:21 says, "Has the potter no right over the clay, to make out of the same lump one vessel for beauty and another for menial use?" Man, as a creation of God, should not protest the Will of his Creator under any circumstance. Therefore, fallen man, who has become devoid of value, is certainly in no position to complain about any treatment by God, who is the very source of his salvation.

In Romans 9:10-13 we read that God loved Jacob and hated Esau, even while they were in their mother's womb, and that Esau, the elder, was to serve his younger brother, Jacob. As will be explained in greater detail in "Abraham's Family in the Dispensation for Restoration," God was working a special will through these brothers. The fact that Jacob was "loved" by God does not mean that he could receive God's grace unconditionally. In order to actually receive God's love, he had to accomplish his responsibility. Even though Esau was "hated" by God (for a special dispensational reason, which will be explained later), if he had accomplished his responsibility, he too would have received the blessing of God's love.

Belief in absolute predestination results from a lack of understanding concerning the relationship between man's responsibility and God's responsibility in fulfilling God's Will for the Dispensation for Restoration. This misunderstanding has led to the belief that God's Will is realized by God's action

alone and to the failure to appreciate the vast importance of
man's responsibility.

CHAPTER SEVEN

Christology

What sort of person is Jesus? What is the relationship between Jesus and God? What is the relationship between Jesus and the Holy Spirit? What is the relationship between Jesus and fallen man? What do trinity and rebirth mean?

Christology deals with these questions. In order to answer them, we must begin by understanding the value of an original, true person. The reason for this is that if Adam and Eve had perfected themselves and had become true human beings, true husband and wife, and true parents, giving birth to descendants who were the embodiments of goodness, there would have been no reason for the Messiah (and thus no Christological discussions).

I. THE VALUE OF A PERSON WHO FULFILLS THE PURPOSE OF THE CREATION

From the following viewpoints, let us discuss the value of a person who fulfills the Purpose of the Creation, that is, of one who attains the value of the perfect Adam.

First of all, what is the value of this perfect person in relation to God? According to "The Principles of the Creation," man is created as the child of God, as the object that substantially resembles the invisible God. When a person fulfills the Purpose of the Creation, he becomes God's body, a being in which the spirit of God dwells (1 Cor 3:16). Naturally he has a divine nature and is one in heart with God. He is a true person, one who is perfect as his Heavenly Father is perfect, as Jesus said (Mt 5:48). Thus, a true person is one who is the visible embodiment of God, is God's true son or daughter, has a divine nature, and fulfills the Purpose of the Creation.

Secondly, what is the value of a perfect person in relation to other people? According to "The Principles of the Creation," God's purpose in creating man is for God to enjoy happiness through him. Therefore, each person is an object substantially resembling the characteristics within God, the subject. Since all human beings resemble the universal aspects of God, all persons share a common nature. However, each individual also resembles certain unique characteristics within God. Thus, no two individuals are the same. If God created, anywhere in his entire Creation, two or more individuals whose characteristics were exactly alike, then God's own Creation would be wasteful. Since man is created to be eternal, God's desire to experience stimulating joy through a certain individual is sufficiently satisfied through that one individual. Therefore, a person who fulfills the Purpose of the Creation is a non-duplicable entity, unique in the entire universe, whoever he might be. In other words, a true person, a person who fulfills the Purpose of the Creation, is a unique individual who will never be duplicated throughout eternity, so he has an innate unique value, which cannot be denied.

Thirdly, what is the value of a perfect person in relation to the rest of the Creation? According to "The Principles of the Creation," man was created to rule the invisible spirit world by means of his spirit self and the physical world by means of his physical self. Man then functions as the medium through which these two worlds interact. A person who fulfills the Purpose of the Creation is to rule the entire cosmos (Gen 1:28).

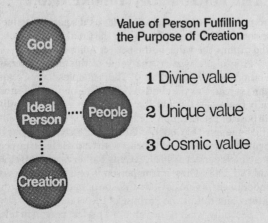

Value of Person Fulfilling
the Purpose of Creation

1 Divine value

2 Unique value

3 Cosmic value

Man's spirit self is to be the microcosm of the entire spirit world and his physical self is to be the microcosm of the entire physical world. A true human being, one who fulfills the Purpose of the Creation, is the microcosm of the entire cosmos. Man is a microcosm (of the Creation) and has the value of the cosmos. The fact that man is originally of such cosmic value underlies Jesus' saying " 'For what will it profit a man if he gains the whole world and forfeits his life?' " (Mt 16:26).

II. JESUS AND THE PERSON WHO FULFILLS THE PURPOSE OF THE CREATION

A. Jesus and the Perfect Person

As explained in "The Fall," if Adam had become the first man who fulfilled the Ideal for the Creation, he would have become the very Tree of Life referred to in Genesis 2:9, and thus, all of his descendants would have become trees of life. However, because Adam fell, he could not realize the ideal of the Tree of Life (Gen 3:24), and ever since, fallen people have hoped to restore themselves and become trees of life (Prov 13:12, Rev 22:14).

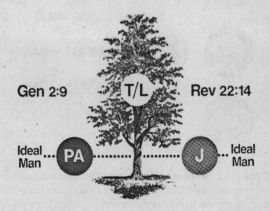

Though fallen man has the "name of being alive," he is, in reality, a false tree of life and dead (Rev 3:1). Since fallen people cannot restore themselves as trees of life by their own power, a Tree of Life—in other words a man who has fulfilled the Ideal for the Creation—must come and graft fallen man to him. The man who comes as the Tree of Life is Christ (Rev 22:14). Therefore, perfected Adam, symbolized by the Tree of Life in the Garden of Eden, and Jesus, who is likened to the Tree of Life in Revelation 22:14, are identical from the standpoint of their both being persons who have fulfilled the Ideal for the Creation.

Then, is Jesus a human being? Yes, he is. He is an example of a person who has fulfilled the Ideal for the Creation; he is a true person, an example of man as he was originally created, and as such his value is not to be compared with the value of fallen man.

As already mentioned, a true person is one who fulfills the Purpose of the Creation, is the incarnation of God, and is perfect as God is perfect, possessing divine value. A perfect person is also a unique, non-duplicable individual who is the lord of the cosmos and has cosmic value. Jesus is a true man, and thus is a person of such value.

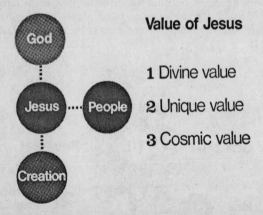

Value of Jesus

1 Divine value

2 Unique value

3 Cosmic value

The Principle does not flatly deny the conventional belief held by many Christians that Jesus is God, because a perfect, true person is one with God. Furthermore, when The Principle asserts that Jesus is a true human being, this does not in any way diminish his value. It is simply that when one examines the value of the perfect person, we find it is equivalent to the value of Jesus. In fact, if the first man and woman had not fallen and had become a man and a woman of such value, then Jesus' coming would not have been necessary. It would be a grave error, indeed, to suppose that the value of fallen man can be compared with Jesus' value simply because Jesus was a human being. He was a true human being. Let us examine the biblical bases for saying this (emphases added):

> For there is one God, and there is one mediator between God and men, *the man* Christ Jesus.
> (1 Tim 2:5)

> For as by one man's disobedience many were made sinners, so by *one man's* obedience many will be made righteous. (Rom 5:19)

> For as by a man [Adam] came death, *by a man* [Jesus] has come also the resurrection of the dead.
> (1 Cor 15:21)

> ... because he has fixed a day on which he will judge the world in righteousness *by a man* whom he has appointed, and of this he has given assurance to all men by raising him from the dead.
> (Acts 17:31)

These passages indicate that Jesus was a man. Jesus also referred to himself as the Son of man in many places in the Bible (e.g., Lk 17:26, 18:8).

B. Is Jesus God?

Up until now, many Christians have believed that Jesus is God, the Creator, based primarily on the following passages from the Bible.

When Philip asked Jesus to show him God, Jesus replied, " 'He who has seen me has seen the Father; how can you say, "Show us the Father"? Do you not believe that I am in the Father and the Father in me?' " (Jn 14:9,10). However, this does not mean that Jesus is God. As clarified above, Jesus was a visible manifestation of the invisible God and is one with God in heart; yet, this does not mean that he is God. Philip asked Jesus to show him God. But God can only be experienced so completely by a person who is perfect. Philip was not yet perfect, and so Jesus had no choice but to show only himself.

Again, the Bible says, "He [Jesus] was in the world, and the world was made through him, yet the world knew him not" (Jn 1:10). Based on this passage, Christians have believed that Jesus is the Creator.

The center of God's Ideal for the Creation is man, and the cosmos is so designed and created as to be the domain which each ideal person is to rule. Thus, God established the person who fulfills the Purpose of the Creation as the highest ideal. From the lowest being to the highest, God created all of them, and then he finally created Adam as lord over all. Then, Jesus, as a person who was fulfilling the Purpose of the Creation, was the ideal person God had envisioned before the Creation was created. In this sense, Jesus existed from the beginning.

Some try to identify Jesus with God on the basis of the quote in John 8:58, in which Jesus said, " '. . . before Abraham was, I am.' " But Jesus didn't mean that he was God. Rather, Jesus could say this because, although on the basis of his genealogy Jesus was a descendant of Abraham, in fact he is the ancestor of Abraham because he came to give rebirth to all mankind from the position of the perfect Adam, that is, from the position of a True Parent, a True Ancestor of all mankind.

If Jesus had been God, then in the spirit world, after his resurrection, he would be one and the same with God, rather than in a position "next to" God. However, in the spirit world, Jesus is said to be at the right hand of God, interceding for us (Rom 8:34). Jesus was born on earth as the Son of man and had a human external appearance like anyone else. In the spirit world he lives as a spirit person just as his disciples do, the only difference being that his spirit self is without original sin and shines brilliantly.

If Jesus were God, how could he intercede with himself? When he prayed, he made it clear that he was not God by calling God Father (Jn 17:1). If Jesus were God, how could he be tempted (Mt 4:1) and tortured and driven to the crucifixion by Satan? It is especially evident that Jesus is not God when, on the cross, he cried out, " 'My God, my God, why hast thou forsaken me?' " (Mt 27:46).

C. Jesus and Fallen Man

A fallen person is not comparable to Jesus. A fallen person

does not fulfill the Purpose of the Creation, and is far from the
Heart of God. What is more, because he has original sin, he is
in such a miserably low state that he even envies the angels,
who were created to be man's servants, and he cannot free
himself from Satan's accusation. Thus, fallen man is very
different from Jesus, who was a perfect, true person. However,
though fallen man has no worth, by being spiritually reborn
through Jesus, who was to be the True Father, a fallen person
will be restored as a spiritual child and will come to resemble
Jesus. Then Jesus becomes the head of the Church (Eph 1:22),
and fallen people are his body and members (1 Cor 12:27).
Jesus is the main temple and we are the branch temples; Jesus
is the vine and we are the branches (Jn 15:5). In order to
become true olive trees, we, as wild olive shoots, should be
grafted onto Jesus, who is the true olive tree (Rom 11:17). Thus
Jesus called us his friends, and John said that when Jesus
appears, we shall be like him (1 Jn 3:2). The Bible also says
that Christ is the "first fruits," and we shall be the next (1 Cor
15:23).

III. REBIRTH AND TRINITY

A. The Meaning of Rebirth

Jesus told Nicodemus, a ruler of the Jews, that unless one is
born anew, he cannot see the Kingdom of God (Jn 3:3). Then,
why must man be reborn?

If Adam and Eve had fulfilled the Ideal for the Creation
and had become true human beings, a true couple, and the
True Parents, and had given birth to true children (without
sin), the Kingdom of Heaven on earth would have been realized. However, because of their fall, they became false parents,
and their descendants have original sin and have realized the
Kingdom of Hell on earth. Therefore, fallen persons cannot
see the Kingdom of God unless they are reborn as heavenly
children, free of original sin.

We cannot be born without parents. Fallen persons absolutely need parents of goodness who can give them rebirth as
children without original sin, enabling each to enter the Kingdom of God. Jesus was the True Father who came to give us
rebirth as children of goodness. Therefore, 1 Peter 1:3 says,
"Blessed be the God and Father of our Lord Jesus Christ! By
his great mercy we have been born anew to a living hope

through the resurrection of Jesus Christ from the dead. . . ."
This shows that Jesus is the source of rebirth. He is also called
the "last Adam" (1 Cor 15:45) and the "Everlasting Father" (Is
9:6) because he was to be the True Father, which Adam failed
to become.

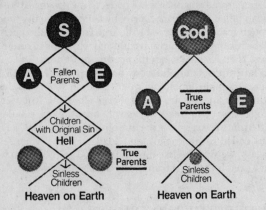

However, to give fallen persons rebirth as children of
goodness, there must be not only a True Father, but also a True
Mother. The Holy Spirit is the one who works as the True
Mother with the resurrected Jesus. This is why Jesus told
Nicodemus he must be born again—born of the Holy Spirit
(Jn 3:3-5). Since the Holy Spirit came as the True Mother, or
second Eve, there are many who receive revelations indicating that the Holy Spirit is a female spirit. The Holy Spirit
works to console and move the hearts of the people (1 Cor
12:3-10). Jesus has been working in the spirit world, while the
Holy Spirit has been working on earth to cleanse the sins of
mankind. When we believe in Jesus, we enter the love generated by the cooperative relationship between the resurrected
Jesus and the Holy Spirit, who are the spiritual True Father
and spiritual True Mother, respectively. Being born again by
believing in Jesus and receiving the Holy Spirit means that
one's spirit is made new and one receives true life through the
love of the spiritual True Parents. This is spiritual rebirth.
However, since man fell both spiritually and physically, each
person must be reborn both spiritually and physically. This is
the reason for the Second Coming.

B. The Meaning of the Trinity

Up to the present, in accordance with Christian theology, Christians have understood that the God who has worked for the salvation of man is a Triune God and have believed that when he reveals himself he appears as one of three persons: Father, Son, or Holy Spirit. When he reveals himself as the Creator, he is in the person of our Heavenly Father; when he reveals himself as the Savior, he is in the person of the Son; and when he reveals himself as the peacemaker, he is in the person of the Holy Spirit.

The theory of the Trinity has caused much debate throughout history. Let us look at this in light of The Principle. If the Fall of man had not occurred, God would not have had to have Jesus and the Holy Spirit work for the salvation of man. If Adam and Eve had perfected themselves as God's son and daughter, each becoming an embodiment of God's divine nature, then they would have been " '. . . perfect, as [their] heavenly Father is perfect' " (Mt 5:48), and they would have attained the ideal of union with God (Jn 14:20). Then Adam would have become God's holy son, and Eve, his holy daughter. They would have become true husband and wife, centered on God. If Adam and Eve had then become one as the True Parents, centered on God, together with God they would have been the *original Trinity*, a trinity centered on God's Heart and ideal.

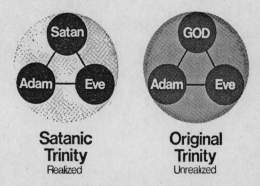

Satanic Trinity
Realized

Original Trinity
Unrealized

This is the fundamental condition for realizing the Three Blessings and the Four Position Foundation which fulfill God's Purpose for the Creation. Yet, because of the Fall, Adam

and Eve became the false parents of man, and failing to fulfill
the Purpose of the Creation, formed a trinity centered on
Satan. Therefore, in order to fulfill the Purpose of the Creation, God had Jesus and the Holy Spirit take Adam's and Eve's
places, as the second Adam and second Eve and as the True
Parents. However, in establishing the spiritual trinity centered on God, Jesus and the Holy Spirit accomplished only the
mission of the spiritual True Parents. Therefore, the Lord of
the Second Coming comes to be the True Father who is to
establish the trinity both spiritually and physically.

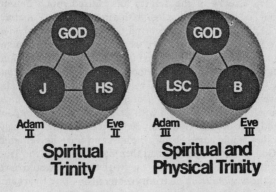

Spiritual   Spiritual and
Trinity   Physical Trinity

CHAPTER EIGHT

Overview of the Principles of Restoration

I. HISTORY FROM THE VIEWPOINT OF THE DISPENSATION FOR RESTORATION

As explained in "The Principles of the Creation," God created man to live in his love for eternity—first, in the Kingdom of Heaven on earth, and later, as a spirit person, in the Kingdom of Heaven in the spirit world. However, because the first man and woman fell (during their growing period), they embodied sin and were dominated by Satan. But God could not leave his original Ideal for the Creation unaccomplished. In Isaiah 46:11 God said, " 'I have spoken, and I will bring it to pass; I have purposed, and I will do it,' " showing that he will definitely carry out his original plan. He is determined to save man. His dispensation to save fallen man consists of restoring man to his original state. Let us examine how God has worked for man's salvation throughout history.

History does not consist solely of who did what, when they did it, and where it was done. It is man's experience that that he can barely shape the course of his own personal history. From God's viewpoint, man's history is the record of

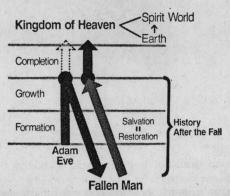

God's dispensation for salvation—that is, of His dispensation for the restoration of fallen man, who is under the dominion of Satan. Human history is the manifestation of God's work to fulfill the purpose of restoration. Thus, it is the history of God's Dispensation for Restoration.

The goal of God's Dispensation for Restoration is the restoration of fallen man to the position where he fulfills the Purpose of the Creation and the restoration of the cosmos as it was originally created. Therefore, the history of mankind can be defined as the history of God's dispensation for re-establishing the Purpose of the Creation in man's life.

A. Fallen Man is the Womb of Good and Evil

A person who fulfills God's Purpose for the Creation becomes God's temple, where God's spirit dwells (1 Cor 3:16). Such a person would have a divine nature and would be " '. . . perfect, as [his] heavenly Father is perfect' " (Mt 5:48). And God would always be the center of the thoughts, actions, and life of such an individual. The personal history of such a person would be good; and the histories of the families of such individuals, and of the nations and world populated by such individuals, would be nothing other than good. Therefore, the ideal history of mankind as conceived of in the mind of God can be stated in one word: goodness.

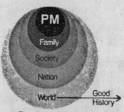

**Ideal Conceived
by God**

Perfect Man
God's Temple
Divine Nature
God's Thoughts, Actions

However, because of the Fall, man did not become God's temple. To the contrary, he became the dwelling place of Satan, and by becoming one with Satan, man came to have an

evil nature instead of a divine nature. As a result, Satan is
" '. . . the ruler of this world . . .' "(Jn 12:31) and ". . . the god of
this world . . ." (2 Cor 4:4) and controls fallen man's thoughts,
activities, and life. Consequently, the history of mankind has
been evil. The histories of such fallen individuals, of the families of such individuals, and of the nations and world populated by such individuals, could be nothing other than evil.
The history of mankind began as a history of sin and evil and
has continued as such.

The Result of
Man's Fall

Fallen Man
- Dwelling of Satan
- Evil Nature
- Satan's Thoughts, Actions

As was already explained in "The Fall," man fell during
the time he was growing toward perfection. Such perfection
means becoming the embodiment of the Ideal for the Creation. However, as a result of the Fall, fallen man became the
embodiment and womb of good and evil.

Adam and Eve had grown to a certain stage centered on
God, and therefore they had within themselves a base of goodness resembling God, although it was not fully developed.
Additionally, they developed a base of evil within themselves
by receiving evil elements from the archangel. The evil element received from the fallen archangel is Original Sin.
However, the degree of good and the degree of evil operating in
fallen man are not equally developed. The base of evil is highly
developed and has borne fruit and thus is easily activated and
expressed. On the other hand, man's foundation of goodness is

only germinal, and so unless conscious effort is made to encourage it, it is extremely difficult for that goodness to bear fruit.

B. The Struggle between Good and Evil—The Hidden Dimension of History

In order to realize the Purpose of the Creation in the midst of the fallen world, which Satan rules, God consistently carries out the Dispensation for Restoration by separating good from evil. As a result, most of human history is composed of struggles between good and evil. Fallen man unites with Satan in his mind and commits sins through his body. Yet, man still has within himself the Original Mind created by God, and it always remains directed toward God.

In the Dispensation for Restoration, there is an unseen struggle between God and Satan. And man, being the embodiment of good and evil, is caught in the middle of that struggle—between God, working to win man to his side through the base of goodness (the Original Mind) within man, and Satan, working to keep man on his side through the base of evil (the evil mind) within man. Without understanding the unseen causal dimension of God and Satan, human history cannot be properly understood. It cannot be understood simply by examining the superficial activities of man on earth.

There is continuous conflict between the evil sovereignty of Satan, who is trying to hold on to man, and the good sovereignty of God, who is trying to recover man and restore

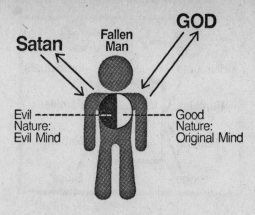

him. This is reflected in the battles between the good and evil in this world. In this struggle between God and Satan lies the reason for the first bloodshed recorded in the Bible, that in which Cain killed Abel; and in this same struggle lies the reason that the history of mankind has been marked by conflict and war, regardless of whether one looks to the East or to the West. Whether the leading roles in these struggles are played by individuals, families, tribes, nations, or blocs of nations, these struggles all amount to a struggle between God, working on the side of goodness, and Satan, working on the side of evil. Accordingly, it is God's work and Satan's work that are behind any type of human conflict, whether it is a struggle

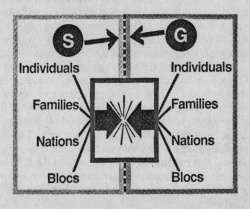

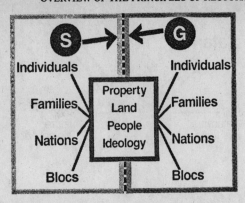

between one individual and another, one family and another, one tribe and another, one nation and another, or one bloc of nations and another.

At times, the struggle has centered on property, land, or people; at other times, on ideologies and beliefs. But actually all of these are just reflections of the struggle between God and Satan. God is trying to restore man to the purpose of goodness, and Satan is trying to maintain his evil position and power. This struggle then manifests in the world as the conflicts recorded in human history.

C. The Cause of the Development and Progress of History

Then, what is the real driving force of history? When we say that all of history is the reflection of God's dispensational work, does it mean that history advances solely by the plan and work of God? Even though the goal of history is to restore the Purpose of the Creation, do the conflicts between good and evil automatically and naturally progress toward that Purpose? If so, then how can we explain the many injustices and tragedies in history, such as the prevalence of evil or the suffering of righteous people, things which could hardly be thought of as the work of an almighty God of goodness?

In the beginning, God gave the first man and woman a commandment which they were to obey until they perfected themselves. The realization of the Purpose of the Creation is possible only if man and woman accomplish their responsibility, by obeying the commandment. The Purpose of the Creation is not to be accomplished simply by concern and action on the part of God. Although man's responsibility may seem infinitely small, it is a principle of the Creation that man's responsibility is a necessary element. Thus, in order to restore the lost Purpose of the Creation, man's portion of responsibility is also absolutely essential—it cannot be done by God's power and dispensation alone.

Accomplishment of the Purpose of Creation

⬆

Man's Obedience to Commandment
(Man's Responsibility)

The Plan and Work of God
(God's Responsibility)

But it is possible for man either to fulfill his responsibility or not to fulfill it. When a person does fulfill his responsibility, God's Will is manifested in history through that person, and God's dispensation is concretely accomplished and restoration progresses. But when a person fails to fulfill his responsibility, God's dispensation through that person is frustrated, and Satan's will comes to be reflected in history instead. Thus, man can make God happy, by fulfilling his responsibility, or sad, by failing in his responsibility. The reason that human history appears to be nothing but a constant re-enactment of sinful history, with the prospect of an ideal world seemingly so distant, is not because God is impotent, or because he is not absolute, but because man has not fulfilled his responsibility to carry out God's Will. God is absolute, eternal, and omnipotent; therefore, the accomplishment of his Purpose for the Creation and of his purpose of restoration are also absolute. God's will for restoration will definitely be accomplished (Is 46:11). Therefore, when the person carrying out the will does not fulfill his responsibility, God, after a period of time re-

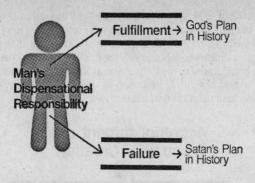

stores the same foundation and conditions as before, and chooses another person to carry out the same mission. This is precisely the reason that we see very similar incidents and events recurring throughout the long history of God's dispensation, even after periods of two to four thousand years. We call this recurrence of similar events or periods, Dispensational Time Identity. (For a full explanation, refer to "Dispensational Time Identity.")

II. THE PRINCIPLES OF RESTORATION

A. The Dispensation for Restoration and the Messiah

What are the specific principles of God's dispensation for the restoration of fallen man? At the completion level of the growth stage, man fell and thus came under the dominion of Satan. In order for God to restore fallen people, God must first separate them from Satan. This is because as long as man remains an object to Satan, or remains under his influence, the Purpose of the Creation cannot be fulfilled. In order to be completely separated from Satan, leaving no basis by which Satan can invade again, a person must be cleansed of Original Sin, because it is the root of all the bases by which Satan accuses and invades fallen man. However, Original Sin cannot be removed unless man is reborn through the Messiah, who comes as the True Parent. Only the Messiah can eliminate the Original Sin.

The Messiah, who is thus the most indispensible central person in the Dispensation for Restoration, is the model of a true person, and it is through him that God creates true indi-

viduals, families, tribes, nations, and a world that fulfill the
original Ideal for the Creation. So, God cannot send the Messiah to the world without preparing it. Preparation is necessary because, ever since the Fall of man, mankind has been
serving the false master, Satan, and if the Messiah were sent
without a prepared environment, there is the danger that the
satanic world would try to eliminate him. Therefore, from the
midst of the evil people who are serving the false master, God
first chooses one individual who will honor and obey him.
Based on this individual, God creates families and nations
separated from Satan's side, families and nations which then
can serve as a foundation of faith upon which the Messiah can
come.

Since at the beginning of God's Dispensation for Restoration the Messiah had not yet come, fallen man had to meet the
condition of symbolically restoring himself to the level from
which the first man and woman had fallen. That is, man had
to meet the condition of symbolically restoring himself to the
completion level of the growth stage. Man thus establishes the
foundation to receive the Messiah. To begin this process, man
must go through a course of separation from Satan. And as a
result of this process, fallen man receives the Messiah, who
comes as the True Parent, and is reborn. Through this rebirth,
a person is restored to the position of Adam or Eve before the
Fall. Since the level from which the first man and woman fell
was the completion level of the growth stage, the completion
level of the growth stage is also the level at which he is born
again in the course of restoration. Consequently, the completion stage still remains to be gone through. Man grows
through this stage by following the Messiah, finally reaching
the position where he fulfills the Purpose of the Creation.
Originally, man's responsibility during his growing period is
only to follow the *Way of The Principle*. However, fallen man is
required to pass through *two* courses on his way to perfection:
(1) the first course is the *Way of Restoration*, which includes the
course he must follow until the Messiah's coming and his
rebirth through the Messiah; (2) the second course is the
original Way of *The Principle*, which is the path he must follow
through the remaining stage of the growing period, namely,
the completion stage. Fallen man does this by following the
Messiah.

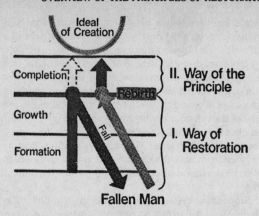

If Adam and Eve had perfected themselves, thus becoming the True Parents and True Ancestors of the human race, their children would have followed the Way of *The Principle* under the guidance and protection of their parents. After being born again through the Messiah, the Way of *The Principle* requires man to be completely obedient to the Messiah and to rely on him while growing to perfection, for he stands as the True Parent.

B. Restoration through Indemnity

Then, what is the Way of Restoration which must be followed until the Messiah comes? In other words, what are the principles of God's dispensation until he sends the Messiah? These questions can be answered by understanding what is involved in preparing for the Messiah. Since the Messiah comes in the position of Adam (1 Cor 15:45), he cannot appear at just any time; he can only appear when man has been restored to the position that Adam had reached just prior to the Fall, that position being the completion level of the growth stage. That is, the Messiah can appear only when there is a foundation for him to stand on in the position of the original sinless Adam. However, fallen man cannot reach that state on his own because he has Original Sin. Therefore, God requires that fallen man meet certain conditions—conditions such that man can be considered as having been symbolically restored to this level—in other words, such that man has restored the completion level of the growth stage in form. Therefore, God's dispensation prior to the Messiah's coming may be summarized as mankind's restoring the foundation upon which the Messiah can appear. Consequently, in the Way of Restoration, man's responsibility is to restore the foundation for receiving the Messiah.

What does 'restoration through indemnity' mean? In order for something to be restored to a position or state which it has lost, certain conditions must be met. To meet these conditions is to *indemnify* the loss of the original—and thus, to *restore through indemnity.*

Man lost his original state and position because of the Fall. In order for him to restore that original position and state, he must meet certain conditions. Since meeting these conditions indemnifies the loss, returning to the original state by meeting the required conditions is called restoration through indemnity. The conditions that need to be met for this process of restoration through indemnity are called *indemnity conditions.* The dispensation to restore fallen man's Original Nature through fulfilling indemnity conditions is called the Dispensation for Restoration through Indemnity.

Next, we need to understand the different kinds of indemnity conditions. The first kind is the *indemnity condition of an equal amount,* such as that found in Exodus 21:23-25: " 'If any harm follows, then you shall give life for life, eye for eye, tooth for tooth, hand for hand, foot for foot, burn for burn, wound for wound, stripe for stripe.' " This means that the original state is restored by paying indemnity of a value that is identical to the loss or damage.

The second kind of indemnity condition is the *indemnity condition of a lesser amount.* In this case, the original state is restored by paying indemnity of a value that is less than that which was originally lost. For example, we receive the great benefit of Jesus' resurrection from the dead by meeting the very small indemnity condition of 'having faith in redemption through the cross'. Other examples of indemnity conditions of a lesser amount are baptism and holy communion. Through baptism we meet the condition of having to be cleansed of sin, and in holy communion we meet the condition of having to be one in spirit and body with Christ.

The third kind of indemnity condition is the *indemnity*

condition of a greater amount. When a person fails to fulfill his responsibility to meet an indemnity condition of a lesser amount, then he must restore the original state by meeting an indemnity condition of a greater amount. For example, when the Israelites' forty days of spying in Canaan (at the time of Moses) failed to meet with God's approval, the duration of the indemnity condition was increased to one year for each of the original days. Instead of suffering for forty days in the wilderness, they had to suffer for forty years (Num 14:34).

Next, what is the method involved in meeting an indemnity condition? An indemnity condition is the condition that must be met in order for something to be restored to its original position or state. An indemnity condition achieves this by being the reversal of the process which led to the loss of the original position or state. Because the first man and woman failed to fulfill their responsibility and fell away from God, their descendants have been required to fulfill the indemnity conditions required in the Way of Restoration.

C. The Foundation for the Messiah

As was explained earlier, although God sends the Messiah out of his grace, in order to receive the Messiah, man must fulfill his responsibility, by meeting the indemnity conditions.

What are the indemnity conditions needed to establish the *Foundation for the Messiah?* Since indemnity conditions must reverse the process by which Adam lost his original position and state, in order to answer this question we must

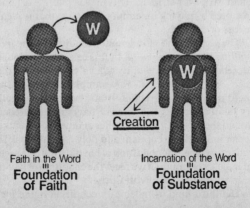

Faith in the Word
**Foundation
of Faith**

Creation

Incarnation of the Word
**Foundation
of Substance**

understand by what process Adam fell—what it is that he did and did not do that left the Purpose of the Creation unfulfilled.

Because Adam and Eve did not believe God's Word, they could not establish the *Foundation of Faith* and they fell. In order to receive the Messiah, fallen man must first restore the Foundation of Faith by indemnifying this failure to believe in God's Word.

After establishing the Foundation of Faith, fallen man must then restore, through indemnity, the *Foundation of Substance*. Let us examine the reasons that this foundation has to be made. If Adam and Eve had established the Foundation of Faith, they would have become perfect incarnations of God's Word. In other words, they would have developed the character of perfected individuals. This perfect incarnation is the ultimate goal in the creation of man. Faith in God's commandment 'not to eat' was necessary for Adam and Eve only until they reached perfection. God's wish was for them to become beings embodying his character and resembling him. When this took place they would have been able rightfully to have dominion over all of the cosmos, including the archangel. But because Adam and Eve did not base their life on an attitude of faith, they lost the basis by which they could embody God's character and resemble him, and instead they came to be dominated by the archangel, who was to have been the servant of God and man. Thus, the Foundation for the Messiah which fallen man must establish requires establishing through indemnity the Foundation of Faith and the Foundation of Substance.

Foundation for the Messiah

1. The Foundation of Faith

First, what are the indemnity conditions that must be met in order to establish the Foundation of Faith? To know what they are, we must understand what Adam and Eve failed to do. Adam and Eve failed to establish this foundation as a result of their not having absolute faith in God's commandment during their growing period.

To indemnify this failure, first of all there must be a central person who can stand in Adam's position and restore the Foundation of Faith. Secondly, to indemnify and restore Adam's and Eve's failure to keep God's commandment, the central person must make the required offering with absolute faith. Thirdly, Adam and Eve did not go through the growing period in accordance with God's Will, thus failing to meet the condition of demonstrating faith. In other words, they did not properly go through the period in which they were to carry out their responsibility—by living in accordance with God's Will.

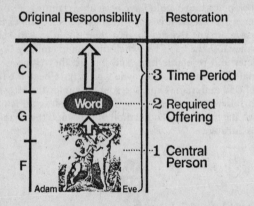

As a result, a numerically determined indemnity time-period became necessary to restore the misused growing period. This period is called the *mathematical period of indemnity.*

The Foundation of Faith is the absolute vertical relationship that man must establish with God. Since man's vertical relationship with God was severed by the first man's and woman's faithlessness toward God, the condition required to indemnify and restore this is called the Foundation of Faith.

The reason that throughout history great men of God such as Abel, Noah, Abraham, and Isaac were required to demonstrate tremendous faith was because they were the individuals responsible to restore through indemnity the Foundation of Faith.

2. The Foundation of Substance

Let us now consider what indemnity is required to restore the Foundation of Substance. If, on the basis of their Foundation of Faith, Adam and Eve had perfected themselves as true children of God, they would have been the perfect incarnations of God's Word and the incarnations of the character of the invisible God. Had this happened, man would have had dominion over all things, including the archangel, thereby fulfilling God's Third Blessing. A Principle relationship would have been established between man and all things, including the angels.

However, Adam and Eve never established a Foundation of Faith, and, consequently, did not establish the Foundation of Substance either. Instead, Adam and Eve were defiled by Fallen Nature and ended up being dominated by the archangel.

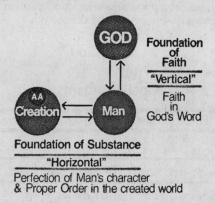

To establish the Foundation of Substance, fallen man must meet the *Indemnity Condition for Removing the Fallen Nature* and restore the proper horizontal order, which was disrupted. This is done by reversing the process through which man acquired the Fallen Nature.

Specifically, what is it that has to be done to remove the Fallen Nature? The first factor in the process of the fall of the archangel lay in the archangel's failure to love Adam, who was receiving more love from God. Fallen man inherited this fallen nature of 'not taking the same viewpoint as God'. To remove this fallen nature, a person in the position of the archangel must love a person in Adam's position, thereby taking the same viewpoint as God.

The second factor in the process of the fall of the archangel was his not wanting to receive God's love through Adam who was closer to God. Instead, the archangel attempted to take Adam's position, and he fell, giving rise to the fallen nature of 'leaving one's position'. To remove this fallen nature, a person in the archangel's position must receive God's love through the person in Adam's position, thus keeping his proper position.

The third factor in the process of the Fall was the archangel's dominating Adam and Eve instead of allowing himself to be governed by them. From this came the fallen nature of 'reversing the order of dominion'. To remove this fallen nature, a person in the archangel's position should be obedient to and submit to a person in Adam's position, thereby establishing the proper order of dominion.

God
↑

Archangel ⟶ Adam

Fallen Nature	Indemnity Condition
1 Not taking God's viewpoint	Love
2 Leaving position	Receive love through
3 Reversing order	Submit to
4 Multiplying sin	Learn God's Way from

The will of goodness not to eat of the Fruit of the Tree of the Knowledge of Good and Evil should have been received from God by Adam, from Adam by Eve, and from Eve by the archangel, thus multiplying goodness. However, instead of goodness being multiplied, Eve accepted from the archangel that she could eat the Fruit of the Tree of the Knowledge of Good and Evil, and Adam accepted that direction from Eve, thus multiplying the will for evil and causing them to fall. Thus, the final aspect of the Fallen Nature was created—the nature of 'multiplying sin'. To remove this fallen nature of multiplying sin, a person in the archangel's position must receive the righteous will from a person in Adam's position, restoring the nature that multiplies the will of goodness.

When all these conditions are met, the Indemnity Condition for Removing the Fallen Nature is met, and this constitutes the Foundation of Substance. The Foundation for the Messiah is made by restoring through indemnity the Foundation of Faith and the Foundation of Substance. It is only on this foundation that fallen man can receive the Messiah.

From the foregoing, we can understand that the history of mankind is the dispensational history in which God leads man to prepare himself to receive the Messiah by inducing man to fulfill his responsibility. When man finishes this preparation, God will send the Messiah and conclude his Dispensation for Restoration.

This interpretation of history based on the principles of God's Dispensation for Restoration is called the Restoration View of History or the Unification View of History. Now, let us examine the central history within God's Dispensation for Restoration.

D. The Central and Peripheral Histories in the Dispensation for Restoration

Through the Dispensation for Restoration, God seeks to save all of mankind. His methods for accomplishing the dispensation have varied somewhat according to the different histories, traditions, cultural backgrounds, and living conditions of the people with whom he has been dealing. However, God carries out a model dispensation through one central nation. He works his dispensation in other nations as *peripheral histories*, at some point grafting the peripheral histories to the *central history* in order that all of mankind can receive the benefit of salvation.

As can be seen in the Old Testament, God had to go
through many difficulties in the restoration process before
finding one central nation. From what is recorded in the Bible,
it seems that once God established Israel as the central nation,
he worked only through that nation. And it is true that the
training the Israelites received from God was very strict and
special and that they received special blessings which cannot
be found among other peoples.

However, Jesus did not introduce God only as the God of
the Jews, but as the God of all nations. This is clearly shown in
John 3:16, where Jesus said, " 'For God so loved the world that
he gave his only Son, that *whoever* believes in him should not
perish but have eternal life' " (emphasis added). This means
that anyone can be connected to the central dispensation of
God—even those in the peripheral histories.

As we study the Bible it becomes clear that God has
focused on educating a central individual, family, tribe, and
nation who will take charge of his model dispensation. Yet, he
has also led the peripheral dispensations toward the day when
he would connect those individuals, families, tribes, and nations to the Messiah.

John the Baptist also showed that salvation was within
reach of all when he chastised the Israelites who did not have
sincere faith and arrogantly prided themselves on being God's
only chosen people, saying to them, " '. . . do not presume to
say to yourselves, "We have Abraham as our father"; for I tell
you, God is able from these stones to raise up children to
Abraham' " (Mt 3:9).

God's central dispensation of preparation for the Messiah
is clearly shown in the Old Testament. Right at the beginning,
God's dispensation for Adam's family was frustrated by Cain's
slaying Abel. Ten generations later, God's Will was transferred
to Noah's family. However, because of the disbelief and failure
of Noah's second son, Ham, the family Foundation for the
Messiah was not established. It was not until the time of
Abraham's and Jacob's families that the Foundation for the
Messiah was established (refer to Chapter 11). Based on
Jacob's family, God was able to form the Israelites as the
chosen people. God's dispensation for the Israelites was to
prepare the landing site of faith for the Messiah by having the
Israelites establish the national Foundation for the Messiah.
As was explained in detail in "The Purpose of the Messiah," the

Israelites failed to establish the national Foundation for the Messiah. They ended up committing the historic error of not believing in the Messiah.

Jesus promised a Second Coming. There should be preparation on earth for the Second Coming similar to that made for the First Coming. The past two thousand years of Christian history have had one central purpose—that of establishing the world-wide foundation for the Second Coming of the Messiah. Therefore, the history of Israel before the coming of Jesus and the history of Christianity since his time are the core material of the history of the Dispensation for Restoration.

Looking at history in this way, we can begin to understand the meaning and significance of the events in the history of the Jewish people as recorded in the Old Testament. It is not merely a history of one particular nation, but is rather the model history through which God has worked his dispensation for salvation. The history of the Jewish people, centered on Judaism, and Western history, centered on Christianity, together are the clearest record of God's Dispensation, and, astonishingly, we can see a consistent formula which is applied throughout these two histories.

Since religion guides man's mind and spirit toward accomplishing the restoration of mankind, from the dispensational viewpoint, the history of religion is the central history of God's Dispensation. The other histories, such as the histories of the development of politics, economics, science, and culture can be considered as peripheral.

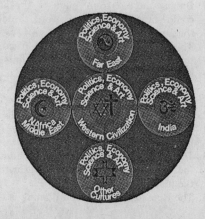

God's Purpose for the Creation is fulfilled in the Three Blessings. First, each individual is to perfect himself. Next, he is to establish an ideal family, an ideal world, and ideal living conditions. Consequently, the first objective in God's Dispensation for Restoration is not to restore man's social institutions, or his living conditions; it is to restore people. Consequently, from the standpoint of the Dispensation, the history of religion is the central history, while the other histories are peripheral.

III. THE COURSE OF GOD'S DISPENSATION FOR RESTORATION

Let us summarize human history from Adam to the present in light of what we have discussed. The entire course of the Dispensation may be divided into three ages of approximately two thousand years each:

    1. The age from Adam to Abraham;
    2. The age from Abraham to Jesus;
    3. The age from Jesus to the Second Coming.

The period after the Second Coming is the new age in which God's Ideal is accomplished in its entirety on earth and in the spirit world.

Now let us examine the contents of the dispensation for each age from several different standpoints. First of all, the ages may be looked at from the standpoint of God's Word of re-creation:

    1. During the age from Adam to Abraham, man could not yet receive God's Word, through which the Dispensation for Restoration is carried out. Through the offerings that God instructed man to make, man was establishing the foundation to receive the Word of God, so this period is called the Dispensational Age of the Foundation for the Word;

    2. The age from Abraham to Jesus is called the Old Testament Age and the formation stage in the history of restoration;

    3. The age from Jesus to the Second Coming is called the New Testament Age and the growth stage in the history of restoration;

    4. The time after the Second Coming is called the

Completed Testament Age and the completion stage in the history of restoration.

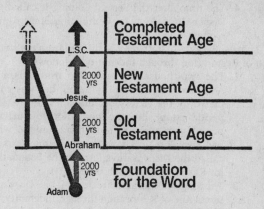

Secondly, the ages can be divided from the standpoint of the dispensation for resurrection. As already explained in "Resurrection," the dispensational history may be divided as follows:

1. The age from Adam to Abraham is the Dispensational Age of the Foundation for Resurrection;
2. The age from Abraham to Jesus is the Dispensational Age of Formation Stage Resurrection;
3. The age from Jesus to the Second Coming is the

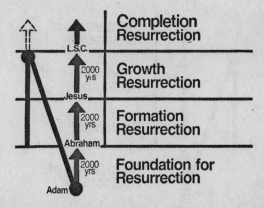

Dispensational Age of Growth Stage Resurrection;

4. The time after the Second Coming is called the Dispensational Age for Completion Stage Resurrection.

Thirdly, the ages of faith may be divided from the standpoint of Restoration through Indemnity as follows:

1. The two-thousand-year period from Adam to Abraham was invaded by Satan, but was completed by the victory of Abraham's family. This period established the foundation to start the period for restoration through indemnity of what had been lost to Satan. Therefore this period is called the Dispensational Age of the Foundation for Restoration through Indemnity;

2. The age from Abraham to Jesus is the Dispensational Age of Restoration through Indemnity;

3. The age from Jesus to the Second Coming came about because the dispensation which was supposed to be fulfilled at the First Coming was extended until the Second Coming because of the chosen people's lack of faith. This period is called the Dispensational Age of the Prolongation of Restoration through Indemnity;

4. The time after the Second Coming is the Dispensational Age for the Completion of Restoration.

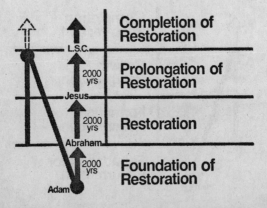

Fourthly, the ages may be divided from the standpoint of the level of the Foundation for the Messiah:

1. In the age from Adam to Abraham, God's dispensation to prepare the Foundation for the Messiah was based on the family. Therefore, this period is called the Dispensational Age of the Family Foundation for the Messiah;

2. The age from Abraham to Jesus is called the Dispensational Age of the National Foundation for the Messiah;

3. The age from Jesus to the Second Coming is the Dispensational Age of the World-wide Foundation for the Messiah;

4. The time beginning with the Second Coming is the Dispensational Age for the Cosmic (i.e., physical world and spirit world) Foundation for the Messiah.

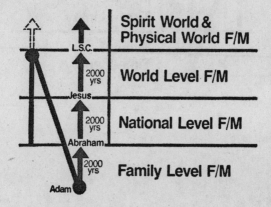

Finally, the ages may be divided according to Dispensational Time Identity, as follows:

1. During the age from Adam to Abraham, man established his faith before God through symbolic offerings, and so this period is called the Age of Symbolic Time Identity;

2. In the age from Abraham to Jesus, man demonstrated his faith in God by offering things in image

form—that is, by offering such things as the tabernacle and the temple, which represented the image of the true human being, which had been lost at the Fall. So this period is called the Age of Image Time Identity;

3. From Jesus' time to that of the Second Coming, man demonstrated his faith through Jesus, the substantial temple. This period is therefore called the Age of Substantial Time Identity.

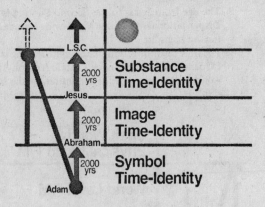

CHAPTER NINE

Adam's Family in the Dispensation for Restoration

God's plan to restore and save man by sending the Messiah existed from the moment the Fall occurred. Thus his dispensation to establish the Foundation for the Messiah began with Adam's family.

I. THE FOUNDATION OF FAITH

Since it was Adam who actually committed the Original Sin, and not Cain or Abel, Adam should have been the one responsible to restore the Foundation of Faith by making the Required Offering to God. Whether or not the Foundation of Faith was accomplished would be decided by whether or not Adam made his offering properly.

A. Separation for the Offering

However, in the Bible there is no record of Adam ever offering a sacrifice. The offerings were made by Cain and Abel. Why is this?

According to "The Principle of the Creation," man was originally created to relate to one lord. Thus, God cannot work a Principle dispensation with a person who has a relationship with two lords. As explained earlier, in the chapter titled "Overview of the Principles of the Dispensation for Restoration," although Adam was created by God, he came to be of Satan's lineage, and thus was in a midway position, relating to both God and Satan.

Since Adam was an embodiment of both good and evil, if God were to try to deal directly with Adam and his offering, Satan would also try to deal with Adam and his offering on the basis of Adam's being of his lineage. If this had happened, Adam would have been in a position to deal with two masters, and thus in a non-Principle position. So God could not work his dispensation through Adam.

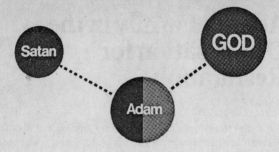

God had no alternative but to separate into two beings the two contradictory natures of good and evil that were embodied within Adam. To this end, God had one of Adam's two sons represent good and the other represent evil.* Then God placed them in the positions where one dealt with God and the other with Satan. In other words, God had them offer their sacrifices from the positions where each dealt with only one lord.

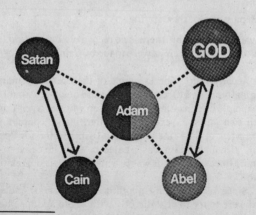

---

* Though Abel and Cain stood on the sides of good and evil, respectively, their positions are relative. Actually, both had Original Sin and Fallen Nature as well as Original Nature—and thus both had natures of evil and of good.

B. The Second Son in God's Dispensation

Both Cain and Abel were sons of Adam. Then which of the two should be the one to represent good, and thus to deal with God, and which should be the one to represent evil, and thus to deal with Satan? Both Cain and Abel were results of Eve's fall, and the question of who would represent which side was decided based on the process of the fall of Eve, who was responsible for the Fail.

Eve was involved in two fallen acts of love (fornication). The first was her relationship with the archangel, causing the spiritual fall. The second was her relationship with Adam, causing the physical fall.

Both of these fallen acts were crimes, but if we think about which of the two was "closer" to *The Principle* and thus more easily forgiveable in the eyes of God, we would have to say that the second fallen act was the more easily forgiveable. The first fallen act was motivated by Eve's excessive desire to have that which was not yet her time to enjoy, that is, it was motivated by her desire to have her eyes opened and to be like God (Gen 3:7)—before she was mature. Also, in the first fallen act, Eve's relationship was with the archangel, who, according to The Principle, was never to have been Eve's spouse. On the other hand, the second fallen act was motivated by Eve's desire to return to God's side after she realized the illicit nature of her first act. Moreover, even though the act was

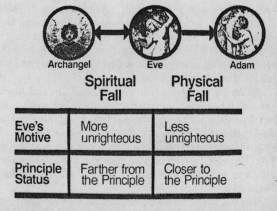

Archangel   Eve   Adam

Spiritual Fall   Physical Fall

	Spiritual Fall	Physical Fall
Eve's Motive	More unrighteous	Less unrighteous
Principle Status	Farther from the Principle	Closer to the Principle

committed prior to the time God had set, it was a relationship with Adam, who, in God's plan, would ultimately have been her spouse.

Because Cain and Abel were the results of Eve's illicit love, God placed them in positions representing evil and good based on her two acts of fornication. Cain, as the first result of the Fall, represented Eve's first fallen act, the relationship with the archangel, and thus he was placed in the position to deal with Satan. Abel symbolized the second fallen act, that between Eve and Adam, and thus he was placed in the position to deal with God.

Satan gained control of God's Creation before God did, and because Satan is a non-Principle being, he brought about a pseudo-Principle world before God could realize a Principle world. Therefore, God began his dispensation by placing the first son, who symbolized the first fallen act, on Satan's side and the second son, who symbolized the second fallen act, on his side. God said to Cain, " '. . . Why are you angry, and why has your countenance fallen? If you do well, will you not be accepted? And if you do not do well, sin is couching at the door; its desire is for you, but you must master it' " (Gen 4:6,7). This shows that Cain was in a position to have to deal with Satan.

When the Israelites fled from Egypt, God smote all the first-born of the Egyptians, and also of their cattle (Ex 12:29). Also, the Bible says that God "loved" the second son, Jacob, and "hated" the first son, Esau, even while they were still in their mother's womb (Rom 9:13). And in the case of Jacob's blessing of his grandsons, Ephraim and Manasseh, Jacob blessed them by crossing his hands so that the right hand lay on the head of Ephraim, the second son (Gen 48:14). In each of these cases is an example of how God placed the second-born child in the favored position.

Based on this principle, God placed Cain and Abel in positions where each could deal with only one master, and then had each make an offering. God could accept Abel's offering (Gen 4:4) because he was in a position representing God and had made the offering in an acceptable manner (Heb 11:4). Through this acceptable offering, the Foundation of Faith was established in Adam's family by the second son, Abel, acting in place of Adam.

God did not reject Cain's offering because he hated Cain;

nor was it God's intention to condemn him forever. However, because Cain was in a position to deal only with Satan, God could not work with him unless he fulfilled an indemnity condition by which he could remove himself from the position of relating to Satan. The indemnity condition that had to be fulfilled by Cain is called the 'Indemnity Condition to Remove the Fallen Nature'.

II. THE FOUNDATION OF SUBSTANCE

In order for Adam's family to establish the Foundation of Substance, Cain had to meet the Indemnity Condition to Remove the Fallen Nature. Had he done so, God would have been able to accept his offering joyfully.

Since Cain was representing the side of Satan, he could not be in the object position to God, who is the subject of goodness. Through Cain's meeting the condition required to remove the Fallen Nature, he would then return to the position where God could deal with him. Then, how was this Indemnity Condition for Removing the Fallen Nature to be met?

The first man and woman inherited the Fallen Nature through their relationship with the archangel. The Indemnity Condition for Removing the Fallen Nature must be established by symbolically reversing the process of the Fall.

The archangel, who was created in a position more distant from God than Adam, should have loved Adam as God did, thus taking the same viewpoint as God. He should have related to God with Adam as his mediator, and should have perfected himself by following the heavenly way of humbling himself before Adam and obeying him. But the archangel did not do this. The Indemnity Condition for Removing the Fallen Nature is met by reversing this failure.

After Abel made his offering, Cain was placed in the position of the archangel, and Abel, in that of Adam. From these positions the Indemnity Condition for Removing the Fallen Nature could have been met by Cain's loving Abel, obeying Abel, and humbling himself to Abel. Doing so, he would have come closer to God. But, instead, Cain killed Abel, repeating the process of the archangel's fall. This was not simply the crime of an elder brother killing his younger brother; it meant that the satanic side had struck God's side, God's efforts to separate good and evil in Adam's family had been frustrated, and the side of goodness had been lost.

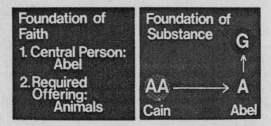

What Cain was supposed to fulfill was the basic indemnity condition that is required for anyone in a position distant from God to come closer to him. Within each person, the mind directed toward goodness (Rom 7:22) is in the Abel position, and the body which tends toward serving "the law of sin" (Rom 7:25), is in the Cain position. Only when the body is subjugated by the mind and obeys it will each individual become good. However, in the actual life of fallen man, the body repeatedly rebels against the directions of the mind, acting as Cain did in killing Abel, thus fostering the evil within each individual.

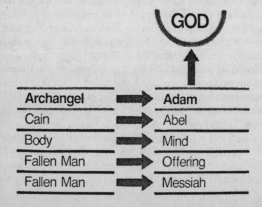

As fallen people, we are in the Cain position to the Messiah. Therefore, by our humbling ourselves before him, and serving him, obeying him, and loving him, we attain salvation through his mediation (Jn 14:6, 1 Tim 2:5). As Jeremiah 17:9 tells us, man became "... deceitful above all things. ..." Therefore, to come to God, man has had to go through the things of the Creation, which were in the Abel position to him. This is the principle behind God's having man use offerings in the Dispensation.

As explained earlier, the foundation upon which the Messiah can come is the restored Foundation of Faith and Foundation of Substance. In Adam's family, a Foundation of Faith was successfully made by Abel's making an offering which God could accept. Through this, Abel also qualified himself to be the central person for the Foundation of Substance. However, because Cain killed Abel, the Indemnity Condition for Removing the Fallen Nature was not established. Thus, the Foundation of Substance and, as a result, the Foundation for the Messiah, were never made, and God's dispensation was not fulfilled in Adam's family.

III. THE FOUNDATION FOR THE MESSIAH

If Cain had fulfilled the Indemnity Condition for Removing the Fallen Nature by humbling himself before Abel and obeying him, the Foundation of Substance would have been established in Adam's family. This, together with the Foundation of Faith, would have constituted the Foundation for the Messiah. In other words, by Abel's meeting the indemnity condition necessary for restoring the vertical relationship with God, he would have stood on the Foundation of Faith. If Cain had re-established the proper horizontal order with Abel, the Foundation of Substance would have been established. These two foundations together would have constituted the Foundation for the Messiah.

On this foundation, the Messiah would have been able to come. At that stage of human history, God's dispensation was on the family level, so if Abel and Cain had established the Foundation for the Messiah, it would have been on the family level. If Adam's family had made such a foundation, they would have received the Messiah and been reborn through him. In this way, they would have been restored and become

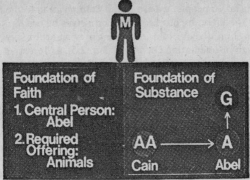

Foundation for the Messiah

the ideal family which God had originally intended, and an
entirely new history would have begun.

Instead, Cain killed Abel, and God's dispensation for
Adam's family was not fulfilled. However, God's will to save
mankind is unchangeable and absolute; so although God may
not be able to continue his work through a person who does
not fulfill his responsibility, he chooses someone from among
that person's descendants to carry on with his Will.

CHAPTER TEN

Noah's Family in the Dispensation for Restoration

God's Dispensation for Restoration centered on Adam's family was not realized because Cain murdered Abel. However, God's Will to fulfill the Purpose of the Creation is predestined as absolute; so on the basis of Abel's heart and loyalty to heaven, God "gave" Seth to take his place (Gen 4:25). Then, from among Seth's descendants God chose Noah and his family to stand in place of Adam and his family, and God began the Dispensation for Restoration centered on Noah's family.

Genesis 6:13 says that ". . . God said to Noah, 'I have determined to make an end of all flesh; for the earth is filled with violence through them; behold, I will destroy them with the earth.' " This clearly shows that God intended to bring about the Last Days at that time. Using Noah's family as the foundation, God intended to fulfill the Purpose of the Creation by sending the Messiah after the Flood Judgment. Therefore, the dispensation in Noah's family was the dispensation to establish the Foundation for the Messiah.

I. FOUNDATION OF FAITH

A. The Central Person for Restoring the Foundation of Faith

In the dispensation centered on Noah's family, Noah was the central person chosen to restore the Foundation of Faith. God found him ten generations and sixteen hundred years after Adam. God blessed Noah as he had blessed Adam earlier, directing Noah to " '. . . be fruitful and multiply . . .' " (Gen 9:7). In the eyes of God, Noah was a righteous man (Gen 6:9),who was therefore qualified to be the central person for the Foundation of Faith.

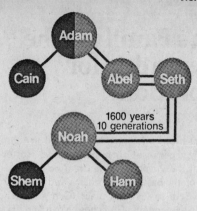

B. The Offering Required in Restoring the Foundation of Faith

The offering which Noah had to make to restore the Foundation of Faith was the ark. What was the meaning of this ark in terms of God's dispensation? Noah was chosen by God to symbolically restore the cosmos, which had been handed over to Satan by Adam's fall. Consequently, Noah had to make an offering which would symbolize a new cosmos, and be acceptable to God. The ark was this offering. After God gave his instructions, Noah spent one hundred twenty years building the ark, enduring all types of ridicule from the evil and sinful world because of his absolute obedience to God.

The three-deck ark symbolized the cosmos which was created through the three growing stages. The eight members of Noah's family who entered the ark were to restore and indemnify the failures of the eight members of Adam's family. Since the ark represented the cosmos, Noah, as the master of the ark, represented God; the members of his family represented all mankind; and the animals in the ark represented the entire Creation. When the ark had been completed, God judged mankind and destroyed the evil through a forty-day flood. According to "The Principles of the Creation," man was created to serve only one master; so God cannot relate as a second master to a fallen person, who already has Satan as his master. If this were to happen, the dispensation would become a non-Principle one. Therefore, in order to establish an object for his dispensation, through whom he alone could work, God brought about the flood to destroy all who remained under Satan's dominion.

What was the dispensational meaning of the forty-day period of the flood? God's Ideal for the Creation is based on the Four Position Foundation. However, the Four Position Foundation was lost to Satan; so God worked his dispensation to restore the Four Position Foundation. Since the number *ten* is the number of return to unity, it symbolizes return to God. Thus, by working to restore the Four Position Foundation in each of the ten generations from Adam to Noah, God was able to establish the condition for restoring the Four Position Foundation to his side. Thus, the period from Adam to Noah may be seen as the indemnity period for restoring the Four Position Foundation to God. Thus, the number *forty* (4 positions x 10 generations) came to represent the return of the Four Position Foundation to God.

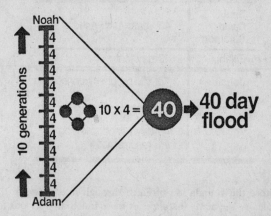

Because of the lust and faithlessness of the people of Noah's time, the indemnity period of ten generations, which was for the purpose of restoring the Four Position Foundation, was invaded by Satan. Consequently, centered on Noah's ark, God set up the forty-day period of the flood as the indemnity period to restore the period from Adam to Noah, which had been invaded. It is based on this that the number 'forty' became necessary in later efforts to separate from Satan and

No. 40 Periods of Separation from Satan

Noah	40 day flood
Abraham	400 years after Noah
Israelites	400 years in Egypt 40 years in wilderness
Moses	40 day fasts

No. 40 Periods of Separation from Satan

Saul, David, Solomon	40 years each as king
Elijah	40 day fast
Jonah	40 day prophecy concerning Ninevah
Jesus	40 day fast 40 day period following the resurrection

restore the Foundation of Faith through indemnity. In the Bible, we see many instances of these indemnity periods for separating from Satan: the four-hundred-year period from Noah to Abraham; the Israelites' four hundred years of suffering in Egypt; their forty years of wandering in the wilderness; Moses' two forty-day fasts; the forty-day period of spying in Canaan; the forty-year reigns of the kings Saul, David, and Solomon; Elijah's forty-day fast; Jonah's prophecy that Nineveh would be destroyed after forty days; Jesus' forty-day fast and prayer; and Jesus' forty-day period after resurrection.

By building the ark in accordance with God's instructions

and faithfully obeying the Will of God throughout the forty-day flood, Noah met the indemnity condition and restored the Foundation of Faith.

II. FOUNDATION OF SUBSTANCE

Noah's family now had to take this vertical attitude of faith which Noah had established toward God and apply it horizontally in their relationships with each other, thus meeting the indemnity condition for establishing the Foundation of Substance. This Indemnity Condition for Removing the Fallen Nature had to be fulfilled by Noah's second son, Ham, and his eldest son, Shem.

In Adam's family, instead of Adam, the second son, Abel, made the offering which was acceptable to God, thus establishing the vertical relationship with God, which is the Foundation of Faith. Therefore, Abel naturally qualified as the central person for the Foundation of Substance.

In Noah's family, however, it was Noah who met the indemnity condition for establishing the Foundation of Faith. Therefore, the position of his second son, Ham, was not yet equivalent to that of Abel after his offering. In other words, Ham had not yet established an absolute and substantial vertical relationship of faith and devotion with God. In order for Ham to be in the central position for establishing the Foundation of Substance, he first had to inherit the foundation of Noah's faith and obedience. For this purpose, it was

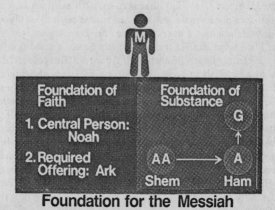

Foundation for the Messiah

essential that Ham forge an unbreakable relationship of heart
with Noah, who had successfully established the Foundation
of Faith. In other words, Ham should have become one in
heart with Noah, obeying him and considering his will to be as
important as life itself.

The Bible records the conditions which God set up to
carry out his dispensation to unite Noah and Ham in heart
(Gen 9:20-25). However, when Ham saw Noah sleeping naked
in the tent, he was so ashamed and displeased that he stirred
up the same shame in his brothers, Shem and Japeth. Recoil-
ing at the thought of their father naked, Shem and Japeth
walked backward and covered him with a garment. This was
such a crime that Noah cursed Ham, saying, " '. . . Cursed be
Canaan; a slave of slaves shall he be to his brothers' " (Gen
9:25).

Judging from Noah's normal conduct, his deep piety, and
the record of his absolute faith, it is not likely that he was
given to intemperate drinking or to improper self-exposure,
which might bring censure. It is natural to think that Noah's
lying naked was at least an impropriety, yet the curse fell not
on Noah but on Ham, who thought that Noah's act was shame-
ful and instigated Shem and Japeth's covering of Noah. The
reason is directly related to God's dispensation.

Why was Ham cursed? This question can be answered by
understanding why Ham's actions were sinful. An act is sinful
when it gives Satan a condition, or basis, to invade, creating
an object for Satan to work through. Satan's power to act
depends upon Give and Take Action with such an object.
Satan does not have the power to act unless he finds an object
with which he has a basis for Give and Take Action.

Then what did Ham do that gave Satan a condition to
invade? Immediately after the Fall, Adam and Eve covered the
sexual part of their bodies, indicating their having entered
into a blood relationship with Satan. Upon seeing his father's
nakedness, Ham was similarly ashamed and covered him up.
From the dispensational viewpoint, the fact that Ham felt
ashamed of his father's nakedness and directed his brothers to
cover him was an admission that he had a blood relationship
with Satan, just as Adam's family had had. Satan, who had
been separated out by the Flood Judgment, was brought back
by Ham's act, and Ham stood in a position to be one with him.
Thus, he was cursed.

Is it a sin to regard the naked human body with a sense of shame? No. However, Noah's family was chosen by God to stand in place of Adam's family, and it therefore had the mission to remove all the conditions by which Adam's family had allowed Satan to invade mankind—conditions which only Noah's family was in the position to remove. It was in accordance with God's dispensation that the righteous Noah became drunk and lay naked in his tent. God had him do this so that Ham, by showing trust, could become one in heart with Noah, who had already established the Foundation of Faith. Everything that Noah did was exactly in accordance with God's dispensation.

Though externally Ham's mistake was only that he harbored shame and displeasure over his father's naked body, dispensationally he was cursed for the mistake of making a base for the influence of Satan, who had been separated out by the Flood Judgment. Therefore, Ham could not possibly stand as the victorious second son and be the center of the Foundation of Substance. Thus, we find nothing recorded in the Bible about Ham and Shem working to meet the conditions for removing the Fallen Nature or establishing a Foundation of Substance.

God could not intervene in the indemnity condition that Ham had to meet, because it was Ham's responsibility. Therefore God did not directly instruct Ham to believe in his father and become one with him no matter what the circumstances.

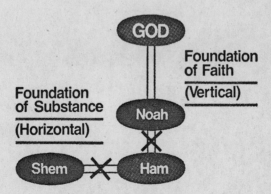

Through Ham's experiences with the flood and Noah's building of the ark, it should have been quite clear that his father was a man representing God's Will. Therefore, after the flood, it was Ham's responsibility to maintain absolute faith in Noah and to obey him in all circumstances.

CHAPTER ELEVEN

Abraham's Family in the Dispensation for Restoration

As a result of Ham's lack of faith, the Dispensation for Restoration was not successfully carried out in Noah's family. However, God has absolutely predestined his Will to fulfill the Purpose of the Creation. On the basis of the loyal and devoted heart of Noah, God called Abraham to carry on the Dispensation. So Abraham had to establish the Foundation for the Messiah, which Noah's family had failed to do.

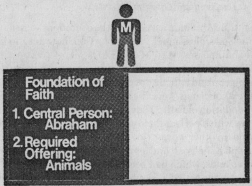

Foundation of Faith

1. Central Person: Abraham

2. Required Offering: Animals

Foundation for the Messiah

I. THE FOUNDATION OF FAITH

A. The Central Figure for Restoring the Foundation of Faith

In the Dispensation for Restoration centered on Abraham's family, the central person for restoring the Foundation of Faith was Abraham. After an indemnity period of four hundred years and ten generations from the time of Noah, God chose Abraham to take Noah's place. Abraham was the son of

Terah, an idol worshipper, and therefore loved by Satan. God
took Abraham as indemnity to restore Satan's having taken
Ham, the second son, who had been in a position to be loved by
God. Because Abraham took the place of Noah, and thus the
place of Adam, God also blessed Abraham, saying that Abraham "would be a blessing" and that he would make Abraham's descendants into a great nation (Gen 12:2). "And he
brought him outside and said 'Look toward heaven, and number the stars, if you are able to number them. . . . I am the LORD
who brought you from Ur of the Chaldeans, to give you this
land to possess' " (Gen 15:5-7). This was God's promise of
blessing to Abraham.

B. The Offering Required in Restoring the
   Foundation of Faith

1. The Symbolic Offering

At that time Abraham asked what the conditions were for him
to gain God's blessing: " '. . . O LORD GOD, how am I to know
that I shall possess it?' " (Gen 15:8).

God asked him to sacrifice a heifer, a ram and a she-goat,
and a pigeon and a turtle dove (Gen 15:9). These three kinds of
sacrificial offerings were the offerings required for restoring
the Foundation of Faith. They symbolized all the things of the
cosmos, which perfect themselves through the three stages of
growing. In other words, God had Abraham sacrifice a heifer,
a ram and a she-goat, and a pigeon and dove as symbols of the
entire cosmos, which had been lost because of the Fall. Thus,
this offering is called a 'symbolic offering'. In addition, these
three sacrifices on the altar were intended to represent and
restore *horizontally* the invaded conditions of the three generations of the *vertical* dispensation—those of Adam, Noah, and
Abraham.

How did Abraham make this significant symbolic offering? We read in Genesis 15:10-13 that Abraham cut the offerings in two and laid one half against the other, except for the
birds, which he did not cut in two. Birds of prey came down
upon the carcasses, and Abraham drove them away. That
evening at sunset, God appeared to Abraham and said, " '. . .
Know of a surety that your descendants will be sojourners in a
land that is not theirs, and will be slaves there, and they will

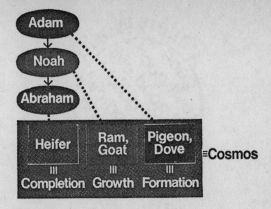

be oppressed for four hundred years . . .'" (Gen 15:13). The birds of prey came down upon the carcasses because Abraham did not cut the birds in two. This caused the Israelites to suffer four hundred years of oppression. Then let us inquire into the meaning of the birds of prey descending upon the offering.

Ever since the Fall of the first man and woman, whenever God works to carry out his Will, Satan moves to block God's way. When Cain and Abel offered sacrifices, Satan was ". . . couching at the door . . ." (Gen 4:7). In Noah's time, the raven symbolized Satan, who was looking for an opportunity to invade Noah's family right after the Flood Judgment (Gen 8:7). Similarly, at the time of Abraham's symbolic offering, the fact that Satan invaded the offering (as a result of the conditions made) is symbolically depicted in the Bible by the birds of prey descending on the offering.

Then what was Abraham's sin? It was his failure to divide the dove and the pigeon. Why should the offerings have been divided? As a result of the Fall, man and his world came to embody both good and evil. The purpose of the dispensation for salvation is the fulfillment of the Purpose of the Creation. God has worked to fulfill the Purpose of Creation by separating good from evil in both man and his world and then destroying the evil and expanding the goodness. In order for God to relate to anything, it must first be symbolically separated from Satan. Thus, the offerings had to be divided.

It was only after the one man, Adam, had been divided in two, in the form of his sons, Cain and Abel, that the sacrificial

offerings could be made. In Noah's time, God's purpose in separating good and evil and then destroying the evil through the flood was to restore the sovereignty of goodness. God intended to have Abraham indemnify Adam's and Noah's failures to separate symbolically the good and evil by having Abraham cut the offerings in two.

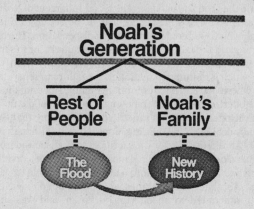

The further significance of dividing the offering was that it would establish the condition of having symbolically separated a world of good sovereignty from the world which is under the dominion of Satan. Also, dividing the offering and draining the blood establishes sanctification by the symbolic removal of the "blood of death," which was inherited through the blood relationship with Satan.

The Significance of Cutting the Animals in Two

1 Cain – Abel Split

2 Separation of Good and Evil through the Flood

3 Separation of the Sovereignties of God and Satan

4 Consecration by removing the "satanic blood"

Not cutting the offering in two was analogous to not having separated Cain and Abel, leaving no Abel-type object for God to relate to. Secondly, it represented the failure to separate the good and evil after the Flood Judgment of Noah's time, as a result of which there was no object of goodness through which God could carry out his dispensation. Thirdly, it represented the failure to meet God's requirement to separate (symbolically) a world of good sovereignty from the world which is dominated by Satan, the failure to separate a world where God can have dominion. Finally, since not dividing the offering meant not removing the "blood of death," it meant the offering was not sanctified and therefore that God could not deal with the offering. Consequently, although externally Abraham did offer the sacrifices to God, viewed from the dimension of dispensational meaning, it was not a divided offering and therefore was not an offering acceptable to God. Because Abraham offered things which were not divided, his offering amounted to an offering to Satan, and was thus deemed sinful.

What were the consequences of his mistake in the symbolic offering? After Abraham failed in the offering, God told him, " 'Know of a surety that your descendants will be sojourners in a land that is not their's, and will be slaves there, and they will be oppressed for four hundred years . . .' " (Gen 15:13). This was a severe penalty. If this was punishment for Abraham's mistake, why did it fall on his descendants, and not on Abraham himself? And why was it for four hundred years?

Because Abraham failed in the symbolic offering, the four-hundred-year period of indemnity that had been necessary to find Abraham as the central person was invaded by Satan. Therefore, from God's viewpoint, making up for the lost four hundred years would require another four-hundred-year period of separation from Satan. This could not be done in Abraham's generation alone. Because of this, his descendants had to restore the lost indemnity period. This was done through the Israelites' four hundred years of oppression in Egypt. Thus, the period of suffering was both the period of punishment for Abraham's mistake in offering the sacrifices and the period to establish the foundation of separation from Satan for the sake of the new dispensation.

If Abraham had offered the three kinds of required offerings in accordance with God's will, in other words, if the symbolic offering had been successful, then the Foundation of Faith would have been restored. Then the work of establishing the Foundation of Substance would have taken place in Abraham's family, centered on his sons. This would have involved an Indemnity Condition for Removing the Fallen Nature between Isaac, the second son, and Ishmael, the first son. There is no mention of this matter in the Bible because Abraham had already failed in his offering, which was to have restored the Foundation of Faith.

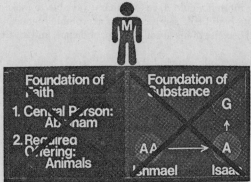

Foundation for the Messiah

2. Abraham's Offering of Isaac

After Abraham's failure in the symbolic offering, God ordered him to offer Isaac as a burnt offering (Gen 22:2), thus beginning a new dispensation. Genesis 22:9,10 states, "When they came to the place of which God had told him, Abraham built an altar there, and laid the wood in order, and bound Isaac his son, and laid him on the altar, upon the wood. Then Abraham put forth his hand, and took the knife to slay his son." With absolute faith, Abraham was committed to offering as a burnt offering his son, Isaac—whom he had received as a blessing. At this moment, the "angel of the Lord" commanded him, ". . . 'Do not lay your hand on the lad or do anything to him; for now I now that you fear God, seeing that you have not withheld your son, your only son, from me' " (Gen 22:12).

In the eyes of God, the sacrifice of Isaac had much more

meaning than just the testing of Abraham's faith. God's dispensation to restore the Foundation of Faith had progressed
through three stages in the families of Adam, Noah, and Abraham. Although Abraham failed in his symbolic offering, it was
God's will that the Foundation of Faith be restored in Abraham's time because it was the third attempt.

Through the offering of Isaac, God unfolded a new dispensation, on a new level. For Abraham, who deeply valued God's
blessing, killing with his own hands and offering the son God
had given him as a blessing pained his heart more than sacrificing himself would have. Abraham was able to make this
extremely difficult sacrifice in an acceptable manner (Gen
22:12) because of his absolute faith, obdience, and loyalty to
God.

When God commanded Abraham to offer Isaac, the situation was already such that the entire Creation, including
Isaac, had fallen into the hands of Satan through Abraham's
failure in the symbolic offering. To separate Isaac from Satan,
God asked Abraham to offer Isaac as a sacrifice. At the point
where Abraham was prepared to make the sacrifice, the absolute faith and obedience within Abraham's heart left no room
whatsover for Satan's accusation. Thus Satan had to leave
Isaac. Separated from Satan, Isaac stood on the side of heaven,
and God ordered Abraham not to kill Isaac. God had now
recovered Isaac, who had been lost. When God says ". . . now I
know . . ." in Genesis 22:12, we can understand that he was
expressing the reproach he felt toward Abraham's failure in
the symbolic offering as well as his joy over Abraham's successful offering of Isaac. Abraham had succeeded despite the
fact that it was much more difficult for him than offering his

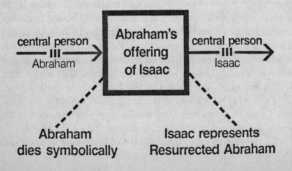

own life as a burnt offering. In offering Isaac, Abraham symbolically killed himself for his failure and made it possible for Isaac to be set up as the resurrected Abraham. Through this offering, Abraham also met the indemnity condition for allowing Isaac to take his place as the central person for the Foundation of Faith. Although the resurrected Abraham and Isaac were two separate individuals, dispensationally they represented one resurrected person. Consequently, the offering of Isaac marks the shift from Abraham to·Isaac as the central person in the Dispensation for Restoration centered on Abraham's family.

II. THE FOUNDATION OF FAITH CENTERED ON ISAAC

A. The Central Person for Restoring the Foundation of Faith

Isaac, who represented the resurrected Abraham, became the new central person. He had been resurrected from the brink of death. Abraham's display of faith in God was highly admirable; but Isaac, himself, had also displayed unshakable faith when, with an obedient heart, he accepted his fate as a burnt offering. It is not exactly clear how old Isaac was at the time of the offering, but from the fact that he carried the wood to be used in it and asked his father where the lamb for the offering was (Gen 22:6,7), it is apparent that Isaac was old enough to understand Abraham's intention to some extent. If Isaac had resisted his father's seemingly irrational plan to kill him for the burnt offering, God would not have been able to accept the offering. Through this we can understand that Isaac was a central person whose obedience was in no way inferior to the loyalty of Abraham.

B. The Offering Required in Restoring the Foundation of Faith

The offering required in restoring the Foundation of Faith was fulfilled by the ram that was offered by Abraham and Isaac: "And Abraham lifted up his eyes and looked and behold, behind him was a ram, caught in a thicket by his horns; and Abraham went and took the ram, and offered it up as a burnt offering instead-of his son" (Gen 22:13).

In place of Isaac, Abraham offered the ram that God had
prepared. It is easy to picture Isaac, caught up in a feeling of
joy and gratitude since he was spared from death, willingly
cooperating with Abraham in sacrificing the ram as a burnt
offering. This was the symbolic offering that restored the
Foundation of Faith centered on Isaac. Even though Abraham
offered the ram, from the dispensational standpoint, Isaac
had become one with Abraham and had inherited his mission;
thus, it was Isaac who restored the Foundation of Faith
through indemnity by successfully carrying out the symbolic
offering, in place of his father.

III. THE FOUNDATION OF SUBSTANCE

Based on the Foundation of Faith which Isaac had established,
the Foundation of Substance now had to be made in order to
complete the Foundation for the Messiah. For this purpose,
Isaac's two sons, Esau and Jacob, had to meet the Indemnity
Condition for Removing the Fallen Nature. If we examine
what is mentioned in the Bible based on outward appearances, the activities of Jacob's family raise many questions.
Why did the twins, Esau and Jacob, fight even while in their
mother's womb (Gen 25:22,23)? Why did God love the second
son, Jacob, while he was still in his mother's womb (Rom
9:13)? Why was Jacob born with one hand grasping Esau's
heel (Gen 25:26)? Why did Jacob have Esau swear to sell his
birthright to him in exchange for some pottage (Gen 25:32-
34)? Why did Jacob cunningly deceive his blind father and
take Esau's blessing (Gen 27:1-36)? Why did God so greatly
love, protect, and bless Jacob throughout his life, despite the
fact that he did so many seemingly questionable things? And
in light of these things, why did God make him the root of the
chosen people?

The record of Esau and Jacob's fighting each other even
while in their mother's womb tells us that their relationship
was not just an ordinary relationship between two brothers.
From God's dispensational viewpoint, Esau and Jacob duplicated his dispensation of separating Cain and Abel, with
Jacob and Esau representing good and evil, respectively. God
"loved" Jacob and "hated" Esau (Rom 9:11-13) even while
they were in the womb because the one represented good and
the other evil.

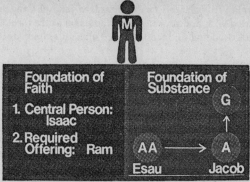

Foundation for the Messiah

Jacob was to be the central person for the Foundation of Substance. First of all, he had to meet the indemnity condition for restoring the position of Abel. Jacob met this condition by restoring the birthright of the eldest son of the family. In other words, because Satan had deceitfully taken control of God's Creation through the position of the elder son, Jacob had to meet certain conditions that would restore the birthright of the first-born to God's side.

Jacob also had to meet conditions that would restore the birthright of the first-born on an individual level. With wisdom and cunning, Jacob took the birthright from his elder brother, Esau, by purchasing it with bread and a lentil pottage (Gen 25:33,34). God blessed Jacob because Jacob realized that the birthright had precious value and did his best to restore it. This is also the reason that God let Isaac give his blessing to Jacob (Gen 27:27). On the other hand, God did not bless Esau because Esau thought lightly of the blessing and sold it for a bowl of pottage.

Secondly, by going through a period of twenty-one years of drudgery in Haran, which symbolized the world of Satan, Jacob met the conditions for restoring a family from the satanic world to God's side.

Thirdly, through the twenty-one years in Haran and his victory in wrestling with the angel, Jacob also met the conditions for restoring dominion over all things (represented by the things and wealth earned from Laban). When Jacob was returning from Haran to the promised land of Canaan, he wrestled with and prevailed over an angel at the ford of the Jabbok. In doing so, Jacob restored man's dominion over the angels.

Restoration of the Birthright

1 Individual: Jacob buys birthright for stew and bread

2 Family: Jacob earns family in Haran

3 Dominion over Creation: Jacob restores material things and subjugates Angel

By restoring dominion over himself, over a family, over the Creation, and especially over the angels, Jacob met the conditions by which God could accept him. Put in another way, Jacob met the conditions necessary to inherit the vertical Foundation of Faith that Isaac had established, and by doing so, restored through indemnity the position of Abel and became the central person for the Foundation of Substance. In this way, Esau and Jacob established the positions of Cain and Abel as they had existed at the time God accepted Abel's offering.

Foundation of Substance

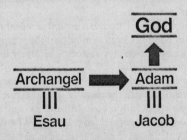

To meet the Indemnity Condition for Removing the Fallen Nature, Esau, who was in the Cain position, first of all had to love Jacob, who was in the Abel position. Secondly, Esau had to accept Jacob as his mediator. Thirdly, Esau had to obey and submit to Jacob and come under Jacob's dominion. Fourthly, Esau had to stand in the position of multiplying (expanding) goodness, by inheriting goodness from Jacob, who had received the blessing from God.

Foundation of Substance

God
↑
Archangel ——→ Adam

Esau   Jacob

Fallen Nature	Indemnity Condition
1 Not Taking God's Viewpoint	Love Jacob
2 Leaving Position	Receive God's Love through Jacob
3 Reversing Order	Submit to Jacob
4 Multiplying Sin	Learn God's Way from Jacob

Jacob's efforts to induce Esau to welcome him back and submit to him of his own will were heartrending. Even when Jacob was returning from Haran to Canaan, Esau still had resentment against Jacob because Jacob had previously taken the blessing from him. So Esau led an army of four hundred men and went to meet Jacob. When Jacob received news of this he prayed to God and did all he possibly could.

Jacob thought, ". . .'I may appease him with the present that goes before me, and afterwards I shall see his face; perhaps he will accept me' " (Gen 32:20). With no reluctance he sent ahead of him as a gift for Esau the more than five hundred livestock that he had earned as a reward for his hard work in Haran. Jacob also formulated an alternative plan, dividing the people and livestock into two groups, so that one might flee if Esau attacked (Gen 32:7,8). When he was about to meet Esau, he deliberately put his beloved wife and child in the very rear, so that he was fully prepared to escape if it became necessary (Gen 33:2). He himself went ahead of them,

bowing to the ground seven times, until he came near to his
brother (Gen 33:3). He greatly humbled himself, saying to
Esau, " '. . . for truly to see your face is like seeing the face of
God, with such favor have you received me' " (Gen 33:10).

Jacob did his best to fulfill God's Will and to change
Esau's heart from one full of hatred to one that would embrace
him with love. Esau was moved by such efforts and sincerity
on Jacob's part and welcomed him. Genesis 33:4 goes on to
say, ". . . Esau ran to meet him, and embraced him, and fell on
his neck and kissed him, and they wept." Since Esau loved
Jacob and welcomed him back, despite the fact that he had
taken the birthright from Esau, the Indemnity Condition for
Removing the Fallen Nature was fulfilled.

A. The Origin of the Chosen People

Jacob's victory was not only an individual victory. He was the
first fallen person to win a victory for God's side. By prevailing
over an angel on his way from Haran to Canaan, Jacob had
met the indemnity condition for restoring man's dominion
over the angels. For this he was named Israel and was selected
as the basis for forming the chosen people (Gen 35:10,11). In
Exodus 3:6, God said, ". . . 'I am the God of your father, the God
of Abraham, the God of Isaac, and the God of Jacob.' " This
means that God's will for Abraham was fulfilled through Isaac
and Jacob and that, from the standpoint of God's dispensation, these three generations are considered as one. Jacob
brought about Esau's voluntary submission so that Esau
could fulfill the Indemnity Condition for Removing the Fallen
Nature. This was the first time that God's side (Abel) had made
Satan's side (Cain) submit.

Jacob $\Longrightarrow$ "Israel"

(Gen 32 : 28)
(Gen 35 : 10 - 11)

Exodus 3:6

The God of:

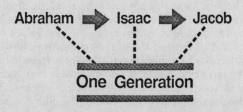

Abraham ➡ Isaac ➡ Jacob

One Generation

In this way, God set up a victorious individual and a victorious family—an individual and family that had met the indemnity conditions for making Satan submit. Then, from this starting point, God raised and developed a chosen people. Viewed in this light, the Israelites' becoming God's chosen people is the result of Jacob's individual victory in subjugating the satanic side.

Jacob's course set the pattern for the subjugation of Satan, and this pattern was to be followed by everyone to come after him. Moses and all the prophets had to go through this model course, and the Israelites as a whole had to go through it. The history of the Israelites provides the historical data which show the model course for subjugating Satan on the national level. Thus the Israelites' history up to the time of Jesus' coming was the central history of the Dispensation for Restoration. This is the reason that the Bible goes into the history of the Israelites in such great detail, though it would seem to have nothing to do with us today.

Now, let us examine the meaning of the verse in Romans 9:13, where we read that God "hated" Esau even while he was in the womb. This verse simply means that God was working to fulfill his Dispensation for Restoration through indemnity according to the principles of the Dispensation for Restoration by placing Esau in the position of Cain. After Esau had completed his responsibility by receiving and loving Jacob, he would have been in the position of restored Cain and would eventually have received the love and blessings of God (Gen 36:7).

B. The Foundation for the Messiah

After the series of delays caused by the failures of the central persons in the Dispensation for Restoration, the Foundation for the Messiah which had been sought ever since Adam's time was finally established for the first time in Isaac's family.

But, because Abraham had failed in his symbolic offering, his descendants still had to go through the indemnity period of four hundred years of oppression. So, though Isaac's descendants had established the Foundation for the Messiah, they could receive him only after they had gone through this indemnity period. Of course, it was impossible that Isaac's family consist of the same individuals for four hundred years. During this time his family expanded and grew into tribes and a nation. After their period of suffering, the descendants of those who had established the family Foundation for the Messiah had to establish it on a national level.

Therefore, the Foundation for the Messiah established in Isaac's family became the basis for starting the course of indemnity which was to establish the national Foundation for the Messiah. In retrospect, Jacob's individual victory led to the establishment of a family to which God could relate. Then, centered on this family, in the next age, God began his dispensation to establish the national Foundation for the Messiah. Internally, God expanded the family Foundation for the Messiah to the national level. Externally, however, Isaac's descendants still had to undergo four hundred years of oppression as indemnity for Abraham's failure.

Foundation for the Messiah
National Level

Foundation for the Messiah
Family Level

Thus, Jacob's twelve sons and the seventy members of the his household went to Egypt, which represented the satanic world, and remained there through four hundred years of oppression. By re-separating them from Satan, who had previously invaded, these events would raise the chosen people to the point where God could deal with them in love. God then planned to bring the chosen people back to Canaan, in order to establish the national Foundation for the Messiah. On that foundation, the Messiah would have been able to come and consummate the Dispensation for Restoration.

God loved and protected the Israelites and sent many prophets to them in order to prepare the Foundation for the Messiah. After the Israelites symbolically gained Satan's submission, God would send the Messiah, who is the fruit of the Dispensation and the true temple. The example set by Jacob, in Abel's position, in bringing about the submission of Esau (in Cain's position) was supposed to bear fruit in the final relationship between the Messiah (Abel) and Israel, representing all mankind (Cain). Thus representing all mankind, the chosen nation was to fulfill its mission by loving, obeying, and serving the Messiah, who is the Abel for all mankind.

CHAPTER TWELVE

Moses in the Dispensation for Restoration

I. GOD USES A MODEL COURSE IN HIS DISPENSATION

The Reason for Establishing the Model Course

The purpose of the Dispensation for Restoration is ultimately accomplished when man fulfills his responsibility and thus obtains Satan's voluntary submission and has dominion over him. However, Satan did not obey or submit to God, and later he would not obey or submit to Jesus, who would come as a First Ancestor and a True Parent. Certainly he would not submit to anyone else. Being man's creator, God therefore assumed the responsibility to make Satan submit.

God established Jacob as the representative through whom he would show the model course for subjugating Satan. This sheds light on the meaning of Amos 3:7, which says, " 'Surely the Lord GOD does nothing, without revealing his secret to his servants the prophets.' " There is far more to the entire course by which Jacob led Esau to submit than Jacob's individual efforts. It is the model course worked by God, through Jacob, to show the way to gain the voluntary submission of Satan, working through Esau. Jacob's course for subjugating Satan is the pattern that Moses followed on the national level. And Jesus, the Messiah, came to teach all of mankind how to elicit Satan's voluntary submission. As man's True Father, or First Ancestor, the Messiah has to pioneer the course that will be the pattern for all mankind to follow in substantially subjugating Satan. Jesus himself substantially subjugated Satan by following the model course that God had already shown through Jacob and Moses. In the same manner, any person can make Satan submit by following the course of Jesus. Acts 3:22 tells us that Moses said, " '. . . "The Lord God will raise up for you a prophet from your brethren as he raised

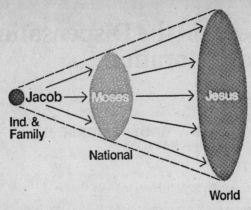

me up. You shall listen to him in whatever he tells you.' ' "
This is a reference to the coming Messiah (Jesus), who was to
follow Moses' course. In John 5:19 Jesus said that he was
following the pattern that God had shown through Moses'
model course: "Jesus said to them,'Truly, truly, I say to you,
the Son can do nothing of his own accord, but only what he
sees the Father doing; for whatever he does, that the Son does
likewise.' " Moses was the model that Jesus followed.

From an external viewpoint, it may seem that Jacob was
merely the head of a family in a tribal age, whereas Moses was
the leader of the Israelite nation, and Jesus was the Messiah.
Yet, these three men did follow similar patterns in their life
courses, because God had set up a model course in his dispensation.

II. MOSES' AND JESUS' COURSES
   FOLLOWED THE PATTERN OF
   JACOB'S COURSE

As already stated, Jacob's course was a course to elicit Satan's
submission. Any course for subjugating Satan must follow the
path which is the reverse of the one by which Satan gained his
wrongful dominion. Let us compare the courses that Moses
and Jesus took with the model course of Jacob.

A. When Adam and Eve did not keep God's commandment and
did not overcome the trials of temptation from the archangel,

they fell. At the ford of the Jabbok, Jacob fought an angel at the risk of his life and gained the victory over him—then receiving the name of Israel (Gen 32:25-28). God tested Jacob by placing the angel in the position of Satan, and consequently the victory in that struggle indemnified the trials which Adam and Eve had failed to pass. The purpose of the trial was not to drive Jacob into misery but to establish Jacob as the person who could complete restoration on the family level by having him restore dominion over the angel. In order for Moses to become the person who could complete the national restoration of Canaan, he also had to overcome a trial at the risk of his life, a trial in which God tried to have him killed (Ex 4:24-26). And in order for Jesus to become the person who could complete the world-wide restoration of Canaan and lead all mankind to the Kingdom of Heaven, he also had to win a fight against Satan at the risk of his life. He did this through his forty days in the wilderness (Mt 4:1-11).

Ⓐ Trial of Faith

Jacob	Struggle with Angel Gen 32:25-28
Moses	God's Attempt to kill Moses Ex 4:24-26
Jesus	Temptations after 40-day fast Matt 4:1-11

B. The Fallen Nature was formed because of the spiritual and physical falls. Jacob and Moses had to meet certain conditions in order to eliminate symbolically the Fallen Nature. In buying the birthright from Esau, Jacob used bread and lentil pottage (Gen 25:34) to initiate the course of indemnity for the Foundation of Substance, the bread and pottage symbolizing the flesh and the spirit. In order to initiate the course for the Foundation of Substance in his course, Moses gave the

Israelites manna and quail, the manna and quail again symbolizing the flesh and the spirit. John 6:49-53 shows that Jesus
followed this model course: " 'Your fathers ate the manna in
the wilderness, and they died. . . . unless you eat the flesh of
the Son of man and drink his blood, you have no life in
you. . . .' " In the world-wide course of restoration, fallen man
can meet the Indemnity Condition to Remove the Fallen Nature only by believing absolutely in Jesus and living as he
instructed (Jn 3:16, Mt 28:19,20).

Ⓑ Flesh and Spirit

Jacob	Bread and Stew Gen 25:34
Moses	Manna and Quail Ex 16:12-15
Jesus	Bread and Wine John 6:48-58

C. Because of the Fall, even man's dead body belongs to Satan.
However, because Jacob was already blessed and sanctified,
when his body was embalmed for forty days and he was
mourned (Gen 50:2,3), the condition for his dead body to be
separated from Satan was also met. Since Moses followed
Jacob's model course, on the foundation of his merits, he also
met the condition for his body to be separated from Satan.
Thus, the archangel fought with Satan for Moses' body (Jude
1:9). And, accordingly, after Jesus' death there were also un-
usual phenomena that occurred concerning his body (Mt
28:12,13).

D. Because of the fall of the first human ancestors (during
their growing period), Satan gained wrongful dominion over
man. To indemnify this, God designed conditions based on the
numbers that represent the length of the invaded period.
Thus, in the process of restoration through indemnity, God

Ⓒ Body

Jacob	Enbalmed for 40 days Gen 50:3
Moses	Dispute between Satan and Michael Jude 9
Jesus	Body Disappeared Matt 28:12-13

Ⓓ Numerical Aspect of Restoration

	3 stages	12 generations	7 days of creation
Jacob	3-day period after leaving Haran Gen 31:22	12 Sons Gen 35:22	70 Family members Gen 46:27
Moses	requested 3-day period Ex 5:3	12 Tribes Ex 24:4	70 Elders Ex 24:1
Jesus	3-day period after crucifixion Luke 18:33	12 Apostles Matt 10:1	70 Disciples Luke 10:1

has worked his dispensation by having man meet the numerical conditions that represent that period.

For example, when Jacob returned from Haran to Canaan, there was a three-day period of separation from Satan (Gen 31:22), that period being the period necessary to initiate a new dispensation. There was a three-day period of the same kind when Moses initiated the course to lead the Israelites out of Egypt into Canaan (Ex 5:3). Also, Jesus spent three days in the tomb (Lk 18:33) to separate from Satan before beginning his world-wide course of the spiritual restoration of Canaan.

Jacob had twelve sons in order to restore in his lifetime (horizontally) the vertical indemnity conditions of the twelve generations from Noah to his time, which had ended up being claimed by Satan. For the same reason, there were twelve tribes under Moses (Ex 24:4), and Jesus had twelve apostles (Mt 10:1).

Satan's wrongful control of the seven-day period of creation was indemnified by Jacob's having seventy family members (Gen 46:27), by Moses' having seventy elders (Ex 24:1), and by Jesus' having seventy disciples (Lk 10:1), each group taking the central role in its respective course of restoration.

🄴 Staff

Jacob	Crossed Jordan river with staff Gen 32:10
Moses	Crossed Red Sea with staff Ex 14:16
Jesus	Rod of Iron (crossing the world of suffering) Rev 2:27, 12:5

E. The staff, which is capable of smiting injustice, pointing out the way, and providing support, is a symbol of God's Word, and thus, a symbol of the Messiah to come. Jacob entered the land of Canaan leaning on his staff as he crossed the Jordan (Gen 32:10), and Moses led the Israelites across the Red Sea with his staff (Ex 14:16). This foreshadows fallen mankind's crossing from the sinful world into the ideal world, led by the Messiah and depending on the Messiah, who smites injustice. Jesus, who smites injustice as the "rod of iron" (Rev 2:27; 12:5), had to lead all mankind from the world of suffering, across the troubled sea of this world, into the ideal world.

F. Eve's sin was the root of sin, which bore fruit when Cain killed Abel. Thus, Satan invaded man and produced the fruit

of sin through a mother and son. According to the principle of
restoration through indemnity, a mother and son should reverse this course, by mutually cooperating to bring about
separation from Satan. Thus, it was by his mother's initiative
and through her cooperation that Jacob received the blessing
and was able to meet the condition for separating from Satan
(Gen 27:43). And through the cooperation of his mother, Moses
came to be in a position to fulfill God's Will (Ex 2:2). Jesus also
was helped by his mother in fulfilling his mission (Mt 2:13).

🅕 Mother-Son Cooperation

Jacob	Rebekah with Jacob Gen 27:43
Moses	Moses' mother saves and raises Moses Ex 2:2-8
Jesus	Mary saves Jesus Matt 2:13

🅖 Satanic World → Heavenly World

Jacob	Haran ➡ Canaan Gen 31:13, 17, 18
Moses	Egypt ➡ Canaan Ex 3:8
Jesus	Egypt ➡ Palestine Matt 2:13

G. The central person in the Dispensation for Restoration must follow a course of restoration that leads from the satanic world to the heavenly world. Jacob walked the course of restoration from Haran to Canaan (Gen 31-33), and Moses walked the course from Egypt to Canaan (Ex 3:8). Jesus also offered his whole life to transform the satanic world into the ideal world.

H. The final goal of the Dispensation for Restoration is to completely demolish Satan. Therefore, Jacob buried idols representing Satan under an oak tree (Gen. 35:4), Moses destroyed the idol of the golden calf (Ex 32:20), and Jesus, through his words and power, was to annihilate the sinful world and gain Satan's surrender.

⒣ Destruction of Evil

Jacob	Buried idols under tree Gen 35:4
Moses	Burned Golden Calf Ex 32:20
Jesus	Subjugation of Satan

III. THE DISPENSATION FOR RESTORATION CENTERED ON MOSES

A. Overview of the Dispensation

The principle of the Dispensation for Restoration was the same in Moses' time as in the previous dispensation, in that he had to restore the Foundation of Faith and the Foundation of Substance in order to establish the Foundation for the Messiah. However, in the Dispensation for Restoration centered on Moses, we discover that there are two differences from the previous dispensations. First, Moses stood on the successful Foundation for the Messiah which had already been established by Isaac's family, and the merit of this completed work applied toward Moses' meeting his own indemnity conditions. Second, the level of the dispensation had expanded from the family level to the national level. God chose Moses to lead the Israelites from the satanic world of Egypt into Canaan, which represented the Kingdom of Heaven. In other words, God worked his dispensation to restore the Kingdom of Heaven (Canaan) on a national level.

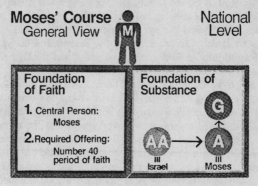

Moses' Course
General View

National Level

Foundation of Faith

1. Central Person: Moses

2. Required Offering: Number 40 period of faith

Foundation of Substance

G

A A → A

III Israel III Moses

Foundation for the Messiah

1. The Foundation of Faith

a. The central person for restoring the Foundation of Faith

Moses was the central person who had to restore the Foundation of Faith. However, God appointed Moses to a dispensational position somewhat different from that held by the previous central persons, Adam, Noah, and Abraham. First of all, Moses stood in a position representing God, even "be[ing] as" God (Ex 4:16; 7:1); secondly, Moses was the model for Jesus. That is, since God's spirit would dwell in Jesus, then God's establishing Moses as his representative means establishing Moses as the model for Jesus.

b. The Required Offering for the Foundation of Faith

Because of his special dispensational position, Moses did not have to make a symbolic offering of things as Abel, Noah, and Abraham did. He was able to restore the Foundation of Faith by fulfilling a forty-based indemnity period of separation from Satan. There are two reasons for this.

First, Moses stood on the foundation of the three successful symbolic material offerings by Abel, Noah, and Isaac. Second, with the establishing of the victorious Foundation for the Messiah by Isaac's family, the age had passed in which a sacrifice was the offering required in place of the Word, and Moses had entered the age in which God's Word was to be received directly. In other words, the Dispensational Age of the Foundation for Restoration had ended and the Dispensational Age of Restoration had begun.

Since the Dispensation had been delayed so long—even from the time of Adam—an indemnity condition was necessary to restore this long span of Satan's invasion. It had to be a condition based on the number forty, which is the number that symbolizes separation from Satan. In the Dispensational Age of Restoration, the Foundation of Faith could be restored through indemnity by man's remaining united with God's Word during a period of separation from Satan, a period based on the number forty, instead of by his making a material offering.

2. The Foundation of Substance

The central person for the dispensation to establish the national Foundation of Substance was Moses himself. As was already explained, Moses was the central person responsible for establishing the Foundation of Faith, which is the vertical relationship with God. In doing so, he was in the position of Jesus, because he was standing as God to the people (Ex 4:16; 7:1). For that reason, Moses was in the position of a parent to the Israelite nation. Yet, as a prophet with the mission of pioneering the way for Jesus, Moses was also in the position of a child to Jesus. Therefore, he was also able to be the central person, or stand in the Abel position, for the national Foundation of Substance. This is the same principle that applied when Abel, in the parent position, successfully made the offering and established the Foundation of Faith which originally should have been established by Adam.

If the Israelites, in the Cain position, had loved Moses and had obeyed him absolutely after he established the Abel position for the Foundation of Substance, then the Indemnity Condition for Removing the Fallen Nature on the level of the nation would have been met, Moses' vertical relationship with God would have been established in the horizontal order among Moses and the people, and the national Foundation of Substance would have been established.

3. The Foundation for the Messiah

If Moses had passed through a forty-period for separation from Satan centered on God's Word, then the indemnity condition to restore the national Foundation of Faith would have been met. If the Israelites, centered on the victorious Moses, had restored the Foundation of Substance, then the national Foundation for the Messiah would have been established. On this foundation, the Israelites were to receive the Messiah and be reborn and cleansed of the Original Sin. Then they would have realized the Original Nature and would have become perfect persons. However, the Israelites did not trust Moses, and the national course of the restoration of Canaan ended up being prolonged two times.

B. The First Course of the National Restoration of Canaan

In order for Moses to become the central person representing the Israelites for the course of indemnity that would restore the national Foundation of Faith, Moses spent forty years in the Pharoah's palace, the center of the satanic world. Although to the world he was a prince because he was raised as the son of Pharoah's daughter (Ex 2:10), Moses was actually raised by his own mother, who lived in the palace as his nurse, and she instilled in him a deep awareness of the God of Israel and of his heritage as one of the chosen people. Finally, he left the palace, preferring to suffer with God's people rather than to enjoy the sinful, ephemeral pleasures of Pharoah's palace (Heb 11:24). Through his forty years in the palace, Moses fulfilled the forty-period of separation from Satan and restored the Foundation of Faith.

In establishing the Foundation of Faith, Moses at the same time qualified himself for the Abel position in the Foundation of Substance. The Israelites, who were in the Cain position, had to faithfully submit to and obey Moses, who was in the Abel position. They would have become one with Moses and they would have inherited God's Will. This would have restored the national Foundation of Substance. If this had been done, the Foundation of Substance would have been established during the period of the Israelites' return to Canaan under the leadership of Moses.

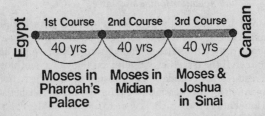

With this purpose in mind, Moses fulfilled the condition for starting the dispensation. Moses confirmed his determination before God and the Israelites when he killed an Egyptian that he saw beating a Hebrew (Ex 2:12).* After seeing Moses act in such a way, the Israelites should have trusted and united with Moses. Then, through Moses, they would have been told by God to travel to the promised land of Canaan by the direct route through the territory of the Philistines, and they would not have had to go the longer way across the Red Sea and through the wilderness of Sinai. By their uniting with Moses during a twenty-one-day journey to Canaan, the Foundation of Substance would have been successfully established, and this course would have indemnified Jacob's twenty-one-year course in Haran. Exodus 13:17 says, "When Pharoah let the

---

* Though Moses had killed someone, he had done so in defense of another person and knowing full well that if found out he would lose his very privileged position and his life. Thus, it was a sign of righteousness and a sign that he was willing to stand with the Israelites.

people go, God did not lead them by way of the land of the
Philistines, although that was near; for God said, 'Lest the
people repent when they see war, and return to Egypt.' " This
passage shows that God's original plan was to have them take
the route through the land of the Philistines, which was a
faster, more direct route.

However, instead of trusting Moses, the Israelites exposed
Moses' killing, and Moses had to escape from Pharoah, as
recorded in Exodus 2:15, "When Pharoah heard of it, he sought
to kill Moses." Moses went to hide in the wilderness of Midian,
and thus the first course of the national restoration of Canaan
could not even begin.

C. The Second Course of the National Restoration of Canaan

1. The Foundation of Faith and the Foundation of Substance

Because the first course of the national restoration of Canaan
could not even begin, the forty-year period of indemnity
which Moses had established for the Foundation of Faith
while he was in Pharaoh's palace was invaded by Satan.
Therefore, Moses had to establish a second forty-year period
of separation from Satan. He did so through his life in exile in
the wilderness of Midian. Through this he was able to restore
the Foundation of Faith for the second national course.

At the end of this period, God appeared to Moses and said,

> . . . I have seen the affliction of my people who are
> in Egypt, and have heard their cry because of their
> taskmasters; I know their sufferings, and I have
> come down to deliver them out of the hand of the
> Egyptians, and to bring them up out of that land to
> a good and broad land, a land flowing with milk
> and honey, to the place of the Canaanites. . . . And
> now, behold, the cry of the people of Israel has
> come to me, and I have seen the oppression with
> which the Egyptians oppress them. Come, I will
> send you to Pharaoh that you may bring forth my
> people, the sons of Israel, out of Egypt.(Ex 3:7-10)

Through his forty years in the wilderness of Midian,

Moses restored the Foundation of Faith and at the same time established his position as the central person for the Foundation of Substance. God's dispensation began with Moses' establishing the foundation to start the course of national restoration by striking the Egyptians with three miracles and ten disasters (Ex 4, 7-11). The Israelites witnessed these and came to realize that Moses was the true leader sent by God. On this basis, the second course of the national restoration of Canaan was finally able to begin. However, the fact that the Israelites were at last following Moses did not mean that the Indemnity Condition for Removing the Fallen Nature was an accomplished fact. Satan was able to invade during this dispensational course and caused this long period to be handed over to him. To restore this lost indemnity period on a national basis, the Israelites, in Cain's position, had to submit to Moses, obey him, and remain one with him throughout the entire period, until their arrival in the land of Canaan. Consequently, the Israelites had to enter Canaan having been obedient to Moses during their entire course in the wilderness. Only then could the national Foundation of Substance have been established.

God already knew that, although the Israelites trusted Moses enough to begin the journey to the land of Canaan, they did not have complete faith in him. God was afraid that if they went via the direct route, their fear of battle (Ex 13:17) would revive their faithlessness, and they might easily return to

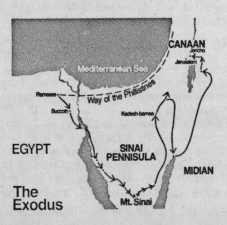

Egypt and leave his dispensation unaccomplished. For this reason, God instead led them across the Red Sea and through the Sinai wilderness, even though it would take more time. God continually showed them his grace by performing miracles. He was trying to make it difficult for them to fall into disbelief and go back to Egypt. As a result, Moses started the Israelites on what should have been a twenty-one month course through the wilderness.

2. The Tabernacle in the Dispensation for Restoration

At the beginning of the third month after the Israelites had left Egypt, they arrived at the wilderness of Sinai. There, God gave Moses special directions. God told him to consecrate the people (Ex 19:10) and reinforce their faith. Then Moses went up Mount Sinai with seventy elders and met God (Ex 24:9,10). There, God showed his glory to his people, as we find expressed in Exodus 24:15-17:

> Then Moses went up on the mountain, and . . . . the glory of the LORD settled on Mount Sinai, and the cloud covered it six days; and on the seventh day he called to Moses out of the midst of the cloud. Now the appearance of the glory of the LORD was like a devouring fire on top of the mountain in the sight of the people of Israel.

This was also to show them that God was personally working with them. God took these measures so that the people of Israel could have absolute trust in him.

God called Moses to the mountaintop and asked him to fast for forty days so that he could receive the two tablets of stone with the Ten Commandments (Ex 24:18). During the time that Moses fasted on the mountain, he received instructions from God concerning the ark of the covenant and the tabernacle (Ex 25-31). When the forty-day fast was over, he received two tablets of stone with the Ten Commandments engraved on them (Ex 31:18). When Moses came down from the mountain, he found that the Israelites had already lost their faith in God and were worshipping a golden calf as their god (Ex 32:2-4). During the forty days that their leader was away from them, the Israelites had lost their faith and rebelled against the very God who had guided them with so many miracles. When Moses saw this, he was greatly angered, and at the foot of the mountain, he threw the tablets to the ground, breaking them (Ex 32:19).

God appeared to Moses again and gave him instructions to cut out of stone two tablets like the first (Ex 34:1). After Moses finished his second forty-day fast, he again received the Ten Commandments, written on the two tablets. The Israelites then built the ark of the covenant and the tabernacle, with the tablets as the core.

a. The significance of the tablets and the ark of the covenant

(i) The significance of the tablets

Adam and Eve were created by the Word. If they had perfected themselves, they would have become perfect incarnations of the Word. However, because of the Fall, they lost the Word.

The tablets inscribed with God's Commandments, which Moses received after the forty-period of separation from Satan, have a special meaning. They are the substantial representation of the Word, symbolically representing the restoration of Adam and Eve from the satanic world. Thus, the two tablets, as symbols of Adam and Eve, also symbolize Jesus and the Holy Spirit, who would come as the substantial incarnations of the Word. This is the reason that Jesus is symbolized as the "white stone" (Rev 2:17) and the "Rock" (1 Cor 10:4).

Moses' receiving the tablets with God's Words also demonstrates that the Dispensational Age of the Foundation of Restoration had passed. In other words, the age during which man could relate to God only through material offerings had passed, and fallen mankind had entered the Dispensational Age of Restoration, in which man could relate to God through the Word.

(ii) The significance of the tabernacle

Jesus compared the temple in Jerusalem to his body (Jn 2:21), and Paul stated that Christians are the temples of God (1 Cor 3:16). The temple is the image-representation of Jesus. However, during their course through the wilderness, the Israelites could not build a temple, and so they built the tabernacle instead. Thus, the tabernacle, which was a miniature type of the temple, was also a symbolic representation of Jesus. For this reason, when God ordered Moses to build the tabernacle, he said, " '. . . let them make me a sanctuary, that I may dwell in their midst' " (Ex 25:8). Accordingly, the tabernacle is the symbolic messiah which the Israelites were to attend during their course in the wilderness.

Messiah   Tabernacle

(iii) *The structure of the tabernacle*

The tabernacle was composed of the Most Holy Place* and the Holy Place (Ex 26:33,34). Only the chief priests could visit the Most Holy Place, and that but once a year, for the offering of sacrifices. Within the Most Holy Place was the ark of the covenant, within which were the two tablets of stone, symbolizing Jesus and the Holy Spirit, and heaven and earth. We can consider the ark, then, in a narrow sense, a microcosm of the cosmos, and also, a microcosm of the tabernacle. The Most Holy Place symbolizes Jesus' spirit self and the invisible substantial world, and the Holy Place, which was the ordinary place for the offering of sacrifices, symbolizes Jesus' body and the visible substantial world.

b. The purpose of the dispensation with the tablets of stone and the tabernacle

From God's viewpoint, once the Israelites had left Egypt it was imperative that they make it to Canaan without turning back; it was necessary to enter Canaan at all cost. To this end, God

---

* Also commonly known as the Holy of Holies

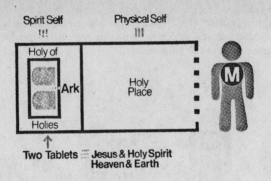

sought to inspire the Israelites to have faith in him by continually performing miracles, beginning right at the start of the dispensation.

After they had set out for Canaan, God guided and cared for the Israelites throughout their course in the wilderness by means of many miracles: guiding them by a pillar of cloud and a pillar of fire (Ex 13:21); dividing the waters of the Red Sea (Ex 14:21); providing manna and quail (Ex 16:12,13,35); having Moses produce water from a rock for the people to drink (Ex 17:6); and defeating the Amalekites with his power (Ex 17:10-13). Despite all of these, the Israelites lost faith in Moses and God numerous times, and in the end there was the danger that even Moses might act faithlessly.

For this reason, God found it necessary to create an object of faith which would never change, even though man might change. If there were even one person among the Israelites who would believe absolutely in this object of faith, then God would be able to carry out his Will by having that person's faith be representative of the Israelites and then passing it from person to person like a baton. That object of faith was the tabernacle, which enshrined the ark and the tablets and symbolized the Messiah. Thus, the Israelites' construction of the tabernacle meant that symbolically the Messiah had come.

Consequently, if, until they entered the blessed land of Canaan, the Israelites had continued to follow Moses and attend the tabernacle with the loyalty due to the Messiah, then they would have established the national Foundation of Substance.

c. The Foundation for the Tabernacle

Since the Messiah's coming must be preceded by the Foundation for the Messiah and the tabernacle was the symbolic Messiah, then receiving it had to be preceded by the Foundation for the Tabernacle. Accordingly, a Foundation of Faith and a Foundation of Substance were necessary for the Foundation for the Tabernacle.

(i) The first Foundation for the Tabernacle

Through Moses' forty-day fast on Mount Sinai (Ex 24:18), God had him establish the forty-period of separation from Satan, thus establishing the Foundation of Faith for the tabernacle. Next, the Israelites were supposed to serve and obey Moses during a forty-day period of separation from Satan and until they had built the tabernacle, since this would establish the Foundation of Substance. However, the Israelites fell into faithlessness and made and worshipped a golden calf (Ex 32:2-4). Because the Indemnity Condition for Removing the Fallen Nature was not fulfilled, the Foundation of Substance was not established. When Moses saw the faithless Israelites at the foot of the mountain, he burned with anger and threw the tablets to the ground, breaking them (Ex 32:19).

Since the two tablets symbolized Jesus and the Holy Spirit, Moses' breaking them in reaction to the people's lack of faith foreshadowed that when Jesus came he could be crucified should the Israelites fall into faithlessness.

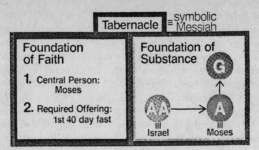

1st Foundation for the Tabernacle

The Possibility of Jesus Crucifixion Foreshadowed

Moses' time: People's lack of faith ➡ Broken Tablets

Jesus' time: People's lack of faith ➡ Crucifixion

(ii) *The second Foundation for the Tabernacle*

After bringing Aaron and the people to repentance, Moses
fasted for forty days and nights a second time, thus re-
establishing the forty-period of separation from Satan. On
this foundation, God inscribed a second set of tablets and
Moses received the Ideal of the Tabernacle (Ex 34:28). The
Israelites not only obeyed Moses during this forty-day period,
but also built the tabernacle according to the directions of
God and Moses. This was the first day of the first month of the
second year since the Israelites had left Egypt. However, the

Foundation of Substance could not be established simply by the Israelites' building the tabernacle; to establish it, the Israelites had to become one with Moses and obey him and had to regard God's Ideal of the Tabernacle as more precious than their own lives.

On the twentieth day of the second month of the second year since the Exodus, the Israelites, revering the tabernacle (Num 10:11,12), left the wilderness of Sinai for Canaan under the guidance of the pillar of cloud. However, they fell into faithlessness and complained to Moses; so God burned an outlying part of the camp (Num 11:1) in an attempt to awaken them. But they still did not awaken to God's Will and continued to complain against Moses and to long for the land of Egypt (Num 11:4-6). In looking back at this, we can see that the successful Foundation for the Tabernacle was invaded by Satan.

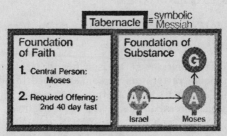

2nd Foundation for the Tabernacle

Thus, God again directed the unfaithful Israelites to establish the forty-day foundation of separation from Satan. He gave them a forty-day period of spying as the condition for accomplishing the second national course of the restoration of Canaan. God chose twelve people to spy for forty days, one person from each tribe (Num 13:1-15). However, except for Joshua and Caleb, all of them returned with faithless reports (Num 13:28-32). The Israelites, hearing these reports, angrily complained against Moses and cried out that they should choose a new leader and go back to Egypt. Then God appeared to all of the people and said to Moses, ". . . 'How long will this people despise me? And how long will they not believe in me, in spite of all the signs which I have wrought among them?' ' (Num 14:11). Then God said, " ' "But your little ones, who you said would become a prey, I will bring in, and they shall know the land which you have despised. But as for you, your dead bodies shall fall in the wilderness. And your children shall be shepherds in the wilderness forty years, and shall suffer for your faithlessness, until the last of your dead bodies lies in the wilderness. According to the number of days in which you spied out the land, forty days, for every day a year, you shall bear your iniquity, forty years, and you shall know my displeasure" ' " (Num 14:31-34).

Thus, the faithless reports led to the failure of the forty-day period of spying, and the Israelites were not able to make the Foundation of Substance at Kadesh-Barnea. As a result, the second national course (the twenty-one-month course in the wilderness) was extended to a third course, a forty-year course, again in the wilderness.

D. The Third Course of the National Restoration of Canaan

1. The Foundation of Faith

Because of the faithlessness of the Israelites, the second course of the national restoration of Canaan ended in failure. Thus, the forty-year period in the wilderness of Midian, through which Moses had established the Foundation of Faith

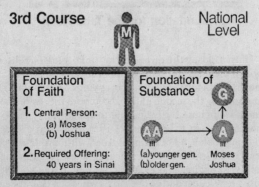

Foundation for the Messiah

for this second course, was also claimed by Satan. With the failure of the forty-day mission of spying in Canaan, Moses began another period of separation from Satan in order to restore the Foundation of Faith for the third course. Thus, he led the Israelites on the forty-year course of wandering in the wilderness, which ended when they returned to Kadesh-Barnea. By exalting the tabernacle with utmost faith and loyalty during this forty years of wandering, Moses re-established the forty-period of separation from Satan.

2. The Foundation of Substance

If, during the forty-year period of wandering in the wilderness, the Israelites had surrendered to and obediently united with Moses, who had exalted and attended the tabernacle with unchanging faith, and they had thus entered the land of Canaan, the Foundation of Substance would have been established in the third course of the national restoration of Canaan. Accordingly, this forty-year period of wandering in the wilderness was the period in which to lay the Foundation of Faith for the third course and to realize the foundation for departing on the third course to Canaan. The third course for the Foundation of Substance was begun centered on Moses, but was completed centered on Joshua. It should be studied in light of these two phases.

a. The Foundation of Substance centered on Moses

Anxious that his people might again fall into faithlessness, God, in his grace, gave the Israelites the ark, the tabernacle, and the tablets of stone with the Ten Commandments. If the Israelites had kept the Ideal of the Tabernacle with absolute faith after they had received this grace from God at Mount Sinai, or during the period of spying, then they would have been able to indemnify the invaded beginning of the second course. In other words, they would have been able to restore their status to that which they had held when they left Egypt, that of being united with Moses after he received the grace of the three miracles and ten calamities. Accordingly, if the Israelites who followed Moses back to Kadesh-Barnea after their forty-year indemnity period in the wilderness had exalted and attended the tablets, the ark, and the tabernacle, then the nation of Israel could have started victoriously for the land of Canaan.

Since the tablets were the microcosm of the ark, and the ark was a microcosm of the tabernacle, then the tablets were also a microcosm of the tabernacle. Thus, the tabernacle or ark can be represented by the tablets, or, further, by the source of the tablets, which is the rock from which they were made. Thus, the Bible records that the beginning of the third course of the national restoration of Canaan centered on the rock at Kadesh-Barnea (Num 20:8-11).

1 Cor 10:4
Rev 2:17

**Rock —
the source
of the tablets**

The Israelites were murmuring in resentment against Moses because they had no water. In order to save the Israelites, who were again falling into faithlessness despite their forty years in the wilderness (Num 20:4-10), God instructed Moses to bring forth water for the people to drink (Num 20:8). Because they were complaining and blaming him for not having water, Moses was so enraged at his people that he twice struck the rock with his rod (Num 20:11). God was displeased, and said, " 'Because you did not believe in me, to sanctify me in the eyes of the people of Israel, therefore you shall not bring this assembly into the land which I have given them' " (Num 20:12).

By striking the rock twice, when he should have struck it only once (as God had had him do earlier at Rephidim (Ex 17:6)), Moses was unable to initiate the dispensation successfully and also prevented himself from entering the blessed land of Canaan, even though it was then in sight (Num 20:24;

27:12-14; Deut 3:23-37). What was the difference between the time when Moses struck the rock at Horeb in Rephidim and this time such that God reproached Moses and prevented him from going into the land of Canaan, which Moses very much wished to enter? After working so devotedly throughout his life, leading his faithless people toward the precious goal, the blessed land, how much must Moses have wanted to enter Canaan! He begged God, " ' "Let me go over, I pray, and see the good land beyond the Jordan, that goodly hill country, and Lebanon" ' " (Deut 3:25). God answered firmly, " ' ". . . speak no more to me of this matter" ' " (Deut 3:26). Though Moses had reached the Jordan, because of the problem in bringing forth the water from the rock he died on Mount Pisgah in the land of Moab without setting foot in Canaan (Josh 34:1-6).

We should learn from Moses' mistake. At both Rephidim and Kadesh, Moses brought forth water after receiving God's instruction. His demonstration of God's power to the faithless people and his use of the rod was the same in both cases. The only difference was that at Kadesh he struck the rock twice. Let us determine why the rock should have been struck only once and why striking it twice was such a sin.

In the Bible, Christ is symbolized as a white stone (Rev 2:17) and as a rock (1 Cor 10:4). Since Christ came as the Tree of Life (Rev 22:14; also see "The Fall"), the Rock also represents the Tree of Life. The Tree of Life in the Garden of Eden (Gen 2:9) symbolized perfected Adam. Since this Tree of Life is also the Rock, the Rock must also symbolize perfected Adam.

In the Garden of Eden, Satan struck Adam and caused the fall of Adam, who was to have become the Rock. Since Adam did not become the Tree of Life (Gen 3:22-24), he failed to become the Rock that would forever give the water of life to his descendants.

Thus, the rock that did not yield water before Moses struck it with the rod represented fallen Adam. God, in accordance with the principle of restoration through indemnity, wanted to establish the condition of having restored Adam as the Rock capable of yielding water, by having Moses strike once the barren rock, which was the symbol of fallen Adam, and bring forth water from it.

Accordingly, God had Moses strike the rock once as the condition for restoring through indemnity the first, fallen Adam into the second, perfected Adam, or Jesus. Therefore, the rock that gave forth water after being struck once symbolized Jesus, who was to come and give the water of life to fallen people ("For they drank from the ... Rock which followed them, and the Rock was Christ" (1 Cor 10:4)). Moses' angry act of striking the rock a second time represented striking Jesus, who was the restored Rock that would give the water of life to all mankind. In other words, Moses' striking the rock twice (in anger at the Israelites' faithlessness) established a basis for Satan to directly confront Jesus, who was the true Rock, if the Israelites were faithless at Jesus' time. This is why Moses' act was so wrong.

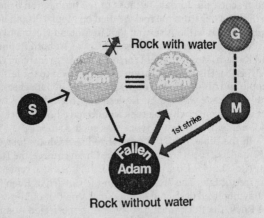

Rock with water

Rock without water

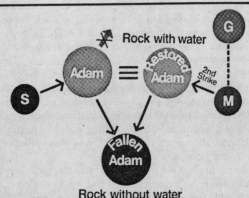

Rock with water

Rock without water

Thus, the foundation for beginning the dispensation, a foundation which was to be based on the rock, was not realized. Instead of Moses, it was Joshua who, with unchanging faith and loyalty, led the new generation into Canaan. He did so on the basis of the foundation he had set for the tabernacle through the forty-day period of spying in Canaan.

b. The Foundation of Substance centered on Joshua

Because of Moses' striking the rock twice, his mission to lead the Israelites passed to Joshua.

> And the LORD said to Moses, "Take Joshua, the son of Nun, a man in whom is the spirit, and lay your hand upon him; cause him to stand before Eleazar the priest and all the congregation, and you shall commission him in their sight. You shall invest him with some of your authority, that all the congregation of the people of Israel may obey."
> (Num 27:18-20)

Joshua was one of the two Israelites who had not fallen into faithlessness during the forty-day period of spying and had stood firmly on the Foundation of Faith which Moses had established for the tabernacle. He was one of the only two who established a foundation for the tabernacle and served it with unchanging faith and loyalty to the end. Although Moses' faith wavered, the Ideal of the Tabernacle remained unchanged on the foundation established by Joshua.

Therefore, God chose Joshua to replace Moses and carried out his dispensation in such a way that in order to begin the third course, the Israelites had to repent and center themselves on the tabernacle (Num 21:6-8). It was now God's intention to establish the Foundation of Substance for the third course using Joshua as the central person by having the Israelites enter Canaan while in absolute obedience to Joshua.

Therefore, God said to Moses,

> ". . . 'he [Joshua] shall go over [into Canaan] at the head of this people, and he shall put them in possession of the land which you shall see.' "
> (Deut 3:28)

Later God said to Joshua:

> ..."Moses my servant is dead; now therefore
> arise, go over this Jordan, you and all this people,
> into the land which I am giving to them, to the
> people of Israel."   (Josh 1:2)

> "...as I was with Moses, so I will be with you; I will
> not fail you or forsake you. Be strong and of good
> courage; for you shall cause this people to inherit
> the land which I swore to their fathers to give
> them."   (Josh 1:5,6)

At the same time, the second generation of Israelites,
which was born in the wilderness, was determined to follow
Joshua at the risk of their lives, saying,

> ... "All that you have commanded us we will do,
> and wherever you send us we will go. . . . Whoever
> rebels against your commandment and disobeys
> your words, whatever you command him, shall be
> put to death. Only be strong and of good courage.
>   (Josh 1:16-18)

They also presented their faithful reports after the spying
at Jericho, saying, ". . . 'Truly the Lord has given all the land
into our hands; and moreover all the inhabitants of the land
are fainthearted because of us' " (Josh 2:24). Thus the second
generation of Israel was completely united with Joshua, who
stood on the Foundation for the Tabernacle in accordance
with God's instruction, and they were led to the Jordan. The
river was running in flood, overflowing its banks. But the
priests bearing the ark waded in as they were instructed, and
the waters stopped, piling up on the upstream side and draining away on the downstream side, and all of Israel passed over
on dry ground to Canaan (Josh 3:16,17).

In taking Jericho according to God's instructions, forty
thousand soldiers proceeded in the vanguard, followed by
seven priets marching with seven trumpets, all preceding the
ark of the covenant, which was carried by the Levite priests.
All the people of Israel marched in the rear (Josh 6:8,9). As God
commanded them, the Israelites marched around the city for
six days, making one tour each day, and on the seventh day,
seven tours. Then at the shout of Joshua and his people the
walls crumbled (Josh 6:20). In this way, the Israelites began

their conquest of Canaan, which was the home they had longed for.

Now, let us summarize what we have learned concerning the Foundation of Substance of the third course of the national restoration of Canaan. Because of the Israelites' faithlessness toward Moses, the Foundation of Substance had not been established centered on Moses, and all of the first generation Israelites, including Moses—all except Joshua and Caleb, who had a steady faith—all died in the wilderness. The second generation Israelites, born in the wilderness, entered Canaan (Num 14:29-38) centered on Joshua, establishing the Foundation of Substance.

Although the national Foundation for the Messiah was established centered on Joshua, it was necessary for the heavenly side to prepare a strong foundation in order for the Messiah to come. This is because fallen man had already built great kingdoms centered on Satan which would oppose the heavenly Dispensation for Restoration.

But, despite their responsibility to establish a heavenly foundation, the Israelites fell into faithlessness even after they came to the land of Canaan, and thus, God's dispensation was repeatedly prolonged until the time of Jesus.

CHAPTER THIRTEEN

Jesus in the Dispensation for Restoration

Jesus had the responsibility for substantially subjugating Satan. To do so he had to follow the model course that God had shown in the symbol and image courses of Jacob and Moses (Deut 18:18, Jn 5:19). But, just as the Israelites under Moses had fallen into faithlessness in the wilderness, the Israelites at the time of John the Baptist fell into faithlessness, with the result that Jesus' world-wide course of the restoration of Canaan also had to progress through three attempts or courses.

I. THE FIRST COURSE OF THE WORLD-WIDE RESTORATION OF CANAAN

A. The Foundation of Faith

1. The Central Person for Restoring the Foundation of Faith

The central person responsible to prepare the foundation for the dispensation of salvation at the time of the Messiah was to "make straight the way of the Lord" (Jn 1:23). This central person was John the Baptist, who was the "greatest born of women" (Mt 11:11). As was already explained in the chapter on Moses' course, the repeated faithlessness of the Israelites had given Satan the chance to invade Jesus' body, which was the incarnation of the rock and the tablets of stone. Therefore, throughout their history, God educated the chosen people to be a people who would not fall into faithlessness. He sent many prophets, especially the prophet Elijah, to teach the people to unite completely, centering on the Ideal of the Temple, which was itself the image of Jesus. However, because the Israelites repeatedly failed to have faith, Elijah's sole purpose, which was to turn the Israelites from their faithless ways back to God, was not fulfilled. Therefore, God said that Elijah would come again—to accomplish his mission (Mal 4:5). The return of Elijah was fulfilled in the person of John the Baptist (Lk 1:17; Mt 11:14; 17:13). He was the person who had the responsibility to establish the base of faith for the Messiah.

2. The Required Offering for Restoring the Foundation of Faith

As was already explained in "Moses in the Dispensation for Restoration," beginning with the dispensation for Moses' age, an indemnity period based on the number forty (referred to as a forty-based idemnity period or a forty-period) became sufficient to meet the condition for separation from Satan. In other words, in place of making an offering, the central person who had to restore the Foundation of Faith could do so by remaining united with God's Word after establishing a forty-based indemnity period of separation from Satan. By meeting this condition, he can meet the condition of indemnity that restores the Foundation of Faith.

John the Baptist was standing on the foundation of a forty-period of separation from Satan, the four-hundred-year Period of Preparation for the Messiah, which had begun with the prophet Malachi. Through his life of asceticism, John was able to separate from Satan and establish the Foundation of Faith. John lived in the wilderness eating locusts and honey, concerned and thinking about God's Will; so the priests and people of Israel looked on his life of faith with the greatest respect.

B. The Foundation of Substance

1. The Central Person for the Foundation of Substance

John the Baptist was also in the Abel position for the Foundation of Substance, that is, he was the central person for establishing the Foundation of Substance. The mission of Moses had passed to Joshua, then to the prophets, including Elijah, and finally to John the Baptist. Therefore, John the Baptist was standing in the position of Moses. Moses had been the

central person for the Foundation of Faith (in the parents'
position) and the central person for the Foundation of Substance (in the position of the second-born). Likewise, John the
Baptist had the dual mission of establishing the Foundation of
Faith and standing in the Abel position as the central person
for the Foundation of Substance.

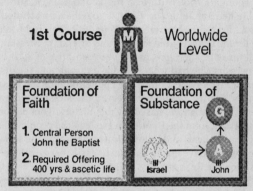

Foundation for the Messiah

2. Establishing the Foundation of Substance

The national Foundation of Substance would have been established by the Israelites' loving and obeying John the Baptist,
who was their national Abel. God had already prepared the
chosen people to believe absolutely in John as a special
prophet of God. Everyone knew that he was a great man of
God, because they had heard of the angel's prophecy about his
birth, of the miracle of his father's becoming mute in the
temple, and of the miracles and signs that had occurred at the
time of his birth. All the people of Judea watched him with
great interest from the time of his childhood. As Luke 1:65,66
says, "And fear came on all their neighbors. And all these
things were talked about through all the hill country of Judea;
and all who heard them laid them up in their hearts, saying,
'What then will this child be?' For the hand of the Lord was
with him." Moreover, John's faith was so exemplary that many
of the chief priests and people of Israel thought that he might
even be the Messiah (Jn 1:19; Lk 3:15). Thus, the people of

Judea, who were in the Cain position, believed in John the Baptist and followed him as if he were the Messiah himself, and thus established the national Foundation of Substance.

C. The Foundation for the Messiah

The Foundation of Faith and the Foundation of Substance established by John the Baptist together constituted the Foundation for the Messiah. The Foundation for the Messiah is people who are prepared to serve and attend the Messiah and fulfill his will. Therefore, as the representative of all the central persons who had worked so hard throughout the dispensational history to establish the Foundation for the Messiah, John the Baptist should have served the Messiah more than anyone. Furthermore, based on this historic Foundation for the Messiah, John the Baptist had to lead the people of Israel to believe in Jesus and follow him, establishing the situation which would have enabled Jesus to easily carry out the Dispensation for Restoration.

However, although John the Baptist had initially established this foundation and had himself testified to Jesus as the Messiah, he did not follow Jesus (Jn 1:29-34). Furthermore, John later even came to doubt that Jesus was the Messiah (Mt 11:3). Also, although he had come as Elijah, he did not understand this and denied it (Jn 1:21). Because the Israelites believed in Malachi's prophecy that Elijah would come before the Messiah, John's denying that he was Elijah confused the people so that they did not know whether to believe Jesus or John and thus had the effect of blocking the way to Jesus for the people of Israel. Therefore, the Foundation for the Messiah that John the Baptist had established did not function as a foundation for Jesus, but in fact became a barrier between Jesus and the chosen people.

The Foundation for the Messiah is the base on which God will completely fulfill the purpose of his Dispensation. Yet, this foundation did not function as the foundation to serve the Messiah, who was supposed to be the center of the Dispensation. As a result, this "foundation" was in reality a failure. Although God had carefully prepared John the Baptist for Jesus, John did not follow Jesus, and thus he lost his qualification as an historic Abel. And as a result, the first course of the world-wide restoration of Canaan ended in failure.

II. THE SECOND COURSE OF THE WORLD-WIDE RESTORATION OF CANAAN

A. The Foundation of Faith

1. The Central Person for Restoring the Foundation of Faith—Jesus Succeeds to the Mission of John the Baptist

Because of John the Baptist's faithlessness toward Jesus, the Foundation of Faith in the first course of the world-wide restoration of Canaan was invaded by Satan. The Messiah came, but the Foundation for the Messiah crumbled, leaving no place for Jesus to stand as the Messiah. Actually, the Messiah can only appear where there is a foundation free from Satan's invasion. Therefore, Jesus was compelled to meet the indemnity conditions that would restore the Foundation for the Messiah by himself, and as he did so, he acted not in the capacity of the Messiah, but in that of John the Baptist.

Since Jesus was the Son of God and was to be the Lord of Glory, he should not have had to walk the path of tribulation (1 Cor 2:8). However, John the Baptist, who was born for the mission of straightening the Lord's way (Jn 1:23; Lk 1:76), failed to accomplish his mission. Therefore, Jesus had to succeed to John the Baptist's mission and himself prepare the foundation for his own appearance as the Messiah. Thus, in the second course of the world-wide restoration of Canaan, Jesus was the central person who had to pay the indemnity to restore the Foundation of Faith.

2. Required Offering for Restoring the Foundation of Faith

The central person responsible to restore the Foundation of Faith could establish it by becoming one with God's Word after first establishing a forty-based period for separation from Satan. To do this, Jesus fasted for forty days and overcame the three temptations from Satan. Jesus met these conditions not as the Messiah, but as a person succeeding to the mission of John the Baptist. In other words, he met these conditions to restore the Foundation of Faith from the position of a central person involved in establishing the Foundation for the Messiah, rather than as the Messiah himself.

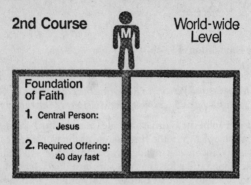

Foundation for the Messiah

Let us look at the reasons for Jesus' forty-day period of fasting and praying and the three temptations. In the course of the national restoration of Canaan centered on Moses, the rock symbolizing Jesus (1 Cor 10:4) had suffered Satan's invasion because of Moses' anger at the faithlessness of the Israelites. This invasion remained as a remote basis for Satan's direct attack on Jesus, the true rock, should the chosen people become faithless again at Jesus' time.

John the Baptist was the central person who could stop this from happening—by fighting against Satan to establish the Foundation of Faith. However, John failed to believe in Jesus. With the faithlessness of John the Baptist as the immediate cause, Jesus could not continue free from Satan's direct attack and he became Satan's constant target. Therefore, Jesus himself had to meet the indemnity condition of the forty-based period for separation from Satan by fasting for forty days and overcoming Satan's attack, which was manifested in the three temptations.

3. Satan's Three Temptations

In Matthew 4:1-10 we read that Satan tested Jesus through three temptations. Satan's original purpose in attacking Jesus with these temptations was not to test any external conditions

or Jesus' power to perform miracles, but was specifically
intended to prevent Jesus from accomplishing his purpose as
the Messiah. Because the Messiah comes to restore the world
intended at the time of creation, which was not established
because of Satan, from Satan's point of view, the Messiah's
fulfilling his purpose would mean Satan's eternal destruction.
Since the Kingdom of Heaven is based on *The Principle*, and
since Adam had failed by not following *The Principle*, Satan's
temptations centered on *The Principle*, and Jesus' answers had
to be based on *The Principle*. More specifically, the world
which the Messiah must create is the world intended at the
time of creation, which is the world based on the fulfillment of
God's Three Blessings. Thus, Jesus had to realize God's Three
Blessings, and Satan's attempt to prevent Jesus from fulfilling
his purpose was through three temptations that were based
on the Three Blessings.

a. The first temptation

In the first temptation, Satan appeared before Jesus and said,
". . .'If you are the Son of God, command these stones to
become loaves of bread' " (Mt 4:3). The stones in Satan's possession represented the broken tablets of stone and the rock
that had been struck twice by Moses. Because of the faithlessness of the chosen people, Moses had broken the tablets of
stones and had struck the rock twice, providing the basis for
Satan to claim the rock. The stones with which Satan tempted
Jesus symbolized Jesus himself as the true rock and the true
tablet of stone (1 Cor 10:4; Rev 2:17).

When the chosen people became faithless, as they had
become in the wilderness, Satan was in a position to attack
Jesus, who was the incarnate Word that had been symbolized
by the tablets of stone. Jesus had to overcome these circumstances. Satan knew well that Jesus had come into the wilderness to restore the rock, so Satan tempted Jesus to change the
rock to bread, because Jesus was as hungry as the faithless
Israelites had been at the time of Moses. If Jesus had become
faithless and had abandoned his purpose of restoring the
stone, choosing instead to command the stone to become
bread in order to fill his hungry stomach, then Satan would
have succeeded in preventing the Messiah from accomplishing his purpose. By keeping Jesus under his sovereignty,

Satan would have had possession of the stone forever.

Jesus' answer to this temptation was, " '. . ."Man shall not live by bread alone, but by every word that proceeds from the mouth of God" ' " (Mt 4:4). This means that even though man's physical body can live by eating bread, his life would not be complete. Man can become whole only if, in addition, he lives by the bread of life, that is, through Christ, who is God's Word made flesh (Jn 6:35,51). Jesus' answer to Satan's first temptation means that even if he were then at the point of starvation, bread for the physical body is not the real issue. Jesus had to triumph over Satan's temptation and become the living bread of God's Word, the bread capable of giving life to all mankind.

Through his triumph over the first temptation, Jesus met the condition for again establishing himself as the true incarnation of the stones which had been lost to Satan in the wilderness because of the faithlessness of the chosen people. In other words, by overcoming this temptation (from the position of John the Baptist), Jesus symbolically restored the position of the Messiah, the model of the perfect person. Through doing this, Jesus established the foundation for restoring God's First Blessing to man, the first step toward accomplishing God's Purpose for the Creation.

b. The second temptation

In the second temptation, Satan set Jesus on the pinnacle of the temple and said, ". . .'If you are the Son of God, throw yourself down . . .' " (Mt 4:6). Jesus referred to himself as a temple (Jn 2:19-21) and believers are also called temples of God (1 Cor 3:16). 1 Corinthians 12:27 tells us that believers are members of the body of Christ. Therefore, we can understand that Jesus is the main temple and the believers are the branch temples. Satan's setting Jesus on the pinnacle of the temple means that, as a result of Jesus' triumph over the first temptation, Satan had to recognize Jesus' authority as the master of the temple. Satan's urging Jesus to throw himself down from the top of the temple was not to test Jesus' ability to perform miracles, but was to tempt him to give up his position as master of the temple, to throw himself down and be as a fallen man, thus putting an end to his restoring people as branch temples. Just as Satan dominated the world as its false master after causing Adam's fall (2 Cor 4:4; Jn 12:31), Satan would have become the master of the temple in place of Jesus, if Jesus (the Second Adam) had succumbed to this temptation.

At this point, Jesus said, " '. . .''You shall not tempt the Lord your God" ' " (Mt 4:7). Satan is a fallen angel; a true human being is to have dominion over the angels. Therefore, a fallen angel was naturally supposed to be under Jesus' dominion. Although Satan may temporarily control the world as its false master, his attempt to stand in the position of the lord of the temple was a non-Principle act. Satan, a fallen angel, should not have tried to tempt God. Yet, he did so by tempting Jesus, for when Jesus had triumphed over the first temptation, he had restored his position as a true person and individual, and thus was the true temple and body of God.

Jesus' answer was a scolding to Satan for his non-Principle act, and it meant that Satan should leave him and stop tempting God's representative and true son. Jesus was the main temple and the True Father of mankind. By overcoming the second temptation, he established the condition that would enable him to restore believers as branch temples, that is, as his children. Through overcoming this temptation, Jesus established the foundation for restoring God's Second Blessing to man, the second step toward fulfilling God's Purpose for the Creation.

c. The third temptation

In the third temptation, Satan led Jesus to a very high mountain and showed him all the kingdoms of the world and their glory. Then he said, ". . . 'All these I will give you, if you will fall down and worship me' " (Mt.4:9). Of course, in reality, there is no mountain where all the kingdoms of the world can be seen. Then, what does Satan's leading Jesus to this very high mountain mean?

Because of his fall, Adam had lost his authority as lord of the Creation and had come to be dominated by Satan; so Satan had naturally become the ruler of the Creation in place of Adam (Rom 8:20). God sent Jesus to be the perfected Adam and, thus, the lord of the Creation (God put all things in subjection under Christ (1 Cor 15:27)). Satan knew this, and since Jesus had been victorious in the first and second temptations, Satan had to place Jesus in the position of lord of the Creation. The was the significance of Jesus' being led to the

mountain where all the kingdoms of the world and their glory
can be seen. Then, Satan tempted Jesus by offering to let
Jesus be lord of the Creation if Jesus would yield to him
(Satan). Satan wanted the second Adam to yield to him as the
first Adam had done in the Garden of Eden.

Jesus replied, " '. . ."You shall worship the Lord your God
and him only shall you serve" ' " (Mt 4:10). Angels were created to be ministering spirits (Heb 1:14), to worship and serve
God. Jesus' answer recalls this principle that Satan, a fallen
angel, should worship and serve God. Naturally, in accordance with this principle, Satan should also worship and serve
Jesus, for Jesus was the temple of God.

By overcoming the first two temptations, Jesus had established the foundation that would enable him to restore to man
God's First and Second Blessings. On this foundation he also
had to restore to man God's Third Blessing, man's dominion
over the Creation. Although Jesus might have gained all of the
kingdoms of the world and their glory if he had yielded to
Satan, his purpose as the Messiah would not have been fulfilled. Jesus answered that although Satan was offering him

1st Temptation	Stones versus bread	1st Blessing	Individual Perfection
2nd Temptation	Temple	2nd Blessing	Multiplication of Children
3rd Temptation	Kingdoms of the World	3rd Blessing	Dominion over Creation

Matthew 4:1-11

sovereignty over the Creation, he would not fall down and
worship Satan, for he (Jesus) was the temple of God. Jesus
responses were based on *The Principle*, and thus he was victo-

rious. By overcoming the third temptation, Jesus was able to meet the conditions for restoring man's dominion over the Creation. In other words, he established the foundation for restoring to man God's Third Blessing. Thus, through enduring the forty-day fast and overcoming Satan's three temptations, Jesus, in place of John the Baptist, established the Foundation of Faith.

B. The Foundation of Substance

Jesus' forty days of fasting and praying for the Foundation of Faith and his triumph over Satan's temptations established Jesus as the central person and Abel for the national Foundation of Substance. Consequently, if the people of Israel, who were in the Cain position, had believed, served, and obeyed Jesus, who was in the Abel position substituting for John the Baptist, the national Foundation of Substance would have been established. This Foundation of Substance and the Foundation of Faith together would have constituted the Foundation for the Messiah, and that would have enabled Jesus to shift from the position of John the Baptist to the Messiah's position.

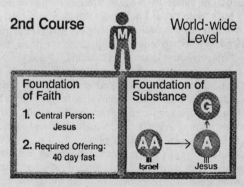

2nd Course   World-wide Level

Foundation of Faith

1. Central Person: Jesus

2. Required Offering: 40 day fast

Foundation of Substance

Israel → Jesus

Foundation for the Messiah

If Jesus had been able to secure this victorious foundation on earth, then he would have been able to give total rebirth to mankind and he would have been able to completely fulfill God's Purpose for the Creation. Therefore, Jesus revealed secrets of the Kingdom of Heaven in his speaking and testified to himself through the performance of miracles—all to make his people believe in him and obey him (Jn 10:38). Because it concerned the Foundation of Substance for the national Foundation for the Messiah, it was very important for the leaders of Judaism and the people to serve Jesus and follow his will, since he was in the Abel position. However, the leaders of the people, such as the priests, the Levites, and the scribes, were in the front ranks of those who became faithless toward Jesus. The general populace also fell into faithlessness and even began to slander Jesus. And even from the early stages of Jesus' ministry, the Pharisees declared that he was a sinner (Jn 9:16,24), though he was actually without fault. On several occasions the people took up stones to throw at Jesus, even though he was teaching them the truth (Jn 8:59; 10:31). Jesus even had to take refuge for some time, because of the people's conspiracies to kill him (Jn 7:1; 8:40).

Meanwhile, Satan, who had been defeated in the temptations, had departed from Jesus "until an opportune time" (Lk 4:13). Satan's departure from Jesus until an opportune time implies that Satan did not leave Jesus completely and would be able to come before Jesus again. Since Jesus had overcome Satan's tests, Satan could no longer attack him directly; so Satan had to try to invade through the people, and he centered on the leaders who had fallen into faithlessness, finally focusing his efforts on Judas Iscariot. 1 Corinthians 2:8 says, "None of the rulers of this age understood this; for if they had, they would not have crucified the Lord of glory." The people's attitude toward Jesus went beyond simple ignorance about him. They developed a strong feeling of disbelief and distrust toward him, to the point where they feared him and wanted to be rid of him, and they crucified him.

Because of this faithlessness of the people, the Foundation of Substance was not established. Accordingly, the Foundation for the Messiah was not established in the second course of the world-wide restoration of Canaan. Naturally, the second course of the world-wide restoration of Canaan also failed.

III. THE THIRD COURSE OF THE WORLD-WIDE RESTORATION OF CANAAN

A. The Spiritual Course of the World-wide Restoration of Canaan, Centered on Jesus

Because of the faithlessness of John the Baptist, the first course of the world-wide restoration of Canaan had ended in failure. Next, Jesus, himself, had tried to establish the Foundation for the Messiah. However, because the people did not follow him, and especially because his disciples became faithless, the second course of the world-wide restoration of Canaan also failed. Therefore, Jesus had to go the way of the cross. In John 3:14, Jesus says, " 'And as Moses lifted up the serpent in the wilderness, so must the Son of man be lifted up. . . .' " When the people with Moses were bitten by fiery serpents and began to die, God directed Moses to raise up a bronze serpent in order to provide a way for the people's salvation. In the same way, when the people at Jesus' time became faithless, God then had to ask Jesus to go the way of the cross.

What is the meaning of the cross? As was already explained in "The Purpose of the Messiah," Jesus' messianic purpose was to complete the dispensation for salvation, that is, to fulfill the Purpose of the Creation.

Man was created with a physical self and a spirit self, and man fell both physically and spiritually. Thus the salvation should also be for both the physical and the spiritual aspects of man. When we say that we absolutely believe in Jesus and we obey Jesus this means that we are fulfilling the ideal of becoming one body with him. Jesus spoke of this when he compared himself to a vine and the believers to branches (Jn 15:5), and when he said, " 'In that day you will know that I am in my Father, and you in me, and I in you' " (Jn 14:20). Unfortunately, the people did not believe in Jesus and did not become one with him. As a result, God had to allow Satan to take the physical body of Jesus to indemnify mankind's sin of faithlessness. Thus, Jesus died on the cross.

Since Jesus is the root of life for all mankind, Satan's invasion of Jesus' physical body means that even saints who

believe in Jesus and become one with him cannot avoid satanic invasion of their physical bodies (Rom 7:22,23). No matter
how faithful believers may be, their bodies are still within the
realm of Satan's invasion. Thus, they have to pray constantly
(1 Thess 5:17), and their children still have Original Sin.

Because of the crucifixion, mankind lost the physical
body of the savior and thus lost its physical object of faith and
could not receive physical salvation. Therefore, the third
course of the world-wide restoration of Canaan could not be
started as a substantial course on both the physical and the
spiritual planes. Instead, this course of the world-wide restoration of Canaan was a spiritual one and was centered on the
resurrected Jesus.

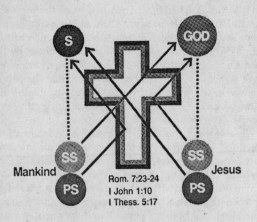

1. The Spiritual Foundation of Faith

The central person responsible for establishing the spiritual
Foundation of Faith was the resurrected Jesus. In fulfilling
that responsibility, he stood in John the Baptist's position.

Although God let Satan take Jesus' body so that man's
faithlessness could be redeemed, the foundation for spiritual
salvation was established when God, using Jesus' absolute
obedience as a foundation, resurrected Jesus' spirit self and
placed him in a position where Satan could not invade.

Jesus said, ". . . 'Destroy this temple, and in three days I
will raise it up' " (Jn 2:19). He was obviously speaking of his

own resurrection in three days. The resurrected Jesus became the central person for establishing the spiritual Foundation of Faith. During the forty days following his resurrection, Jesus established the spiritual foundation of separation from Satan. This also established the spiritual Foundation of Faith for the spiritual third course of the world-wide restoration of Canaan.

Of course the resurrected Jesus was not the same as he was when he had lived together with his disciples before his crucifixion. He was already a spirit person who transcended time and space and could not be seen by means of normal physical sight (Lk 24:16). For example: he once suddenly appeared in a closed room where his disciples were gathered (Jn 20:19); on another occasion he appeared at the sea coast of Tiberia and was not immediately recognized by his disciples (Jn 21:1-4); on still another occasion, he suddenly appeared before two disciples on their way to Emmaus and accompanied them for a considerable distance without their recognizing him (Lk 24:15,16). As a matter of fact, Mary, who was the first to encounter the resurrected Jesus, was also unable to recognize him (Jn 20:14). During the forty-day period on earth following his resurrection, Jesus appeared to his disciples transcending time and space, and thus established the spiritual Foundation of Faith.

2. The Spiritual Foundation of Substance

By establishing the Foundation of Faith, on the foundation of the central person for establishing the spiritual Foundation of Substance, that is to say, he also secured the spiritual Foundation of Power, that is to say, he also secured the spiritual Abel position.

God could no longer deal directly with the Jewish people, for they had betrayed Jesus; so he needed a new Israel, that is a *Second Israel* that would follow the resurrected Jesus with absolute faith. The new Israel, in the Cain position, had to absolutely believe in and obey Jesus, the spiritual Abel, and thus establish the spiritual Foundation of Substance. Jesus made a great effort to establish the spiritual Foundation of Substance, which would establish the resurrected new chosen people who would unite with him in faith.

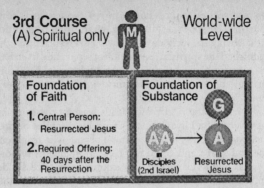

3rd Course
(A) Spiritual only

World-wide
Level

Foundation
of Faith

1. Central Person:
Resurrected Jesus

2. Required Offering:
40 days after the
Resurrection

Foundation of
Substance

Disciples
(2nd Israel)

Resurrected
Jesus

Foundation for the Messiah

Acts 1:3 speaks of Jesus' disciples, saying, "To them he presented himself alive after his passion by many proofs, appearing to them during forty days, and speaking of the kingdom of God." Jesus gathered his disciples, who had scattered after they had lost their faith, and appearing repeatedly before them, taught them to have absolute faith in him as the Messiah.

> And beginning with Moses and all the prophets, he interpreted to them in all the scriptures the things concerning himself.   (Lk 24:27)

> And Jesus came and said to them, "All authority in heaven and on earth has been given to me. Go therefore and make disciples of all nations, baptizing them in the name of the Father, and of the Son, and of the Holy Spirit, teaching them to observe all that I have commanded you; and lo, I am with you always, to the close of the age."   (Mt 28:18-20)

> And while staying with them he charged them not to depart from Jerusalem but to wait for the promise of the Father, which, he said, "You heard from me, for John baptized with water, but before many days you shall be baptized with the Holy Spirit."(Acts 1:4,5)

Jesus performed many miracles (e.g., Jn 20:19; 21:6); he

instilled faith in the faithless Thomas (Jn 20:26-29); he made
Peter pledge absolute loyalty to him (Jn 21:15-18); and he
taught his disciples to be the roots of the new Israel. The
disciples gave their lives to believe, serve, and follow the
resurrected Jesus, unlike the old way in which they had only
weakly believed in him. Thus, they were able to establish the
spiritual Foundation of Substance.

3. The Spiritual Foundation for the Messiah

The Foundation for the Messiah is actually the foundation
upon which the Messiah can save both physically and spiritually. But the resurrected Jesus, who was carrying out the
mission of a spiritual John the Baptist, could restore only the
spiritual Foundation for the Messiah (the Foundation for the
Messiah in the spirit world), first setting up the spiritual
Foundation of Faith (the Foundation of Faith in the spirit
world) and then the spiritual Foundation of Substance (the
Foundation of Substance in the spirit world). Jesus' original
mission was not to carry out the mission of John the Baptist.
Thus, once he established the spiritual Foundation for the
Messiah, he stood as the spiritual Messiah.

No conditions for Satan's accusations exist in the realm of
resurrection which Jesus established (in accordance with the
principle of restoration through indemnity) by letting Satan
take his life. Thus, the Foundation of Faith that the resurrected
Jesus established on the spiritual plane is not vulnerable to
Satan's invasion. The spiritual Foundation of Substance,
established by believing in Jesus in one's own life, is therefore
impregnable to Satan's spiritual attack, and the spiritual
Foundation for the Messiah is thus a sphere which Satan
cannot violate.

The most fundamental role of the Messiah is the role of
the True Father. The resurrected Jesus became the spiritual
True Father by restoring the Holy Spirit. The arrival of the
Holy Spirit recorded in the second chapter of Acts is the
arrival of the spiritual True Mother. The resurrected Jesus, as
the spiritual True Father, and the Holy Spirit, as the spiritual
True Mother, work together to give spiritual rebirth to believers. Therefore, anyone who believes in Jesus and the Holy
Spirit, who are the spiritual True Parents, and spiritually
grafts onto them stands on the spiritual Foundation for the

Messiah and will have spiritual salvation (Jn 3:16).

Spiritual salvation means that believers are restored only as God's spiritual children, through spiritual parents; that is to say, only a spiritual Canaan is restored. Thus, Christians can only receive the benefit of the establishment of the spiritual Canaan, and can still have their physical bodies invaded by Satan, just as Jesus, man's mediator, had his body invaded by Satan. As a result, Original Sin still remains within man (Rom 7:25).

The Messiah must come again in order to complete salvation and restore the substantial Canaan where man can be restored both spiritually and physically as the true children of God. The Israelites, centered on Moses, spiritually entered Canaan; the second generation Israelites, centered on Joshua, substantially entered the national Canaan. (This is explained in "Moses in the Dispensation for Restoration.") Likewise, Christians, centered on Jesus, established the spiritual Canaan world-wide; and at the Second Coming, the Messiah, like Joshua, will lead Christians to establish the substantial world-wide Canaan.

B. The Substantial Course of the World-wide Restoration of Canaan Centered on the Lord of the Second Coming

If, at the Second Coming, those with the mission of John the Baptist fail to fulfill their missions, the Lord of the Second Coming himself will have to assume the role of John the Baptist and establish the Foundation of Faith for the substantial phase of the third world-wide course to Canaan. However difficult a way the Lord of the Second Coming may walk, devout people will gather around him, absolutely believing in and serving him, establishing the Foundation of Substance in the substantial phase of the third world-wide course to Canaan.

The Lord of the Second Coming must come in order to restore all mankind into God's direct lineage, as God's children. Consequently, he must be born on earth, in the flesh, just as Jesus was. He must restore, through indemnity, the tearful course that Jesus had to tread, and, on the basis of the substantial Foundation for the Messiah, he must engraft all mankind both spiritually and physically. Mankind will then finally be in God's direct lineage, having the Original Sin removed through the Lord of the Second Coming.

The spiritual phase of the third world-wide course to Canaan, which began with the spiritual Foundation for the Messiah, has expanded its territory to a global level over the last two thousand years. Just as Joshua succeeded Moses' mission and completed the national course to Canaan, so also

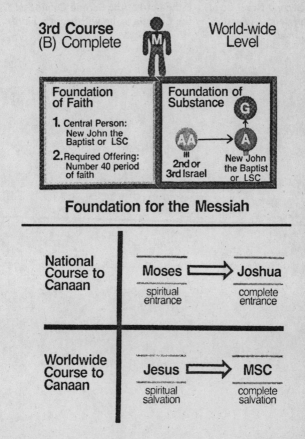

3rd Course (B) Complete — World-wide Level

Foundation of Faith

1. Central Person: New John the Baptist or LSC
2. Required Offering: Number 40 period of faith

Foundation of Substance

2nd or 3rd Israel → New John the Baptist or LSC

Foundation for the Messiah

National Course to Canaan	Moses ⟹ Joshua
	spiritual entrance / complete entrance
Worldwide Course to Canaan	Jesus ⟹ MSC
	spiritual salvation / complete salvation

the Lord of the Second Coming will complete the establishment of the Kingdom of Heaven by completing, on a physical level, the third world-wide course to Canaan which began centered on Jesus.

Just as Jesus walked the bitter path of the spiritual restoration as a result of the disbelief of the chosen people of Israel, so also the Lord of the Second Coming will experience similar tribulations if and when the Second Israel, the Christians, fall into disbelief. And just as Jesus had to abandon the First Israel and begin a new course, centered on the Christians as the Second Israel, so also, if the Lord of the Second Coming experiences rejection by the Christians, he will begin a *Third Israel*.

CHAPTER FOURTEEN

Dispensational Time-Identity

I. INDEMNITY CONDITIONS AND DISPENSATIONAL TIME-IDENTITY

The purpose of the Dispensation for Restoration, which is to fulfill the Purpose of the Creation, will be fulfilled through the Messiah. Fallen man's responsibility is therefore to prepare the foundation necessary for the coming of the Messiah, that is, the Foundation for the Messiah. This responsibility consists of meeting the indemnity conditions necessary to restore the Foundation of Faith and the Foundation of Substance.

What happens if the central person of the Dispensation fails to fulfill his responsibility to meet the indemnity conditions? The goal of the Dispensation for Restoration was conceived in the mind of God, who is absolute, and therefore the goal of the Dispensation is also absolute and must be fulfilled (Is 48:11). Therefore, should a central person fail, God chooses another person to carry out His Will, even though this prolongs the dispensational history. At the time God chooses the new central person, the circumstances, events, and people surrounding the new central person will be similar to those under which God chose his predecessor. Even if there is a two thousand or four thousand year hiatus in the history of restoration, similar circumstances, events, and persons will appear. This reappearance of past circumstances, events, and people is called Dispensational Time-Identity. This phenomenon of Dispensational Time-Identity appears in accordance with God's Dispensation for Restoration through indemnity.

What factors create time-identity in dispensational history? The answer to this lies in the efforts by God and man to restore the Foundation for the Messiah through the indemnity process. In other words, the contents of a time-identity period consist of a central person, the time period, the required offering, the actions by which the central person establishes the Foundation of Faith, and the course though which the

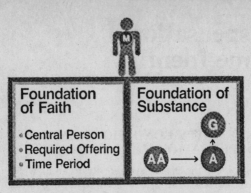

Foundation for the Messiah

central person meets the Indemnity Condition to Remove the Fallen Nature and establishes the Foundation of Substance.

The levels and contents of the Foundation for the Messiah have expanded from those of the family level to those of the national and world-wide levels. Although the Dispensation for Restoration may be prolonged due to man's failure in carrying out his responsibility, God restores all that is lost by expanding his level of activity. For example, when the chosen people who were responsible for the national Foundation for the Messiah failed, God did not choose another nation for another national dispensation. Instead, God began the world-wide dispensation. If the world-wide dispensation is successfully completed, through it the national dispensation will be simultaneously recovered.

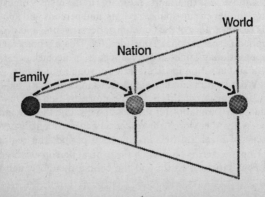

II. DIVISION OF THE DISPENSATIONAL AGES, BASED ON TIME-IDENTITY

A. Division of the Ages

Abraham's family established the family Foundation for the Messiah. For the first time in human history a victorious foundation on which God could work was established on earth. Thus, with Abraham's family, God could begin the Dispensation for Restoration. Then, what is the meaning of the history prior to the time of Abraham?

Since Abraham failed in his first sacrificial offering, history up to Abraham's later foundation of victory was taken by Satan. Therefore, that period of history became only the foundation for the Dispensation for Restoration, with Abraham's descendants becoming the people chosen to carry out God's Will. Viewed in retrospect, the period from Adam to Abraham is the period in which God established the foundation for the Dispensation for Restoration, and thus it can be called the Dispensational Age of the Foundation for Restoration through Indemnity. Seen from the viewpoint of Dispensational Time-Identity it was the Age of Symbolic Time-Identity. In that age, God intended to establish the family Foundation for the Messiah.

Family Level Foundation for the Messiah

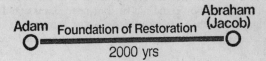

Adam   Foundation of Restoration   Abraham (Jacob)

2000 yrs

Symbol Time-Indentity

The time from Abraham's family to Jesus was the age of God's dispensation to restore through indemnity the lost Dispensational Age of the Foundation for Restoration. This period is called the Dispensational Age of Restoration. From the viewpoint of Dispensational Time-Identity, it was the Age of Image Time-Identity. In this age, God's dispensation was to establish the national Foundation for the Messiah.

National Level Foundation for the Messiah

Abraham (Jacob) — Restoration — 2000 yrs — Jesus

Image Time-Identity

Jesus came to complete the Dispensation for Restoration. If the secular and religious Israelite leaders of Jesus' day had followed him, God's Dispensation for Restoration would have been completely accomplished at that time. Sinful history would have ended, and a new history, centered on God, would have begun, fulfilling the Ideal for the Creation. The new heaven and new earth that the Bible speaks of would have been established at that time. However, because of the chosen people's faithlessness toward Jesus, he was crucified and God's Dispensation could not be concluded. Jesus could do nothing other than promise that he would come again, and Christians have had to wait in hope for the time of the Second Coming.

Consequently, the time from Jesus' crucifixion to the Second Coming has been the age of God's dispensation to restore the uncompleted Dispensational Age of Restoration by means of its prolongation. Thus, this age is called the Dispensational Age of the Prolongation of Restoration. From the viewpoint of Dispensational Time-Identity, it is the Age of Substantial Time-Identity. In this age, God intended to establish the world-wide Foundation for the Messiah.

World Level Foundation for the Messiah

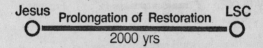

Jesus   Prolongation of Restoration   LSC

2000 yrs

Substance Time-Identity

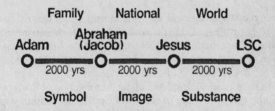

Family	National	World
	Abraham	
Adam	(Jacob)	Jesus	LSC

Adam   2000 yrs   Abraham (Jacob)   2000 yrs   Jesus   2000 yrs   LSC

Symbol   Image   Substance

B. The Parallels among the Dispensational Ages

As explained at the beginning of this chapter, the three dispensational ages are all directed toward the purpose of establishing the Foundation for the Messiah. As a result, similar conditions, events, and persons recur in the course of human history, and the three dispensational ages show direct parallels or time-identity among each other.

The parallels between the Ages of Image Time-Identity (Abraham to Jesus) and Substantial Time-Identity (Jesus to the Second Coming) will be dealt with here, while their parallels with the Age of Symbol Tide-Identity (Adam to Abraham) will be explained in the more advanced *Outline of The Principle, Level V.*

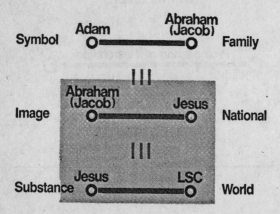

In the Dispensational Age of Restoration, the central nation responsible for God's dispensation was the chosen nation of Israel. The central history, of course, was the history of the nation of Israel, centered on Judaism. The detailed record of that history is found in the Old Testament.

In the Dispensational Age of the Prolongation of Restoration, the central people in charge of God's dispensation was not the nation of Israel, but rather those who believed in and followed Jesus, the Christians. Since the Christians inherited the mission of Israel, they became the Second Israel. As a result, the history of Christianity provides the central historical data for the Dispensational Age of the Prolongation of Restoration.

The Dispensational Age of Restoration is divided into six sub-periods, titled: Slavery in Egypt; Judges; United Kingdom; Divided Kingdoms of North and South; Jewish Captivity and Return; and Preparation for the Messiah.

The Dispensational Age of the Prolongation of Restoration is also divided in a similar manner, producing six sub-periods, titled: Persecution in the Roman Empire; Christian Churches under the Patriarchal System; Christian Kingdom;

Divided Kingdoms of East and West; Papal Captivity and Return; and Preparation for the Second Coming of the Messiah.

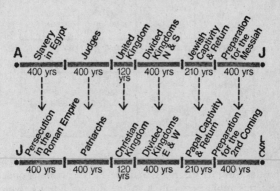

The difference of almost two thousand years is not the only difference between the histories of the Dispensational Age of Restoration and the Dispensational Age of the Prolongation of Restoration—differences in national, environmental, and cultural background are also involved. Nevertheless, each of the six sub-periods in the Age of Restoration is a period of time-identity with its corresponding sub-period in the Age of the Prolongation of Restoration. Each time-identity is described below. The remarkable similarities show that human history has been moving in accordance with the living God's consistent Dispensation for Restoration.

1. The Period of Slavery in Egypt and the Period of Persecution in the Roman Empire

The Period of Slavery in Egypt began as a result of Abraham's failure in the offering. It is the period in which Jacob's twelve sons and seventy kinsmen entered Egypt, which represented the satanic world, and in which their descendants were miserably persecuted by the Egyptians. The Period of Persecution in the Roman Empire began as a result of the Israelites' failure

I. Period of Slavery in Egypt
(400 years)

Jacob 12 sons 70 family Members	Sabbath circumcision sacrifices	after 400 years, entered Canaan	Mosaic Law

I. Period of Persecution in the Roman Empire (400 years) 0-392 A.D.

Jesus 12 Apostles 70 disciples	Sabbath communion & baptism Martyrs	392 A.D. Christianity becomes state religion	New Testament

to believe in Jesus. This is the period in which Jesus' twelve apostles, seventy disciples, and the early Christians underwent miserable persecution in the Roman Empire, which represented the satanic world.

During the four-hundred-year period of oppression in Egypt, the chosen people of Israel maintained their position as God's faithful amidst their suffering by performing the rite of circumcision, offering sacrifices, and keeping the Sabbath. Similarly, for approximately four hundred years during the period of persecution in the Roman Empire, the Christians maintained their position as God's faithful by keeping the Sabbath, living a life of sacrifice, and performing the sacraments of holy communion and baptism.

After the four-hundred-year Period of Slavery in Egypt, God chose Moses to subjugate Pharaoh and lead the Israelites to a new environment, the land of Canaan. Likewise, Christianity, which had been persecuted, gained legal recognition 313 A.D. and was declared the state religion of the Roman Empire in 392 A.D. In this way, Christians came to be restored out of the satanic world into a spiritual Canaan.

After the Period of Slavery in Egypt, Moses received the Ten Commandments on Mount Sinai, setting up the core of the Old Testament. By revering the tablets of stone, the tabernacle, and the ark of the covenant, the chosen people of the First Israel prepared themselves to receive the Messiah. Likewise, toward the end of the Period of Persecution in the Roman Empire, the chosen people of the Second Israel collected

Jesus' words and the writings of the apostles and established the New Testament and churches centered on the Word, thus laying a foundation necessary for the Second Coming.

2. The Period of the Judges and the Period of the Christian Churches under the Patriarchal System

During the four-hundred-year period after Joshua and Caleb led the Israelites into Canaan, the nation of Israel was led by judges. These judges each carried out the multiple functions of prophet, chief priest, and king. During the Period of the Christian Churches under the Patiarchal System, the Christians were led by the patriarchs, whose duties, from the standpoint of the Dispensation for Restoration, corresponded to those of the judges.

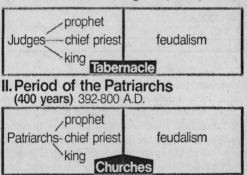

II. Period of the Judges (400 years)

Judges	prophet chief priest king	feudalism

Tabernacle

II. Period of the Patriarchs
(400 years) 392-800 A.D.

Patriarchs	prophet chief priest king	feudalism

Churches

During the Period of the Judges, a feudal system arose in Israel, centered on the judges and based on the new land allotted to each tribe. Likewise, after Christianity's liberation from persecution in the Roman Empire, the Gospel was spread to the Germanic tribes that had moved to western Europe because of the fourth century invasion by the Huns from Mongolia. There, in the new land of western Europe, a feudal system arose.

3. The Period of the United Kingdom and the Period of the Christian Kingdom

With the beginning of the United Kingdom of Israel, the period during which the judges led the First Israel ended, and the mission of the judges was divided among the prophets, the chief priest, and the king. Likewise, with the beginning of the Period of the Christian kingdom, the period of patriarchial

III. United Kingdom (120 years)

prophets chief priests king	Samuel Saul (King)

III. Christian Kingdom (120 years)
800-919 A.D.

monks pope king	Pope Leo III Charlemagne (Emperor)

leadership over the Second Israel ended, and the mission of the patriarchs was divided among the monks, the pope, and the king. As the United Kingdom of Israel had begun when the prophet Samuel anointed Saul as the first king, in accordance with God's command, what in God's dispensation was to have become a united Christian empire began when Pope Leo III crowned Charlemagne emperor of the Franks and Romans.

4. The Period of the Divided Kingdoms of North and South and the Period of the Divided Kingdoms of East and West

The United Kingdom of Israel, which had begun with King Saul, continued under King David and King Solomon; then it was divided into the northern kingdom of Israel, consisting of ten tribes in the Cain position, and the southern kingdom of Judah, consisting of two tribes, in the Abel position.

IV. Divided Kingdoms: N & S
(400 years)

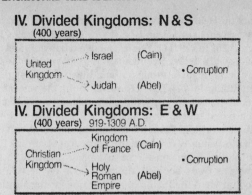

United Kingdom ⤑ Israel (Cain)
⤑ Judah (Abel)
▪ Corruption

IV. Divided Kingdoms: E & W
(400 years) 919-1309 A.D.

Christian Kingdom ⤑ Kingdom of France (Cain)
⤑ Holy Roman Empire (Abel)
▪ Corruption

The Christian Kingdom, which had begun with Charlemagne, was also divided, but into three parts—the East Frank
kingdom (the kingdom of Louis the German), the West Frank
kingdom (the kingdom of Charles the Bald), and the middle
kingdom (the kingdom of Lothair)—because of quarrels
among Charlemagne's three grandsons. However, soon after
the Period of the Divided Kingdoms began under Henry I in
919, Italy came under the control of the East Frank kingdom,
and so the division became one between the kingdoms of the
East Franks, or the Holy Roman Empire, and the West Franks,
or the Kingdom of France, with the eastern kingdom in the
Abel position and the western kingdom in the Cain position.

5. The Period of Jewish Captivity and Return and the Period of Papal Captivity and Return

The northern kingdom of Israel began its faithless ways soon
after the United Kingdom was divided, and it perished as a
result of its disbelief (ca. 722 B.C.). The southern kingdom of
Judah also became faithless. Thus, these kingdoms failed to
unite centered on God's ideal of the temple, and therefore they
failed to establish the Foundation for the Messiah. Therefore,
God allowed them to be taken captive and suffer at the hands
of the Assyrians and the Babylonians, respectively, that is, at
the hands of the satanic world. In the south, Babylon gained
control in 608 B.C., and beginning with Daniel and a few
members of the nobility (605 B.C.), began a series of deporta-

tions of the Hebrews to Babylon, where they had to remain for almost seventy years (Dan 1:1-6; Jer 25:11,12; 29:10; 39:1-10; II Kings 24,25). In 539 B.C., Persia conquered Babylon, and King Cyrus issued a decree freeing the Jews, who returned to their native land in three groups over a ninety-four-year period (culminating in 444 B.C.). However, until the reformation centered on Malachi, they did not establish themselves as a nation based on the Law and did not establish traditions acceptable to God. From the dispensational viewpoint, only when they actually reformed their practices according to the Law could they be considered as having returned (to their position as God's people). The conclusion of the returning period initiated the Period of Preparation for the Messiah.

From the end of the Period of the Christian Kingdom, which was to prepare the world-wide foundation for the Second Coming, until the time when the papacy fell into complete corruption, God sent many signs—such as the defeats in the Crusades—to make the popes and priests repent. But they did not repent, and instead, with the gradual expansion of royal power, conflict developed between popes and kings. Pope Boniface VIII came into conflict with the French King, Philip IV, and was even imprisoned by him for a time. In 1309, Clement V, whose election as the first French pope was arranged by Philip IV, moved the papacy from Rome to Avignon in southern France. There the succeeding popes lived for almost seventy years under the influence of the French kings. In 1377, Pope Gregory XI returned the papacy to Rome, initiating the period of return from exile. For the next one hundred forty years there was much confusion, with even three popes reigning simultaneously for a time. By the end of this period the pope in Rome had regained absolute control in the church.

6. The Period of Preparation for the Messiah and the Period of Preparation for the Second Coming

After returning from captivity in Babylon, the Israelites rebuilt the temple which had been destroyed, and at the urging of the prophet Malachi repented of their past sins of having worshipped foreign gods. They centered on the Law, inspiring a reformation movement and the beginning of the four-hundred-year Period of Preparation for the Messiah.

Period of Preparation for the Messiah (400 years)

> • Religious Reformation ╱ Malachi

Period of Preparation for the Second Coming (400 years) 1517-1918 A.D.

> • Religious Reformation ╱ Luther

After the pope returned to Rome, reformation movements inspired by God began, and the Christian church established a world-wide base of faith for the Second Coming. Through the Reformation, the dark clouds of the Middle Ages were penetrated, and, inspired by a new and passionate faith, a movement to spread the Gospel throughout the world arose. The four-hundred-year period that began with the Reformation is called the Period of Preparation for the Second Coming.

The Old Testament Age was the age in which faith in God was demonstrated through the external response of offerings and compliance with the Law. Therefore, in order to indemnify the entire history since Abraham in the Period of Preparation for the Messiah, the First Israel had to suffer external tribulations under the rule of Persia, Greece, Egypt, Syria, and Rome.

The New Testament Age is the age in which man was to demonstrate faith in God through the internal response of prayer and faith based on Jesus' words. Therefore, in the Period of Preparation for the Second Coming, the Second Israel had to endure internal tribulations. With the rise of humanism (the leading philosophy of the Renaissance), Enlightenment philosophies, and superficially applied freedom of faith after the Reformation, Christianity (the Second Israel) had to endure great chaos and confusion. Christians in that period had to indemnify the entire course of history since Jesus' time by overcoming severe internal trials in their religious lives.

During the Period of Preparation for the Messiah, God prepared the First Israel to receive the Messiah by reforming and renewing Judaism and by having the prophet Malachi prophesy concerning the Messiah's coming. However, although God focused his efforts to prepare for the Messiah on the nation of Israel, he also prepared the rest of the world for the Messiah's coming. Among the Gentiles, God had Gautama Buddha of India (565-485 B.C.) pioneer the base for Buddhism by improving Hinduism, and he had Socrates (470-399 B.C.) pioneer the period of the great philosophers in Greece. In the Orient, God had Confucius (552-479 B.C.) set up a standard of human ethics and morality through Confucianism. God thus had each establish the culture and religion suitable for his

Period of Preparation for the Messiah (400 years)

External response to God:	External tribulations
Offerings Law	Persia, Greece, Egypt, Syria, Rome

Period of Preparation for the Second Coming (400 years) 1517-1918 A.D.

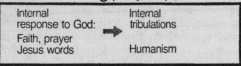

Internal response to God:	Internal tribulations
Faith, prayer Jesus words	Humanism

particular place and people so that they might make the necessary spiritual preparation to receive the Messiah. Jesus, coming on the foundation of this preparation, intended to unify all of the regions and various religions and cultures into one sphere of God-centered culture by absorbing Judaism, Hellenism, Buddhism, Confucianism, and all the religions and cultures that God had prepared.

God also prepared the world for the Messiah's coming by uniting the Mediterranean world and developing the Roman Empire, with its ease of communication in all directions and its vast cultural sphere based on a common language (Greek). With this external foundation already made through God's dispensation, when the Messiah came, his ideology would have been able to quickly expand from Israel to Rome, and from Rome to the whole world.

Similarly, God worked in the Period of Preparation for the Second Coming to prepare the world in addition to

Period of Preparation for the Messiah (400 years)

Environment	
Roman Empire	• Buddha
	• Socrates
	• Confucius

Period of Preparation for the Second Coming (400 years) 1517-1918 A.D.

Environment	
Renaissance	Missionary movement
Industrial Revolution	

Christianity. Prior to the Messiah's birth (two thousand years ago), God had to prepare the different peoples to receive what the Messiah would teach. That preparation was made in Judaism, Buddhism, Confucianism, and the other religions and ethical developments that God stimulated and developed. The ethical, spiritual, and Heart foundation for the Second Coming is made through Christianity. Therefore, God prepared the world for the Second Coming by the spread of Christianity throughout the world.

In the Period of Preparation for the Second Coming, the external circumstances were also greatly developed as a foundation for the Messiah's second coming. God has worked to develop the external conditions to the point where the Messiah will be able to use them to establish the Kingdom of Heaven. The separation of cultures is being overcome by modern developments in communication and transportation that make possible the rapid and frequent interchange of languages, traditions, and cultures. One of the developments which will greatly help the Messiah teach the ideals and ways of heaven is the development of global communications systems. Beginning with the Industrial Revolution, the great developments in almost every area of human concern have prepared nearly everything necessary to produce an ideal environment (e.g., production of food, clothing, medicines, environmental control, and electricity).

We have reviewed the histories of the First and Second Israel as they occurred in different eras and different places and with the key roles played by different people. Yet, we can see an astonishing time-identity when we look at these two histories from the dispensational viewpoint. This time-identity appears because both histories are histories of the central dispensation to prepare for the Messiah and thus both dispensations have been inspired and led by God.

CHAPTER FIFTEEN

Preparation for the Second Coming

This chapter covers the period from the Renaissance to the present day. It includes primarily the Period of Preparation for the Second Coming, which is further divided into three sub-periods: the Period of the Reformation, from 1517 to 1648; the Period of Conflict between Religion and Philosophies, from 1648 to 1789; and the Period of the Maturing of Political Structure, Economy, and Ideology, from 1789 to 1918. It also deals with the World Wars of the twentieth century.

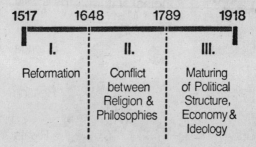

Preparation for the Second Coming

1517	1648	1789	1918
I.	**II.**	**III.**	
Reformation	Conflict between Religion & Philosophies	Maturing of Political Structure, Economy & Ideology	

I. THE PERIOD OF THE REFORMATION

The Period of the Reformation lasted approximately one hundred thirty years, from Luther's call for religious reform in 1517 until the fighting between Roman Catholics and the new Protestant sects and governments ended with the Treaty of Westphalia in 1648.

After the Period of Persecution under the Roman Empire, the Pope and the leaders of the Roman Catholic Church had

the central responsibility for establishing the Foundation for
the Messiah. For this reason, God gave them positions and
authority which had tremendous influence over nation and
society. But, in medieval times their corruption and excessive
intervention in people's lives hindered the establishment of
the Foundation for the Messiah. The misuse of ecclesiastical
authority in the strict medieval feudal system, in addition to
the corruption and immorality among the clergy, stifled man's
attempt to fulfill the desires of the Original Nature with which
he had been endowed at his creation.

The movement to break down the medieval social environment and corrupt religious system sprang out of the
desires of man's Original Nature. Thus this pursuit had a Sung
Sang (internal) aspect and a Hyung Sang (external) aspect
corresponding to the two aspects of the Original Nature of
man. Thus, man sought to satisfy his inner desires, such as
those for a life of faith, honor, duty, piety, and relationship
with God, and his external desires, such as those to develop his
knowledge (through science), his powers of reason, and his
rights.

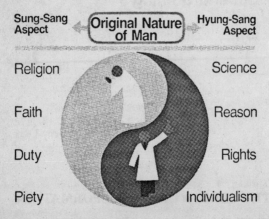

First came the movement to revive Hellenism, which was
a *Cain-type* movement, in pursuit of the objects of man's external desires; and then came the *Abel-type* movement, in pursuit
of the objects of man's internal desires. The movement to
revive Hellenism became known as the Renaissance and

emphasized such humanist concerns as the beauty of nature, the freedom of the individual, and the value of life in this world. The Reformation arose out of man's inner desire to renew a God-centered way of life, and in that the Reformation emphasized man's relationship to God in contrast to the humanistic and worldly emphasis of Hellenism, we can call the Reformation a revival of Hebraism.

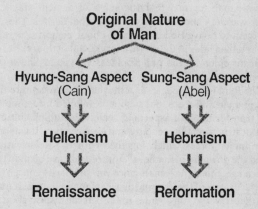

A. The Renaissance

Under the grace of God's Dispensation for Restoration, man has been restoring his Original Nature. The external aspect of man's effort to restore that Original Nature gave rise to the Renaissance.

According to "The Principles of the Creation," man was created to become perfect only by fulfilling his responsibility, through the exercise of free will. Man is created to be free, and thus he continually pursues freedom. Also, a man of perfected character is to have independence as an individual truth body. Thus, man, of his Original Nature, desires to develop a sense of individuality.

Man was created through God's Word (the Logos) to resemble God's nature. Because of this, man, of his Original Nature, desires to develop his intellect and powers of reason. Man was also created to have dominion over the Creation. Thus, man, of his Original Nature, values science and an

understanding of nature and desires to develop his environment. However, the desires of the external aspect of man's
Original Nature were being suppressed within the feudal system of the Middle Ages. This caused people to pursue even
more ardently such things as freedom, individualism, and
respect for reason.

The pursuit of these external desires was precipitated by
the importing of ancient Greek classics during the Crusades.
Medieval man learned that the spirit of ancient classical
Greece was very similar to his own external desires. Thus, a
movement to revive Hellenism came about, centering first in
Italy, and then later in the rest of Europe. Out of this revival of
Hellenism emerged the philosophical viewpoint known as
humanism.

The Renaissance began as a movement to recapture the
spirit of ancient Greece, but it soon developed into a movement transforming all aspects of society, including culture,
political structure, the economy, and even religion. It was one
of the major forces which together with the Reformation
caused the downfall of medieval culture and gave birth to the
modern age. Since the Renaissance was primarily concerned
with the desires of the external aspect of man's nature, it may
seem that it would run counter to God's basic dispensation to
restore man's spirit. However, in order to accomplish the goal
of restoring man's original value, a phase of restoring the
external aspect of man's nature is necessary. By all means, all
dimensions of man's value must be restored. This means that
each person must be perfected as a unique individual, integ-
rating both the inner and outer aspects of his being. With this
in mind, God brought about the Reformation on the foundation of the Renaissance.

B. The Reformation

The corruption of the medieval Catholic Church was counter
to God's dispensation for the Second Coming, and the
Church's abuse of ecclesiastical authority and its formal
ritualism caused many people to call for drastic reform. And
as a result of the Crusades, the "Babylonian Captivity," the
Great Schism, and the Renaissance, papal power and authority were greatly diminished, and the cry for reform became
increasingly militant. As the influence of humanism grew,

opposition to the Church's restrictive measures against man's freedom and self-government began to gain hold among the people.

In the 14th Century, John Wyclif, a professor of theology at Oxford University in England, translated the Bible into English, insisting that the criterion by which one's faith is to be measured is not the Pope or the priests, but the Bible itself. He further argued that many of the Church's rituals, laws, and traditions had no basis in scripture. Many others criticized the Church's exploitation of the people and the priests' irreligious attitudes, and also called for reform. However, none of them succeeded, and some were executed.

In 1517, Pope Leo X began to sell indulgences in order to raise funds for construction of Saint Peter's Basilica. The reaction against this practice ignited the Reformation, beginning with Martin Luther, a professor of biblical theology at the University of Wittenberg in Germany. This revolutionary movement developed rapidly in Germany, France, and Switzerland, centered on Luther, Calvin, and Zwingli.

The conflict which erupted over the Protestant movement was not only a religious conflict—it expanded into an international war among the countries with different interests in the success or failure of the Reformation. The conflict lasted for over a hundred years, until the fight between the old and new religious traditions was finally settled by the Thirty Years' War. This war, waged primarily in Germany, finally ended in 1648 with the Treaty of Westphalia. It ended with the victory of Protestantism in northern Europe, and the Reformation was successful.

II. THE PERIOD OF CONFLICT BETWEEN RELIGION AND PHILOSOPHIES

The Period of Conflict between Religion and Philosophies lasted slightly more than one hundred forty years, from the Treaty of Westphalia, in 1648, until the beginning of the French Revolution, in 1789. Through the influence of the Renaissance and Reformation, man entered into the full pursuit of satisfying the external and internal demands of his Original Nature, and because of the freedom given to religious and philosophical thought man could not avoid the divisions in doctrine and the conflicts among philosophies.

The Dispensation for Restoration is characterized by the separation of the *Cain-type and Abel-type views of life.* At the consummation of history, this same principle of separation must again be applied, with the world being divided into Cain-type and Abel-type factions. The Cain-type world is the world of atheism-communism, and the Abel-type world is the religion-supporting democratic world, these two being comparable, on the world level, to the "goats" and "sheep" that Jesus spoke of in Matthew 25:32. These two worlds are based on two different views of life.

A. The Cain-type View of Life

The emphasis on fulfilling the desires of the external aspect of man's Original Nature led to the sprouting of the Cain-type view of life, which makes light of faith in God and religious dedication and has tended to think of everything in terms of nature and humanism. This tendency became more pronounced in reaction to the medieval view of life, in which people considered the human body and the material world in general as base and were so awed by God and submissive to religious leaders as to often disregard reason. Influenced by this, many began to look at nature and life in light of reason and their own direct experience, independent of theological preconceptions. The rationalists, such as Descartes, and the empiricists, such as Locke, abandoned the attitude of regarding God as the cause of all things and insisted that truth can be known only through reason or experience. Rationalism tended to disregard history and tradition, and value only human reason. Empiricism, on the other hand, was centered on man's five senses and argued that knowledge is only gained through experience and direct observation, devoid of any a priori conceptions. So, both rationalism and empiricism came to reject mysticism, visions, and revelations. The more these two philosophies emphasized rationalism and the experiences of the five senses and limited their focus to nature and man, the more they separated man from God.

In the 18th century, the Cain-type view of life evolved into the thought of the Enlightenment, which can be considered the second stage of the Renaissance. The Enlightenment evaluated every human endeavor from the perspective of reason and how closely it resembled the order of nature. It affected every aspect of life and resulted in the breaking down of a great many of the existing traditions. Because they stressed only the rational aspects of life, Enlightenment thinkers thoroughly rejected whatever seemed to be arrived at by other than a rational process or which seemed not true to life. As a result, man went beyond the stage of being independent from God and came to the extreme of denying him.

Cain-type View of Life

- **Rationalism**/Descartes

- **Empiricism**/Locke

- **Deism**/Herbert

- **Left-wing Hegelianism**
  Straus, Feuerbach

- **Marxism**/Marx, Engels, Lenin

Influenced by this Cain-type view of life, the doctrine of Deism was born. Deists preferred to believe in theology based on reason and excluded such experiences as revelation and miracles. Deists conceived of God as an impersonal creator who was not involved in history and believed that man could derive his moral standards from nature without revelation from God. Left Hegelianism (Strauss and Feuerbach), together with the philosophy of the French socialists, provided the foundation for the birth of the Communist ideology. That is, under the influence of these ideologies, Karl Marx and Friedrich Engels developed their doctrine of dialectical materialism. Communism may be seen as the synthesis of atheism and materialism, and is the last major ideology which denies God.

B. The Abel-type View of Life

When we superficially examine the transition from medieval society to the modern world we may be inclined to regard that transition as the process of separating man from God and

religion. This is because medieval man's expression of the
external aspects of man's Original Nature in this transitional
period produced such a profound development in society.
However, careful observation will lead us to understand that
there is another major aspect in the transition from medieval
society to modern society. Medieval man's expression of the
internal aspects of the Original Nature gave rise to the movement reviving a *Hebraistic* view of life. This movement ma-
tured as the Reformation. Through this movement, philosophy and religion developed the vertical view of life, which is
the Abel-type view of life, and led medieval man to develop a
closer relationship with God.

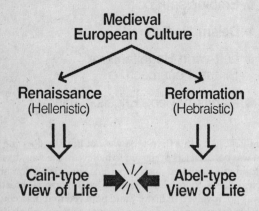

In the 17th and 18th centuries, new movements emerged,
movements emphasizing mystical experiences, a Christian
life, and moral conduct. The religious world, which had been
influenced by the general trend toward rationalism, was in
serious need of this movement emphasizing religious passion
and man's inner life as opposed to doctrines or formalities.
Pietism in Germany (centered on Spener); Methodism, which
aroused a great revival in England (centered on the Wesley
brothers); and Quakerism (founded by George Fox) are all
examples of this movement. They all emphasized faith based
on personal religious experiences and the mystical or spiritual aspects of man's life, which cannot be explained in pure-
ly rational terms; they emphasized a view of life based on

relationship with God. In the realm of philosophy, the Ideal-
ists, such as Kant, Fichte, Schelling, and Hegel, in opposition
to the rationalistic and materialistic views of the Enlightenment, expounded views of life that gave greater emphasis to
spirituality and morality—that is, views that were basically
of the Abel-type.

Abel-type View of Life

- **Pietism**/Spener

- **Methodism**/ Wesley

- **Quakers**/Fox

- **(American) Great Awakenings**
  Edwards

- **German Idealism**/Kant, Fichte,
  Schelling, Hegel

III. THE PERIOD OF THE MATURING OF POLITICAL STRUCTURE, ECONOMY, AND IDEOLOGY

This third period lasted one hundred thirty years. It began
with the French Revolution in 1789, continued through the
Industrial Revolution, and ended with the conclusion of the
First World War. Based on the Cain-type and Abel-type views
of life which had emerged prior to this period, separate Cain-
type and Abel-type worlds began to form. The dispensational
significance of this one-hundred-thirty-year period lies in the
development of political structure, economy, and ideology to
the stage at which the Messiah can be received and at which
he can transform them to establish the ideal world as originally conceived of by God.

A. The Development of Modern Political Systems

Political power, which had been decentralized under the feudal lords during the Middle Ages, was consolidated by the kings

to form absolute monarchies by the middle of the 17th century. Then, beginning in the late 18th century, the system of absolute monarchy was transformed into Cain and Abel types of democracy, originating in the Cain-type and Abel-type views of life. Under the influence of Enlightenment ideals, people aimed to establish liberty, brotherhood, and equality as realities in human affairs—but did so in France through struggles of an external and brutal nature, thus establishing a Cain-type democracy. The Abel-type democracies which developed in England and the United States and other countries were largely based on the Abel-type view of life, which accounts for the much more humane character of their revolutions. Out of these two traditions have developed the Communist and democratic worlds.

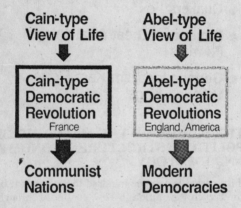

As was explained in "The Principles of the Creation," the Creation was made with the structure of the perfect human being as the model. The ideal world, consisting of perfect persons, would also have resembled the structure and function of a perfect human being. Just as the cells and organs of a human body move according to the command of the brain, the people and organizations in the ideal world would work in accordance with the Will of God. Just as no part of the body rejects the commands of the brain, it would not be difficult for an ideal human being to follow the Will of God. Just as commands from the brain are transmitted to all the parts of the body through the peripheral nervous system, centered on the spine, the directions from God will reach the entire society through the saints, centered on the Messiah, who comes as a True Parent.

Ideal Person ≡ Ideal Society

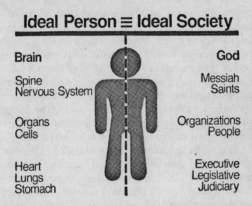

Brain	**God**
Spine Nervous System	Messiah Saints
Organs Cells	Organizations People
Heart Lungs Stomach	Executive Legislative Judiciary

In the ideal society, the harmony among the legislative, executive, and judicial branches of the government corresponds to the harmony among the three major organs of the body—the lungs, heart, and stomach (and the respiratory, circulatory, and digestive systems, respectively). Just as these three organs (and systems) in the human body work smoothly when they work according to the commands of the brain, in the ideal world, the three main branches of government will also work in harmony because they operate according to the Messiah and the Will of God.

For a period in the development of political structure in western Europe, the king controlled all functions of government: legislative, executive, and judiciary. However, after the era of the French Revolution, these three powers began to be separated. Thus, externally, at least, the pattern of the ideal political structure began to be realized. This means that some political systems of the present externally resemble the structure of a human body. However, because political leaders neither understand God, nor carry out God's Will, the system cannot function harmoniously as originally intended. The Messiah must come to teach man God's Will and show him how to embody it within himself.

B. The Industrial Revolution and the Maturing of the Economy

According to "The Principles of the Creation," God blessed man to have dominion over the Creation (Gen 1:28) upon his attaining perfection, thus to create and enjoy a pleasant environment. God has been directing the dispensation toward the improvement of the material environment through influencing the development of industry and commerce, which is based on the progress of science. Although man is fallen, he must use the creative ability that God gave him to develop inventions which will create the living environment suitable for the Messiah to realize the ideal society. The Industrial Revolution, beginning in England, occurred to create the basis of the ideal environment for God's ideal society.

In the economic structure of the ideal society, production, distribution, and consumption would be well harmonized under God's Will. Therefore, production in accordance with man's needs, fair distribution, and consumption in accordance with the purpose for the whole would exist. Although currently science and the economy are quite advanced, in much of the world, production is still not able to meet the demand, consumption is often insensitive to long range and ethical considerations, and the injury caused by inequities in distribution is serious. Only when the whole is well harmonized by the Messiah, in accord with God's Will, can the ideal economic structure be established. After the Industrial Revolution, mass production required many developing countries, such as England, to settle vast colonies in order to expand their markets and sources of raw materials. However, most of the developing countries were Christian nations, and this pioneering of colonies for economic reasons provided the external foundation for the internal spreading of the Gospel. The Industrial Revolution has had considerable significance in terms of fulfilling Jesus' prediction that the Gospel would be preached to the ends of the earth in preparation for the Messiah (Mt 24:14).

C. The Stages of Revolution in Politics, Economy, Ideology, and Religion

As discussed above, the anti-medieval movement to revive

Hellenism, known as the Renaissance, was a Cain-like trend reviving humanism. The Renaissance further developed its Cain-like nature and evolved into the Enlightenment, which can be regarded as a second Renaissance. Then the Enlightenment further developed its Cain-like nature and gave birth to the age of Communism, the third and culminating "Renaissance."

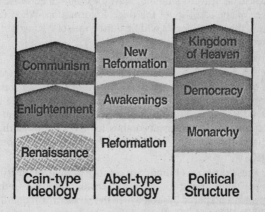

Cain-type Ideology	Abel-type Ideology	Political Structure
Communism	New Reformation	Kingdom of Heaven
Enlightenment	Awakenings	Democracy
Renaissance	Reformation	Monarchy

Satan knows God's plan and always moves to establish things on his side before God can accomplish them. Thus, what Satan has worked to accomplish is similar (in form, not in content) to what God's dispensation will later bring about. Thus, beginning with the Renaissance, three periods of Abel-type revolution followed each of the three phases of Cain-type revolution in religion, politics, and industry. The first Abel-type period was the Reformation, which began with Luther, following the Renaissance. Then, during and following the Enlightenment, a second spiritual awakening occurred, amidst great persecution, based on Fox, Spener, John Wesley, and Jonathan Edwards, and it expanded to become the second Reformation. Based on these events and on the understanding of the above principle of evil preceeding good, the third Reformation is to be expected following the third Renaissance. In fact, the state of today's Christianity reveals an urgent need for such a reform.

Three stages of reformation have also occurred in the area

of politics. The medieval feudal society collapsed under the influence of the (first) Renaissance and the (first) Reformation, while the absolute monarchies collapsed under the influence of the "second Renaissance" (Enlightenment) and the "second Reformation." Finally, on the satanic side, the Communist society was formed by political revolution based on the "third Renaissance." Now, it is essential that the democratic world on heaven's side subjugate the Communist world by means of the ideology of the third Reformation. When this occurs, these two worlds will be united into one Kingdom of Heaven on earth.

We also notice that the Industrial Revolution has also proceeded through three stages. The first phase of the revolution occurred based on the development of steam-generated energy. Immediately afterward, the second phase of the Industrial Revolution took place based on the development of electricity and the internal combustion engine. Now, a third Industrial Revolution is in the making, based on atomic energy.

These three revolutions are coming to their maturity in this period of preparation for the Second Coming. Together they form a prepared base on which the Messiah can come and fulfill God's Purpose for the Creation. The maturing of religion and ideology is for the dispensation directed toward the full perfection of man's Original Nature, while the maturing of politics and economy is for the dispensation that will develop the structure and environment for the ideal world.

IV. THE WORLD WARS

A. The Dispensational Causes of the World Wars

Of course, wars do break out as a result of political, economic, and ideological causes. However, in addition to such external causes, there are internal causes, that is, dispensational causes in accordance with the principle of restoration through indemnity. The basic cause of the world wars is the conflict between the good sovereignty of God, who is trying to restore man to his side, and the evil sovereignty of Satan, who is trying to preserve his domination of man—a conflict in which man is caught in the middle. Let us examine this in more detail.

Internal Causes of the World Wars

1 Satan's last struggle

2 Restore three blessings

3 Three temptations

4 World-wide Cain/Abel conflict

First of all, the world wars break out because of Satan's last struggles to preserve his sovereignty against his opponent. Because of the Fall, man realized the non-Principle world, and serves Satan as his master instead of God. So God has been working the dispensation to restore his *Principle* world by establishing a territory of goodness within the non-Principle world, under satanic dominion, and then gradually expanding that territory. Christ, in particular, at the Second Coming, comes to end the world of evil sovereignty and to realize the world of good sovereignty centered on God. Therefore, the time of the Second Coming is Satan's last chance to keep from losing his sovereignty, and consequently, his struggle becomes more desperate and total, with the result being the three world wars.

Secondly, Satan realized a world based a non-Principle pattern of the Three Blessings; so in order to restore the fallen world in accordance with the principle of restoration through indemnity, God has to have man meet, on a world-wide level, indemnity conditions to receive the Three Blessings. Although man fell, God could not stop him from realizing an imitation of the blessed world which God originally intended to build, and fallen men have developed a Satan-centered, non-Principle world based on imitations of God's Three Blessings to man. Thus, a non-Principle world has been established in which the individual nature is centered on Satan, the family and society are centered on Satan, and dominion of the created world is centered on Satan. Therefore, in order to meet, world-wide, the indemnity conditions for receiving the Three Blessings, it is inevitable that man be faced with three world-wide struggles, in which the side representing *The Principle* and heaven must be victorious over the non-Principle, satanic side.

Thirdly, the world wars must occur in order for the world to meet the condition of having to overcome Satan's three temptations to Jesus. Jesus' course is the course through which Chistians must pass. Therefore, the three temptations that Jesus faced must be overcome by all mankind on the individual, family, national, and world-wide levels. Accordingly, three world struggles must emerge so that mankind, on a world level, can overcome the three temptations of Jesus.

Fourthly, the world wars must take place in order to meet, on the world level, the indemnity conditions for restoring heavenly sovereignty. God has been moving the Dispensation for Restoration through Indemnity ahead by dividing the fallen world into two types: the Cain-type and the Abel-type. Attacks by the Cain-type, satanic side against the Abel-type, heavenly side are the process of restoration. The Abel-type, heavenly side establishes the foundation of goodness through its sacrifices. The last struggles must occur to restore through indemnity, on the world level, the act of Cain's having killed Abel. The Cain world strikes the Abel world first, yet the result is that the Abel world wins the victory over the Cain world.

B. The First World War

During the last stage of preparation for the Second Coming, God carried out his dispensation by dividing mankind politically, economically, and ideologically into two worlds: the Abel-type, heavenly side, and the Cain-type, satanic side. The heavenly side and the satanic side are determined according to their direction relative to God's Dispensation for Restoration. Taking the same direction as that of God's dispensation, or acting in concert with that direction, even in an indirect way, determines a thing as being on the heavenly side. A position contrary to the direction of God's dispensation, even indirectly, determines a thing as being on the satanic side.

All religions having goodness as their purpose are on the heavenly side. However, when a certain religion blocks the way of another religion closer to God, the former religion stands on the satanic side. Since Christianity was established as the central religion for fulfilling the purpose of all other religions, in the Dispensation for Restoration, it stands the closest to God. Therefore, in the First World War, the leading Allied nations, England, America, France, and Russia, were Christian nations. Thus, they belonged to the heavenly side. On the contrary, the two leading nations of the Central Powers, Germany and Austria-Hungary, not only supported Turkey, a Moslem country which was persecuting Christianity, but were also extremely authoritarian countries. Thus, they belonged to the satanic side. In the First World War, the heavenly side was attacked by the satanic side, but eventually achieved the final victory.

With this foundation of victory, the heavenly side met, on the world level, the formation stage indemnity condition for the restoration of God's Three Blessings. Seen from the standpoint of the world's having to overcome Satan's first temptation to Jesus, the indemnity condition for restoring God's First Blessing to man was met. In other words, the indemnity condition for restoring the blessing of individual perfection was met. Furthermore, the formation stage of the foundation for restoring heaven's sovereignty was established. Also, with the victory of the heavenly side in the First World War, the foundation was established upon which the Messiah could be born (as the example of a true human being).

Results of World War I

1 Formation stage world-wide condition for restoring the 3 blessings

2 Condition for restoring the 1st blessing

3 Formation stage foundation for restoring the Heavenly Sovereignty

4 Foundation for the birth of the Messiah

C. The Second World War

The Second World War was the war in which democracy established the growth stage foundation of victory by conquering fascist totalitarianism. In the Second World War, the United States, England, and France, as democratic nations, represented God's side. Germany, Japan, and Italy, as totalitarian nations which stood opposed to Christianity, stood on Satan's side.

It was due to the fall of three beings, Adam, Eve, and the archangel, that God's blessings were not fulfilled. The participation of three beings—an Adam-type being, an Eve-type being, and an archangel-type being—is necessary in order to restore the Three Blessings. Accordingly, the wars by which the world was to meet the indemnity condition to restore the blessings had to be a confrontation between three nations representing Adam, Eve, and the archangel, standing on God's side, and three nations representing those same positions on Satan's side. In the Second World War, Adam, Eve, and the archangel on God's side were represented by the United States, England, and France, whereas Germany, Japan, and Italy represented those positions on Satan's side.

Why did the Soviet Union, which was a nation on the satanic side, cooperate with the heavenly side during the Second World War? When any social structure or governmental system becomes an obstacle to God's fulfilling his Dispensation for Restoration, he works to break down and destroy that obstacle. Likewise, in order to move forward ahead of God and achieve his own ultimate goal, which is the realization of the non-Principle world, Satan works to break down any obstacles in his path. At times the obstacle obstructs both God's and Satan's efforts; at that time both the heavenly side and satanic side move so as to break down and destroy them.

Both the Cain and Abel sides each worked to destroy the medieval feudal society. Also, the heavenly side and satanic side each worked to break down the monarchic society. Likewise, during the Second World War, fascist totalitarianism became an obstacle to the heavenly side, and to the satanic side, and thus each worked to destroy it. God let the Soviet Union cooperate with the nations on the heavenly side in breaking down the other totalitarian nations, even though it meant that the Communist world would be established.

The Second World War ended with the victory of the

nations on the heavenly side. Through this, the growth stage world-wide indemnity condition for restoring God's Three Blessings to man was met. Seen from the standpoint of over-coming, world-wide, Satan's temptations to Jesus the indemnity condition for restoring world-wide God's Second Blessing, which is to multiply children of goodness, was met. Therefore, after the war, work for the Second Coming was developed to the stage of furthering religious development. Furthermore, the growth stage foundation to restore heavenly sovereignty was established.

Results of World War II

1 Growth Stage world-wide condition for restoring the 3 blessings

2 Condition for restoring the 2nd Blessing

3 Growth stage foundation for restoring the Heavenly Sovereignity

D. The Third World War

God originally intended to complete the Dispensation for Restoration in Adam's family, through Cain and Abel. However, his work to separate good from evil ended in failure due to Cain's killing Abel. Since that time, God has worked continually to separate good from evil, expanding in stages from the family level to the tribal, national, and world-wide levels. At the consummation of human history, both the heavenly side and the satanic side have come to operate on the world-wide level. Thus, the two worlds of democracy and Communism coexist. But after the third world struggle, these two worlds will be united. Seen from God's dispensation, the Third World War will inevitably take place. However, there are two ways for that war to be fought.

First, the satanic world could be subjugated by a wholly internal fight through ideology. God does not desire judgment or destruction (Ezek 33:14-16), but salvation. Thus he desires to induce Satan to submit ideologically, and with the least amount of external sacrifice. If this fails, the satanic side will inevitably attack the heavenly side. The heavenly side must then defeat the satanic side by force. The manner in which the Third World War takes place depends on how these two worlds, which bear the responsibility of the Last Days, carry out their tasks.

Whatever the manner in which the war is fought, there must be a fundamental ideology by which mankind can be led to the ideal world. This is so, because even if the submission of the satanic world is gained through an external fight with weapons, the ideal world can only be realized through an ideology of a higher dimension, one which all people can follow freely and with joy.

Ideology is the driving force which will establish the ideal world of the family of man. Thus, the ideology needed must be an ideology of true love which can break down barriers between tribes and nations and solve the serious problems among races and cultures. Furthermore, this ideology must be able to give mankind hope and conviction concerning the realization of the ideal world. It must also be an ideology that can bring spiritual inspiration and a change in character and give the youth a positive viewpoint toward life. It must com-

Results of World War III

1 Completion stage world-wide condition for restoring the 3 blessings

2 Condition for restoring the 3rd blessing

3 Completion stage foundation for restoring the Heavenly Sovereignty

pletely reveal the falseness of other ideologies, especially that of the Communist ideology, Marxism-Leninism, which is the culmination of all the Cain-type views of life.

If the Third World War ends in victory for the heavenly side, the indemnity condition for the restoration of God's Three Blessings will have been met. The heavenly side will have overcome, on the world-wide level, Satan's third temptation of Jesus, thus, establishing through indemnity the complete foundation for the restoration of God's sovereignty.

If this takes place, the work of Christ at the Second Coming will bring about on earth the ideal world of God's sovereignty, and man's dominion over the Creation will be completely restored. The ideal world which God had originally conceived of at the time of creation, which he has been painstakingly trying to establish on earth through the long period of history since the Fall of man, will be the result. This ideal world is the world in which man and the entire cosmos attend God and become harmonious with each other. This ideal world is called the Ideal World of Cosmic Ideology.

CHAPTER SIXTEEN

The Second Coming

Jesus definitely spoke of a Second Coming (Mt 16:27). Yet, there has been no clear understanding concerning the Second Coming. We need to know how, when, and where the Second Coming will take place. Some people believe that the Second Coming takes place when Jesus enters the heart of an individual (Jn 14:20) through the descent of the Holy Spirit (Acts 8:16,19). However, this is not The Principle view. Ever since the descent of the Holy Spirit at Pentecost (Acts 2:4), many believers have experienced the presence of Jesus within themselves. If this were the Second Coming, then we would have to say that the Second Coming already took place two thousand years ago. However, we know that the Second Coming does not take place in this way because Christians have continued to wait for the Second Coming even after the descent of the Holy Spirit on the day of Pentecost.

On the other hand, some people believe that Jesus will return spiritually. Other facts indicate that this will not be so. Ever since the resurrection of Jesus, the appearance of Jesus in spirit has been possibile at any moment, and has frequently occurred. Yet, Christians still eagerly wait for the day of the Second Coming. From this, we know that what they have been waiting for was not a second coming in spirit. Jesus often met the apostle John in spirit, yet Jesus told him, " 'Surely I am coming soon' " (Rev 22:20).

I. HOW WILL CHRIST COME AGAIN?

A. Lessons Based on the Second Coming of Elijah

Then how will the Second Coming of Christ take place? In considering this, let us first look at the second coming of Elijah. In fact, the second coming of Elijah is the clearest example that God has given us related to how Christ will come again.

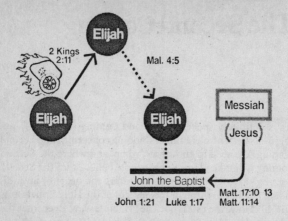

Through the prophet Malachi, God promised to send Elijah again, before the coming of the Messiah (Mal 4:5). So Israelites of that time who were waiting for the Messiah were actually waiting for the second coming of Elijah, because he was to precede the Messiah. Because the second coming of Elijah was to be the return of the Elijah who had ascended into heaven, the people believed that Elijah would surely descend from heaven. Yet, Jesus clearly declared that John the Baptist, who was born on earth, was Elijah (Mt 11:14; 17:13). However, that the second coming of Elijah took place through John the Baptist does not mean that Elijah, himself, was born again as John the Baptist. Elijah was in the spirit world, helping John the Baptist, who was on earth, since John was born with the same mission (Lk 1:17). So, although the mission was the same, the person was different.

Through this lesson learned from the second coming of Elijah, we can understand that the Second Coming might possibly take place by the Lord's being born on earth. We can also understand that though at the Second Coming, the Lord, as the Messiah, will have the same mission as Jesus, he may not have the same appearance as Jesus (Jn 14:16,17; 16:12; Rev 19:12; 2:17).

B. Lessons based on the First Coming

In the Old Testament, we find two contradictory prophecies concerning the coming of the Messiah. In Daniel 7:13, we find the prophecy that the Lord would come on the clouds: "I saw in the night visions, and behold, with the clouds of heaven there came one like a son of man. . . ." However, the prophet Micah prophesied that the Messiah would be born in Bethlehem (Mic 5:2). Which of these two contradictory prophecies did the Israelites believe?

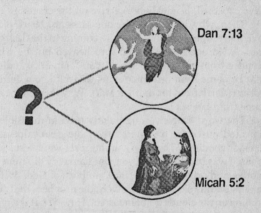

Dan 7:13

Micah 5:2

Knowing the influence of the two prophets Daniel and Micah on the Israelites, and knowing that the Israelites had great faith in God, we know that they were waiting for the Messiah to come from heaven.

It was for this reason that even after the crucifixion of Jesus, an anti-Christian movement arose saying that Jesus could not have been the Messiah because he was born in the flesh on earth. This can be understood in the warning by the apostle John: "For many deceivers have gone out into the world, men who will not acknowledge the coming of Jesus Christ in the flesh; such a one is the deceiver and the antichrist" (2 Jn 7:8).

There are some people who insist that Daniel 7:13 is a prophecy of what is going to happen at the Second Coming. However, from the following passages, we can see that the Old Testament Age was to end with the coming of Jesus: " 'For all the prophets and the law prophesied until John . . .' " (Mt 11:13) and "For Christ is the end of the law, that every one who has faith may be justified" (Rom 10:4). The situation was such that no one ever imagined a second coming of the Messiah until Jesus himself, toward the end of his ministry, said that the Lord would come again. As a result, no Israelite at the time of Jesus would have thought that the prophecy of Daniel 7:13 was concerned with a second coming. They would have believed it applied to *the* coming of the Messiah, and they would have acted as though it did. (In other words, they would have expected *the* Messiah to arrive on the clouds.)

Then, why, in sending the one Messiah, Jesus, did God give this prophecy of the Messiah's coming in the flesh? Jesus said, " 'No one has ascended into heaven but he who descended from heaven, the Son of man' " (Jn 3:13), indicating that he came from heaven. Yet, as we well know, Jesus was born on earth from his mother, Mary. Why then did he say he came from heaven?

The word 'heaven' is frequently used in the Bible. It is repeatedly used as a metaphor to connote great value, sacredness, or goodness. Thus, we can interpret what Jesus said to mean 'I was born like all of you, but I am very different in the motive and origin of my birth; I am born of God'. With this understanding of the word 'heaven', the prophecy that Jesus is coming on the clouds is not incorrect. However, it is a mistake to interpret it literally.

In a similar way, John the Baptist, who was born in the family of Zechariah according to God's special dispensation, was not merely born of this earth, but had a great mission (Lk 1:15-17,76). Regardless of the form of his birth, God was the direct cause, and thus John had "come down from heaven" representing Elijah, and had the same mission as Elijah.

C. The Second Coming of Christ Takes Place through his Birth on Earth

From what is shown in the examples of Elijah's second coming and Jesus' coming, both of which were the direct work of God, one cannot help but give serious thought to the prophecies for the Second Coming.

In summary, the New Testament not only contains prophecies that say Christ will come as a judge amidst glory on a cloud from heaven, but also some that say he will come again just as he did the first time, quite contrary to the other type of prophecy of his coming on the clouds.

We read in Luke 17:24,25 that Jesus, anticipating what was going to happen at the Second Coming, said, " '. . . so will the Son of man be in his day. But first he must suffer many things and be rejected by this generation.' " If the Lord should come again amidst power and glory, with the trumpet call of the archangel, who would dare deny and persecute him? Would you persecute him?

Today, many faithful Christians and churches are looking up to the sky, waiting for the Lord to come on the clouds. If he were to come on the clouds, there would be no reason for him to be persecuted. However, if he does not come on a literal cloud, and instead comes in the flesh, as at the First Coming, then it becomes apparent why Jesus said he would first suffer before finally being recognized (Lk 17:24,25).

Revelation 12:5 says, ". . . she brought forth a male child, one who is to rule all the nations with a rod of iron, but her child was caught up to God and to his throne." The man who will rule the world with a rod of iron is the coming Lord. In this verse, it says that he will be born of a woman. When the Pharisees wanted to know the time of the Second Coming, they asked Jesus when the Kingdom of God was coming, and he answered, ". . .'The Kingdom of God is not coming with signs to be observed . . .' " (Lk 17:20). Everyone can gaze up at heaven, but Jesus said that the coming of God's Kingdom, in other words, the Second Coming will not be visible. Why is that so? It is because the Messiah does not come on a literal cloud. In Luke 18:8, Jesus said, " 'I tell you, he will vindicate them speedily. Nevertheless, when the Son of man comes, will he find faith on earth?' " Jesus was prophesying that he would not find faith on earth at his second coming. This means that when he comes, there will be almost no one who will be saved by their complete faith. Why is this so?

Of course, not all believers on earth have perfect faith, but there are people all over the world who are going the way of true faith. Then why did Jesus imply that he would not find faith? Furthermore, who would fail to recognize the Lord coming on a literal cloud? Certainly even non-believers would recognize him and have faith in him. Will people lack faith because someone will prevent them from having it? Certainly not. Difficulties do not necessarily weaken a person's faith. We interpret Jesus' saying that he would not find faith on earth to mean that he is going to come in the same manner as at the first coming.

When Jesus came two thousand years ago, there was great faith—of a sort—among the people. Some prayed day and night in the temple, and they memorized the command-ments. They tried hard to keep all of the commandments and laws that God had ordered them to keep. They faithfully offered their tithes, and they fasted. In this sense, they had great faith in God, yet there was no true faith. Why didn't they have a faith that would allow them to believe in Jesus as the Messiah sent by God?

From this viewpoint, Jesus could not find any faith on earth! Similarly, today there are millions of good Christians waiting for the Lord to appear—on the clouds; but if he comes in the same way as he did before, will he find the faith that will enable Christians to recognize him?

To emphasize once again, based on the Bible passages quoted above and on the lessons learned from God's work in history, the Second Coming will occur as the first coming did, with the Messiah's being born in the flesh on earth. Indeed, he comes as the Son of man.

D. The Principle Point of View

According to "The Principles of the Creation," God's purpose in creating Adam and Eve was to be fulfilled through their fulfilling the Three Blessings on earth. In other words, they were to perfect themselves as ideal individuals, become true parents, who are the origin of the ideal family, and establish the Kingdom of Heaven on earth. Then, as God's representa-tives, they were to rule the Creation in love. However, because they fell, they could not become the True Parents and they created an evil world.

Jesus, who came as the Second Adam (1 Cor 15:45), was to transform this world into the ideal world that had been plan-ned at the time of creation (Mt 4:17). Since God's Three Bles-sings still remain unfulfilled, even after the dispensation for salvation through Jesus' cruxifixion and resurrection, the Messiah, the sinless Third Adam, must come to fulfill God's Purpose for the Creation.

The Messiah must be born on earth as a substantial, physical being since he must be the example of the ideal

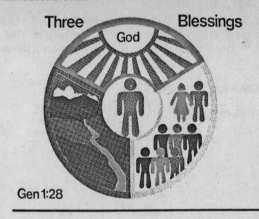

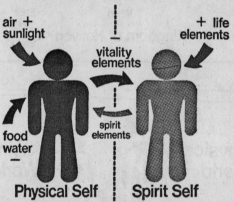

person, the person who has perfected his character, and thus, who has fulfilled the First Blessing. He can only carry out this responsibility in the flesh. He must also realize the ideal family that God has desired, and thus become the True Parent, one who has realized God's Second Blessing. His parental heart will emplant God's Heart and love in the hearts of everyone following him and will help them to perfect themselves by giving rebirth to them and showing each one how he himself can also accomplish the true purpose of life. He will be a perfect person and will become the lord who governs the spirit world and physical world in perfect love, fulfilling God's

Third Blessing. People will be grafted to him (Rom 11:17) and become one with him by believing and attending him. Thus, the Lord will lead them to become persons who control things

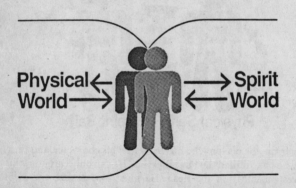

through love, realizing God's Third Blessing. Therefore, he must be born in the flesh, on earth, as at the first coming.

The main mission of Judaism was not only to receive Jesus but also to follow him and help him fulfill his will after he came. Likewise, the mission of Christianity, in addition to establishing the world-wide foundation for the Second Com-

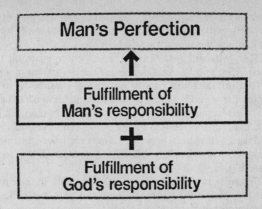

ing, is to help the Lord accomplish his mission when he comes.

The Kingdom of Heaven on earth which Christ is to build is not to be a Kingdom of Heaven in fantasy. The Kingdom of Heaven cannot be realized by supernatural miracles but only by man's fulfilling his responsibility to solve all of the problems in a realistic way, in accordance with God's guidance.

Salvation cannot take place in those who do not respond to God's work. However, it is God's desire for all mankind to be saved because he is the God of righteousness and love. Since God's Ideal for the Creation is not fulfilled with the perfection of an individual's character, God's dispensation for salvation also does not end with the salvation of the individual. Therefore, Christ, who at the Second Coming will completely fulfill God's ideal, will not be bound by any particular denomination of Christianity, but will transcend all denominations. He will work to establish one world under God, transcending tribal, national, and racial boundaries.

E. The Meaning of the Clouds

If the Lord is to appear on earth in the flesh, then what is the meaning of coming on the clouds? What is meant by clouds? Clouds are vaporized water. Regardless of how dirty water might be, when it evaporates into a cloud, it becomes purified. According to Revelation 17:15, water symbolizes fallen or sinful man. Then, clouds signify the people resurrected or reborn as saints from among the fallen people. The metaphor that Christ will come on the clouds means that he will come again among the saints that God prepares.

Then why did Jesus say he would come again on the clouds? First of all, it was to prevent the deceptions of antichrists. Until the actual time of his coming, it was better to let people believe that he would come on the clouds. If it had been clearly explained that Christ would appear in the flesh on earth, the confusion caused by the claims of many antichrists could hardly have been prevented. However, when the time is imminent, God will surely tell us how the Messiah is to come (Amos 3:7).

Secondly, it was to encourage the disciples in their religious life, which was to be a difficult course. Actually, Jesus said several things about the Second Coming that do not seem completely understandable. Revelation 22:20 says, " 'Surely I am coming soon.' " Matthew 10:23, Jesus said, " '. . . for truly, I say to you, you will not have gone through all the towns of Israel, before the Son of man comes.' " In Matthew 16:28, he said, " 'Truly, I say to you, there are some standing here who will not taste death before they see the Son of man coming in his kingdom.' " In John 21:18-22, he also spoke as though he would come again during John's lifetime. In all of these passages Jesus emphasized that the Second Coming would take place soon (relative to his time). Yet, it did not happen. Then why did Jesus say it would? What was Jesus' reason for speaking that way?

Jesus foresaw the persecution by the Roman Empire, so he had to educate, encourage, and give hope to his disciples in such a way that Christianity would survive the miserable persecution and quickly prepare the world-wide foundation for the Second Coming. The early Christians were able to remain enthusiastic and zealous because they believed that Jesus' second coming was imminent and that he would come from heaven on clouds in the power and glory of God. Because of this belief, they had the strength to withstand the oppression and persecution of the Roman Empire and thus establish the early Christian Church.

II. WHEN WILL CHRIST COME AGAIN?

Then when will Christ come again? In Matthew 24:36, Jesus

said, " 'But of that day and hour no one knows . . . ,' " indicating that it would be fruitless to speculate as to the time of his return.

However, that same verse in Matthew says that the Father knows, and Amos 3:7 says, " 'Surely the Lord GOD does nothing, without revealing his secret to his servants the prophets.' " Thus, we can understand that through prophets God will surely let people know about Christ's Second Coming. Many examples of God's foretelling what he would do can be cited in the course of restoration: God forewarned Noah of the Flood Judgment and Lot of his destruction of Sodom and Gomorrah; and God revealed the time of the Messiah's birth the first time. God revealed the time of Jesus' birth to the family of John the Baptist (Lk 1:41-45); to the wise men of the east (Mt 2:1-12); to Simeon (Lk 2:26-32); to shepherds in the field (Lk 2:8-12,15); to Anna (Lk 2:38); to Joseph (Mt 1:20-22); and to others. In the entire history of God's dispensation, can there be any more important time for God than that of the Messiah's coming? How can God not let the people know when the Son of God, himself, comes to earth to fulfill the lost Purpose of the Creation?

God reveals his plans (Amos 3:7)

Noah · · · · · · · · · · · the flood

Lot · · · · · · · · · · · · Sodom & Gomorrah

John the Baptist, wise men, others · · · Jesus' birth

? · · · · · · · · · · · 2nd Coming

On the other hand, Jesus also said that he will come like a thief (Rev 3:3). But then, he also said that he would not come like a thief to those who are in the light (1 Thess 5:4-6) and to those who remain awake (1 Thess 5:4-6, Rev 3:3). So it is clear that to those believers who always pray and are awake and in the light, God will foretell the advent of the Lord so that they can prepare for him (Lk 21:34,35).

Since God's Dispensation for Restoration is consummated through the Messiah, the Messiah is the most precious fruit of the entire history of God's Dispensation for Restoration. The foundation prepared for this precious Messiah was Judaism and the Israelites, which began with Jacob's family. However, as was already explained, the people of Israel did not believe in Jesus, and thus God developed a multi-racial Second Israel (Christianity) of those who believed in Jesus.

God's dispensational formula which is found in the history of Israel must also be found in the history of Christianity, because God prepared Christianity to be the world-wide Second Israel in place of the lost First Israel. The history of the First Israel, which began with Jacob, and the history of the Second Israel, Christianity, which began at Jesus' time, must both follow the same process for fulfilling the purpose of preparing for the Messiah to be received on earth.

The history of Israel and the history of Christianity differ in terms of their historical eras and events and their geographical settings and cultural backgrounds. However, the role of central history in God's Dispensation for Restoration was passed on from one to the other. Since both of these dispensations were to prepare the Foundation for the Messiah, the purpose underlying them was one and the same.

We have already compared these two histories from the viewpoint of God's Dispensation for Restoration. Let us consider the time of Christ's coming on the basis of that comparison.

The history of Israel from Jacob to Jesus was divided into six major sub-periods: the Period of Slavery in Egypt; the Period of Judges; the Period of the United Kingdom; the Period of the Divided Kingdoms of North and South; the Period of Jewish Captivity and Return; and the Period of Preparation for the Messiah. These six sub-periods actually comprise one dispensational age of nineteen hundred thirty years, during which God desired to consummate the Dispensation for Restoration. But when the First Israel could not fulfill its responsibility to believe in the Messiah, God had no alternative but to prolong the Dispensation for Restoration. The period from Jesus to the Second Coming is also divided

into six major sub-periods: the Period of Persecution in the
Roman Empire; the Period of the Christian Churches under
the Patriarchal System (the Period of the Patriarchs); the
Period of the Christian Kingdom; the Period of the Divided
Kingdoms of East and West; the Period of Papal Captivity and
Return; and the Period of Preparation for the Second Coming.
These six sub-periods also span a period totalling nineteen
hundred thirty years.

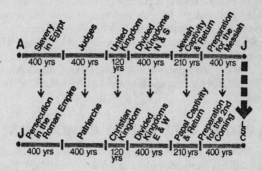

The year 1930 is not a time which we have to wait for with
hope and expectation—it has already occurred. Then why
haven't we on earth witnessed the Final Judgment and the
glory of the Second Coming? If the Second Coming is supposed to take place in the air, then the Lord's glory already
would have been brightly spread all over the world. However,
as explained earlier, the Lord will not come on literal clouds;
the Second Coming will take place by the Messiah's being
born in the flesh on earth. Then, is 1930 the precise year the
Messiah was born? The year cannot be pinpointed so exactly
because a difference of up to ten years was often observed
throughout the dispensational history. For instance, the
Period of Persecution in the Roman Empire was to be four
hundred years, but actually lasted only until 392 A.D. The
Period of Preparation for the Second Coming began with the
Reformation in 1517 and ended four hundred years later.
Based on this, the Second Coming should have occurred in

1917. Thus the birth of Christ should have taken place some-where between 1917 and 1930.

When Jesus came two thousand years ago, he did not immediately proclaim his messiahship and thereupon promptly begin the Judgment. There was an unseen and un-heard, yet steady preparation period of private life, and then a period of public ministry to prepare the foundation for fulfill-ing the Messiah's purpose. At the Second Coming, the Lord must also go through a similar course of preparation after his birth. By understanding what took place during the Dispensa-tion for Restoration, we can understand that this present period is the time of preparation for the Lord's appearance. We call the time of Christ's second coming the Last Days. It has already been explained in "Consummation of Human His-tory" that the present days are the Last Days. Consequently, it can be said that the present days are the time when Christ will appear.

III. WHERE WILL CHRIST COME AGAIN?

Then, if Christ is again to be born as a man in the flesh, he must be coming to a particular place in a particular nation. Which nation is it?

Two thousand years ago in Judea, Jesus said that he would come again, but will he come again among the people of Israel? In Matthew 21:33-43, in the parable of the vineyard, Jesus clearly indicated that he would not come to the land of Israel again. In this parable, God is the owner of the vineyard, the vineyard represents the work of God to accomplish the Ideal for the Creation, the tenants are the chosen nation of Israel, the servants are the prophets, the owner's son is Jesus, and the nation producing the fruits means the nation that will receive the Lord at the Second Coming. Jesus said that he would not come again to the people who had killed him. Moreover, he said he would take their right to be the chosen nation and give it to a nation and people who would be fruitful for the Second Coming.

Then, how should we take the Bible passage which speaks of the coming of the sons of Israel? Revelation 7:4 says that at the time of the Second Coming, one hundred forty-four thousand would be drawn from the tribes of Israel and sealed. What does this mean?

The name 'Israel' was originally received by Jacob after he prevailed over the angel at the ford of the Jabbok (Gen 32:28) and means 'he who has strived with God'. In other words, 'Israel' means the people of God who have triumphed in faith and does not necessarily mean the lineal descendents of Jacob. This is borne out in the words of John the Baptist in Matthew 3:9 " '. . . do not presume to say to yourselves, "We have Abraham as our father"; for I tell you, God is able from these stones to raise up children to Abraham.' " It is again borne out by St. Paul when he said in Romans 9:6, "For not all who are descended from Israel belong to Israel. . . ."

Then who would be the chosen people of "Israel" after Jesus' death on the cross? They are the devout Christians who believe in the Lord. Romans 11:11 says, ". . . through their [the Israelites'] trespass salvation has come to the Gentiles, so as to make Israel jealous." This indicates that the center of God's Dispensation for Restoration has shifted from the Israelites. Then God will work his central dispensation not among the lineal descendants of Abraham, but among the devout Christians who have taken up the faith of Abraham. But to precisely which country will the Lord come?

When asked by a disciple where he would come again, Jesus replied metaphorically in Luke 17:37, " 'Where the body is, there the eagles will be gathered together.' " Jesus did not specify which country he would come to. But Revelation 7:2-4 says that an angel would ascend from the rising of the sun, in other words, from the east, and would seal one hundred forty-four thousand chosen servants of God on their foreheads. Then what country does this refer to?

That nation of the East is Korea. When a farmer transplants a tree, he carefully digs up the soil and waters it to prepare for the tree. How could God, who is expecting the fruit of human history, send the Messiah without preparation? From this perspective of the foundation prepared by God, let us further consider the idea that Korea is the land which is to receive the Lord.

First of all, the nation to which the Messiah comes must be the object of God's Heart. Based on this view, Korea is the land God has prepared. From the Fall of the first man and woman until today, God has lived in deep despair and has felt unfulfilled. Often we refer to God as a being of utmost glory who is so far above us. But this is because we do not know

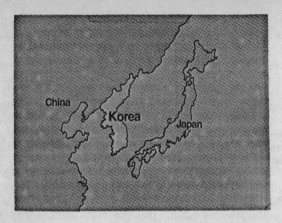

God's Heart. Because of the Fall of Adam and Eve, who were
God's only children, God has been grieving with the heart of a
parent who has lost his children, and he has wandered
through the sinful world of Hell in search of them, longing to
save his rebellious children. Therefore, the individual, family,
or nation which fights against Satan in God's place can hardly
avoid the path of tears and suffering. How could filial and
faithful children, who would share the agony of their parent's
heart, lead an easy life? Since the Messiah is the one who bears
the grieving heart of God, and is to relieve God's sorrow, he
cannot come to a people who are satisfied by their material
abundance. Since the nation that is to receive the Messiah
must be the object of God's Heart, that is, since its people must
be sons and daughters who have the same Heart as God's, that
nation cannot avoid the way of suffering.

The First and Second Israel both had to walk the path of
suffering and hardship. As the nation which is to receive the
Messiah, Korea also had to walk that same path. Thus, in its
recent history Korea has had to undergo a course of the most
extreme suffering. Even while undergoing suffering and misery, Korea has faithfully developed the good traditions of filial
piety and loyalty. Even at the height of its national power, it
never provoked or first invaded another nation. God's strategy
has been to win victory *after* being attacked, quite different
from Satan's strategy of invasion. The Korean people's maintaining their homogeneous lineage, unique language and tra-

ditional national spirit, and the integrity of their own distinct culture despite numerous invasions over nearly five thousand years is a record that may well be unparalleled in world history. Even in the midst of its persistently sorrowful history, the Korean nation has cherished righteousness and peace and was being educated to be God's object.

Secondly, it is significant that Korea is a nation bearing the fruits of many religions. Koreans have a strong inclination toward religious life; they revere God and a spiritual way of life. Thus, many of the world's great spiritual and ethical teachings, such as Buddhism and Confucianism, have flourished in this land, and it is centered on these spiritual

Qualifications of the chosen nation

1 Have experiences similar to those of God

2 Many religions

3 Front-line of God and Satan

4 National indemnity period

5 Messianic prophecies

traditions that the Korean national culture became fruitful. Within the last few centuries, Christianity arrived and achieved the highest pinnacle of Christianity. Religion has blended deeply with daily life in exquisite harmony. A nation matching this description is hard to find anywhere in the world.

The Lord does not come to save Christians alone. While Christians are the central nation in God's dispensation, all people are to be God's children, and God, himself, has created and guided all of the major religions toward the restoration of the people of their particular region, time period, and circumstances. Therefore, the Messiah, who is to accomplish the ultimate purpose of God's dispensation, must simultaneously fulfill the purpose of all other religions. In this light, the nation suitably prepared to receive the Lord would be a nation bearing the fruits of all the major religions.

Thirdly, the nation to which our Lord comes must be the front line of both God and Satan. God told Adam and Eve, " '. . . do not eat of the fruit . . . for in that day you will die.' " From these words, we can understand that the point where they fell became the dividing line between heaven and earth, between life and death, and between good and evil. Thus, the Lord must come to the same type of point, where life and death and good and evil again confront one another. He must then go on to actually solve the problems of the world and conclude the dispensational history.

God's dispensation to restore to his side the world begun by Satan is based on, and may be summarized as, the separation of Cain and Abel. The separation of the Cain and Abel worlds before the coming of the Messiah is manifested in the Communist and democratic worlds. This is a horizontal development of the vertical dispensation which God has worked throughout history. Therefore, the Lord will appear where the two powers of democracy and Communism confront one another, that is, at the focal point of both God's love and Satan's hate. That line of confrontation is the 38th parallel in the Korean peninsula. The 38th parallel in Korea has this dispensational meaning to it. It is not only the front line of democracy and Communism; it is also the front line of God and Satan.

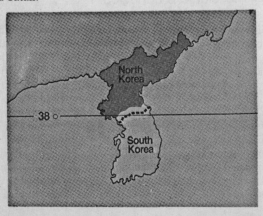

When God works to accomplish his Will, Satan works to oppose and prevent God's work. Thus, God's front line becomes Satan's front line. Of all the efforts of God, Satan would most oppose the preparation of the nation which is to receive the Messiah. Since the core element in the process of restoration is religion, in the world-wide Dispensation for Restoration, God works to prepare for the Messiah based on the fruits of the world's religions, and Satan works to crush all religion. In preparing Korea for the Messiah, God sought to foster religion throughout Korea—Satan wanted to totally eradicate it. Thus, the Korean War which broke out along the 38th parallel, and the resulting division of Korea, were not merely the results of a nation's civil conflict due to territorial separation. It was the confrontation between the democratic and Communist blocs, and furthermore, between God and Satan. The fact that many nations (16) not immediately concerned with the conflict nonetheless participated and helped the Dispensation for Restoration has divine significance.

Fourthly, the nation to which the Lord comes must establish a national foundation for the Dispensation for Restoration. In order for Korea to be the nation to receive the Messiah, it had to establish the national foundation of separation from Satan, just as Israel and the Early Christians did. The Israelites had to meet the condition of separating from Satan by suffering for four hundred years in Egypt, which represented the satanic world. The Second Israel established the condition of separation from Satan by enduring persecution for nearly four centuries under the Roman Empire, which also represented the satanic world. Thus, at the time of the Second Coming, in order to separate from Satan, Korea must also endure suffering at the hands of a nation on the satanic side. In this case, the nation on the satanic side was Japan, and for forty years it brought unimaginable torment upon Korea. In the name of the Eulsa Protection Treaty, Japan forcibly deprived Korea of its diplomatic rights and national sovereignty from 1905 until 1945, when Japan was defeated in World War II. During this period, the Korean people were completely deprived of their freedom by Japan, and countless numbers were imprisoned and slaughtered and underwent all sorts of extreme persecution. Beginning in 1910, when Japan annexed Korea, the persecution of Christianity, which was the foundation of Korea's independence movement, was unparalleled in its cruelty. While under God's dispensation, Christianity was enjoying its freedom around the globe, the Korean nation, with its Christians at the forefront, suffered greatly and thus paid the national indemnity that qualified it as the nation which would receive the Messiah.

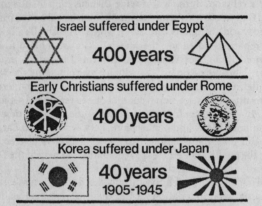

Israel suffered under Egypt
400 years

Early Christians suffered under Rome
400 years

Korea suffered under Japan
40 years
1905-1945

Fifthly, this nation must have a history of relevant prophecy. When God sends his beloved Son, how can he do it quietly? Certainly he would reveal it to all those on earth who are spiritually prepared; certainly he would hand them the good news and have them prepare to receive the Messiah. Just as the Israelites knew through the prophets that the Messiah would come as a king and save them, the Korean people have waited for a king of righteousness. For five hundred years, Korea has also had a strong messianic expectation as a result of the Chung-Gam-Nok, a book of prophecy. It is quite characteristic of the Korean people to have had this type of unique messianic thought even before they were actually able to receive the benefits of God's dispensation for salvation through Jesus. Many spiritually gifted clergymen and laymen have received specific revelations regarding the Second Coming of the Lord in Korea; and many deeply religious people have had the common revelation that Korea will be the center of world salvation.

The fulfillment of God's Dispensation for Restoration is focused primarily on restoring man and secondarily on restoring the environment of the Kingdom of Heaven. God has worked through religion to restore man; God has developed civilizations in order to restore the environment of the Kingdom of Heaven. He has worked to create the most ideal culture and civilization for the Second Coming. The Second Coming will bring harmony between religion and science, between the spiritual aspects and the material aspects of civilization, and between East and West. All will be blended in harmony, giving birth to the new culture of Godism. The Korean peninsula was a hidden area of the Orient for a long time; however, western culture came to the East and finally reached Korea.

New Culture of Godism

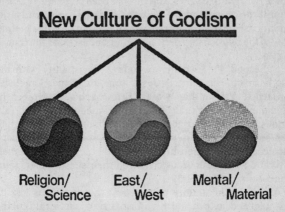

Religion/   East/   Mental/
Science   West   Material

God trained the Korean people for five thousand years to have deep faith and love, and on that basis Christianity was received. When God sent Christianity to the Korean people, he made his final preparation for them to receive the Lord of the Second Coming, and made Korea the world representative of Christianity. Although Korea is a small nation, it has consistently played a significant role in modern history, as if it were the nucleus of the leading international political trends.

Jesus' Age and the Present Age from the Standpoint of Time-Identity

Jesus' age and the time of the Second Coming are periods of dispensational time-identity. Thus, God's dispensation for the

Second Coming, which is centered on Christianity, is similar
to that for Jesus' time.

First, let's look at these two ages from the viewpoint of the
central nation for the dispensation. God's plan was to have his
dispensation expand from Jesus to the nation of Israel, from
Israel to Rome, and from Rome to the rest of the world.
Assuming that the central religion at the time of the Second
Coming is Christianity, and that the Israel is Korea, then
which nation would be in the position of the Roman Empire?
The present day Rome is the nation which God developed as
the leading nation of the world, based on Christianity. For
over two hundred years, America has been prepared by God to
fulfill the purpose of the Second Coming. Consequently, the
relationship between Korea and America in our time is similar to the relationship between Rome and Israel at the time of
Jesus.

Second, let us compare today's Christianity with the
Judaism of Jesus' time. At Jesus' time, Judaism in Israel was
attached to the authority of the priests and to the rites of the
temple; their spiritual life was corrupted. The Jewish religious leaders had forgotten the traditional piety which had
passed from Abraham to Jacob and Moses and the prophets.
Instead, their relationship to God had become only a formality, and as a result Jesus criticized their substanceless faith
many times (Mt 23:1-39).

Today, Christianity must repent that it too has lost its
content and has become mere formality. When we think of the
passion and faith of the early Church, we can say that today's
Church has become too formal and has departed greatly from
the original purpose of the faith. Many people consider themselves Christian, but in reality are living a life far distant from
the teachings of Jesus.

Just as Jesus poured out all of his effort to reform the
corrupted Judaism of his time, at the Second Coming, he will
also fundamentally reform Christianity to make it a true
church which reveres God and will also inspire Christians to
be those who practice God's Will and Jesus' teaching.

At Jesus' time, Judaism did not recognize the true value of
Jesus; the Jewish leaders turned their backs on God's Will and
the reformation which Jesus was teaching and persecuted
him. Likewise, at the Second Coming, the new teachings and
reformation activities of Christ will be opposed by believers

who refuse to make the effort to reform Christianity, and by
the Church, which is attached to its traditional authority and
rites.

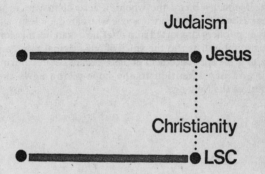

At Jesus' time, the words of the Messiah were not received
by the leaders of Judaism. Rather, they were received by
simple lower class Jews and Gentiles who were thirsty for
spiritual life, or who were troubled by their guilty conscien-
ces. Similarly, at the time of the Second Coming, laymen who
are trying hard to live God's Word, or even non-Christians,
may be the first to accept the teachings of Christ, rather than
the leaders of Christianity. This is why Jesus, in sorrow, said
that those who would enjoy the marriage feast which he
would prepare might not be those invited, but those called in
at random from the street (Mt 22:8-10).

The people of Jesus' time were born to lead lives of dispensational significance, for they were to attend the Messiah and
help him to realize his will. They were not ordinary individuals, but had the historic responsibility of living at the
most important time in dispensational history. Similarly, all
people today, and especially Christians, have the responsibility to attend the Lord and establish the world that realizes the
Ideal for the Creation. We are living at a point in time unlike
any since the beginning of history.

At the Second Coming, Christ will proclaim God's Will,
which must be realized on the earth, and he will educate

people to carry it out. True people of faith should search for and attend him, and follow God's Will, which is revealed through him. In Matthew 2:3, the Bible says that upon hearing of the Messiah's birth, the whole of Jerusalem was in an uproar. However, was there any one who cared for Jesus as a baby, or publicly supported him after he began his mission? Let us humbly listen to the voice of our original mind and search for the announcement of the Messiah. Let us calm our mind and pay attention to the hope-giving news that announces the New Age.

NOTES:

NOTES:

NOTES:

NOTES:

NOTES:

NOTES:

NOTES:

NOTES: